FRANCE DURING THE SOCIALIST YEARS

France During the Socialist Years

Edited by
GINO RAYMOND
University of Bristol

Dartmouth

Aldershot • Brookfield USA • Singapore • Sydney

Published by
Dartmouth Publishing Company Limited
Gower House
Croft Road
Aldershot
Hants GU11 3HR
England

Dartmouth Publishing Company
Old Post Road
Brookfield
Vermont 05036
USA

British Library Cataloguing in Publication Data
France During the Socialist Years
　I. Raymond, Gino G.
　944.083

Library of Congress Cataloging-in-Publication Data
France during the socialist years / edited by Gino Raymond.
　　　p.　　cm.
　　"This book developed from a one-day conference which took place in the French Department of Bristol University in November 1991"–Acknowledgements.
　　　ISBN 1-85521-518-7
　　　1. France–Politics and government–1981- 2. Socialism–France. 3. France–Social policy. 4. France–Cultural policy. I. Raymond, Gino.
JN2594.2.F69　1994
944.083'8–dc20
　　　　　　　　　　　　　　　　　　　　　　　　　　　94-15661
　　　　　　　　　　　　　　　　　　　　　　　　　　　CIP

ISBN 1 85521 518 7

Contents

Main Abbreviations

CDS	Centre des Démocrates Sociaux
CERES	Centre d'Etude de Recherche et d'Education Socialistes
CAP	Common Agricultural Policy
CAPES	Certificat d'Aptitude au Professorat de l'Enseignement du Second Degré
CDN	Centre Dramatique National
CES	Collège d'Enseignement Secondaire
CES	Contrat Emploi-Solidarité
CIR	Convention des Institutions Républicaines
CSG	Contribution Sociale Généralisée
DDC	Direction du Développement Culturel
EAC	Etablissement d'Action Culturelle
EC	European Community
EMU	Economic and Monetary Union
EMS	European Monetary System
FGDS	Fédération de la Gauche Démocrate et Socialiste
FN	Front National
IUT	Institut Universitaire de Technologie
MRG	Mouvement des Radicaux de Gauche
MRP	Mouvement Républicain Populaire

PCF	Parti Communiste Français
PR	Parti Républicain
PS	Parti Socialiste
PSD	Parti Social-Démocrate
PSU	Parti Socialiste Unifié
RMI	Revenu Minimum d'Insertion
RPR	Rassemblement pour la République
SEA	Single European Act
SFIO	Section Française de l'Internationale Ouvrière
SNES	Syndicat National de l'Enseignement Secondaire
TUC	Travaux d'Utilité Collective
UDF	Union pour la Démocratie Française
URC	Union du Rassemblement et du Centre
UPF	Union pour la France

Preface

The three sections in which the contributions to this book fall highlight the attempt to give a broad overview of the way the uninterrupted decade of socialist presidency which began in 1981, and a near-uninterrupted decade of socialist government, ending in the resounding failure of the *Parti socialiste* in the legislative elections of March 1993, impacted on France. The scale of the collapse of electoral support for the Socialists prompted comparisons with historical landslides going back to the *chambre introuvable* of 1815, dominated by the royalist right of the Bourbon restoration. Immediate analyses of the failures of the left in present-day France adduced the obvious weaknesses which undermined their support electorally and reduced them to a fraction of their former presence in a National Assembly dominated by a centre-right with 80 per cent of the seats: weaknesses like the failure to address economic and social problems such as unemployment; the taint left by numerous political and financial scandals; and that rather vague but nonetheless significant factor called 'l'usure du pouvoir'. However, instead of focusing narrowly on the ambitions and inevitable failures of the actors, this study attempts to adduce the dialectical relationship between socialist ambition and the reality of France as polity, culture and society, illuminating the way in which the two terms of this progression informed each other and the compromises which ensued.

In Part I, John Gaffney analyses the presidential discourse of François Mitterrand to illustrate the extent to which the credibility of Mitterrand rested on the presidential persona, concomitant with a move away from an ideologically-based defence of socialist government and in the direction of a renewed sense of republican virtue. As Helen Drake explains, during the socialist years, France's policy vis-à-vis the European community was indelibly stamped with Mitterrand's determination to make that policy the embodiment of his presidential authority at home, and France's key role within the Community. The weight of presidential authority was keenly felt by the *Parti socialiste* during the first term of Mitterrand's mandate, but as Alistair Cole explains, Mitterrand's re-election in 1988 was followed by a resurgence of the factionalism that had been characteristic of the PS before its accession to power. The consequent loss of credibility for the party was part of a general tendency, examined by Gino Raymond, which led to the decline of France's party political establishment.

In Part II, David Looseley documents the unfolding cultural project of the Socialists, and weighs their debt to the policies of previous, right-wing governments, against their own innovations. The electoral triumphs of the Socialists were destined to render somewhat problematical the position of a significantly left-leaning intellectual elite, as John Flower suggests. While Nick Harrison focuses specifically on the issue of blasphemy, illustrating how an ostensibly pluralistic and libertarian government failed to analyse the underlying issues sufficiently for it to rise fully above the reflex reactions of the right.

In Part III, Linda Hantrais explores the paradox which characterized the attempts of the Socialists to pursue social policies commensurate with their ideological convictions, while transforming themselves into the accomplished managers of French capitalism. A sense of enduring realities, and specifically enduring inadequacies, is what emerges from Peter Collier's chronicling of the great educational non-debate under the Socialists. A deeper sense of impending crisis provides the disturbing undercurrent to Jim Shield's examination of the immigration issue, and the way the Socialists exhibited a tendency to conform to a pattern of policy options more reminiscent of conservatism than of a socialist commitment to equality and fraternity. Finally, Gino Raymond probes the manner in which the socialist government was caught in the sweep of cultural and social shifts which call for a fundamental re-examination of the relationship between the governing and the governed.

Acknowledgements

This book developed from a one-day conference which took place in the French Department of Bristol University in November 1991, entitled 'France During the Socialist Years'. In addition to the versions of the papers given at the conference, contributions from Alistair Cole of Keele, Helen Drake of Aston and Jim Shields of Warwick have greatly enhanced the depth and coverage of this book.

The burden of indebtedness incurred through the help and encouragement of colleagues and institutions, both in France and England, is too great to be discharged within these few lines. However, I wish to express particular thanks to the following: the Department of French of Bristol University for affording me the time to pursue this project, more specifically Dany Hinett and Judith Hurley for their generous secretarial support; Tim Hooton of Aston University for his remarkable patience in taking me over the hurdles involved in accessing contributions on different disks with different programmes; the British Academy, whose material support was invaluable in the realization of this project.

Last but not least, I wish to thank my wife Svetlana for her gracious acceptance of my absences as this project was brought to fruition.

PART I
POLITICS

1 From the *République Sociale* to the *République Française*

JOHN GAFFNEY

Introduction

This chapter examines the changing relationship between socialism and republicanism in France in the 1980s, and the crucial role played in this by the President of the Republic, François Mitterrand. Mitterrand, the Socialist Party (PS) candidate in the 1981 presidential elections, won the presidency from Valéry Giscard d'Estaing, bringing the left to power for the first time in the Fifth Republic. In the ensuing legislative elections the PS won an absolute majority in the National Assembly, thus ending 23 years of right-wing control of both the executive and the legislature. The Socialist Party governed from 1981 to 1986 and again from 1988 until 1993. François Mitterrand remained President throughout the entire period.

The Socialist party's increasing pragmatism during the 1980s and the concomitant loss of revolutionary language has been dealt with elsewhere.[1] What we shall do here is examine how the rhetoric of French socialism changed, and what the effects of this were not only upon French socialism itself, but also upon the Republic and upon French political culture more generally. In order to analyse these issues we shall examine François Mitterrand's discourse. Let us first, however, look briefly at how French socialism moved away from its earlier commitment to, if not a revolutionary socialism, then at least a quasi-revolutionary rhetoric which marked it off radically from most of its sister parties in Western Europe (and even from several communist parties) at the end of the 1970s.

From the break with capitalism to the break with socialism

An assumption generally held by observers is that the winning and exercise of power in 1981 rapidly brought to an end the more unrealistic aspects of the earlier PS promise to 'break' with capitalism. The realization that the policy of 'socialism in one country' was not possible in the context of an international environment which was in recession has been thoroughly catalogued.[2] The economic policies of the Socialist governments of the 1981–84 period were failures (in that they failed to control inflation, unemployment and so on). More than this, however, they were never revolutionary.[3] It was not, therefore, a question of revolutionary policies having to be abandoned in the face of harsh realities; the policies applied were mildly reflationary, even though these policies too had to be revised and, from 1982, austerity measures implemented. What therefore is of interest to us is the initial rationale for the revolutionary rhetoric, given that few, if any, revolutionary policies were ever really contemplated, let alone passed into law and applied.[4] Why was it that the PS felt it necessary to deploy a highly rhetorical discourse throughout the 1970s? And if it is the case that such a rhetoric had little to do with the intention to effect dramatic socialist change (state intervention on a decisive scale, the redistribution of wealth, the social ownership of the means of production and so on), what was it for? In part, it had to do with welding the various left and centre-left currents in the party around a common interest, and with maintaining a rhetorical style which would enable the PS to match the strong Communist Party's rhetoric to its left, and thereby protect the PS from any siren calls from the right or centre-right. Yet why this particular kind of rhetoric and one which had so little relation to reality? A first point to make is that an examination of the party's literature of the 1970s reveals not simply a revolutionary rhetoric but also the existence of an already developed, and contrasting, 'culture of government' style: many of the texts are detailed, and practical (although this does not mean of itself that

4

they were capable of implementation). It is not, therefore, as has often been claimed, that the PS had lyrical illusions and lost them after 1981; it in fact had two approaches, two registers, two discourses. What is it then in French socialism and French political culture more generally which encouraged, if not required, a party on the threshold of power to be both 'revolutionary' and 'realistic' at the same time?

Towards republicanism

In terms of the possibility of republicanism as a discourse replacing socialism within the PS, a first point to note is that both possess this strange quality of being able to accommodate a revolutionary discourse (i.e. destructive of institutions) as well as a pragmatic discourse (i.e. creative of institutions). A second point to make here is that in all the literature of the PS throughout the 1970s, the Republic as a reference point, though not actively nurtured (it was abandoned as a major theme quite soon after the establishment of the Fifth Republic in the late 1950s) was never challenged.[5] In leftist thought generally, established political institutions were (especially in the 1960s) often equated with capitalism itself and were depicted as 'fronts', or legitimating institutions for an inegalitarian society which they maintained and nourished. In France, however, and no matter how radical the rhetoric became, the institutions themselves were never the target that other democratic institutions were in the discourse of the left in other countries which deployed a revolutionary discursive register. On the other hand, republicanism itself (in part because it had become so intertwined with de Gaulle's Fifth Republic) was rarely actively defended, promoted or used as a symbol: not, that is, until the 1980s. It is as if from the late 1950s to the early 1980s, republicanism existed as a latent though unvoiced element within socialist discourse.

In the early 1980s, the Socialist government moved decisively towards what we might call centrist policies. The party rhetoric reluctantly followed, but one of the results was that socialism as a complex philosophy of reference gradually diminished to the point where, by the late 1980s, it barely existed at all within the party's discursive framework. During the 1980s, apart from a brief rhetorical flirtation with 'modernisation' as a mobilizing theme,[6] little took its place. Politically, there was a clear shift

5

to the centre in terms of policies and rhetoric, and, after 1988, various moves or potential moves to the centre in terms of political alliances and governmental strategy. The harsh realities of government seem to have made of 'socialism' one of the left's first and lasting casualties. In the course of the 1980s, myriad books and articles talked unendingly of the *vide idéologique* which had opened up in the party. By the end of the 1980s and into the 90s, 'Europe' was rapidly filling this gap at the level of explicit discourse and of policy. Such a shift was encouraged, not only by the apparent absence of alternative doctrinal reference points, but also by the increasing references to Europe by President Mitterrand. Here we may observe that throughout the 1980s in the PS there were a few rearguard attempts to defend Socialism, a half-hearted commitment to modernisation, and later a belated enthusiasm for 'Europe'. What of republicanism? Before answering this question we should first ask what we would expect a declared commitment to republicanism as a mobilizing force to look like and where on the Left we would expect to see it emerge. Since the 1848 revolution, and especially since the defeat of the Commune in 1871 and the setting up of the Third Republic, socialism was seen both before and after the 1917 Revolution in Moscow as an advance upon republicanism. *La république sociale* was often used as a slogan to distinguish left-wing republicanism from other forms, but generally speaking, 'socialism' itself was seen as that which, without necessarily destroying the Republic and its advances, would, nevertheless, transcend it, put paid to any complicity between republicanism and capitalism, and see the eventual 'conquest' of power rather than its mere 'exercise'.

In the 1980s, with the double blow to socialism of, first, its apparent impossibility in practice (even with an absolute majority in the National Assembly and a Socialist President), and, second, its philosophical degeneration, one would assume that republicanism and reference to it would come from the right of the party; a right that would use reference to a kind of safe Third Republicanism (equality of opportunity, rational government, education and training, incrementalist social advancement and a moderate redistribution of wealth) to mark its triumph over the left of the party, and that gradually such a rhetoric would fill the discursive or ideological void as the left of the party faced the facts and accepted the clear impracticality of its own notions of the break with capitalism. In fact, the right of the party, represented by Michel Rocard and his followers,

6

spoke little of republicanism, and scarcely more boldly of the social-democracy that had been so calumnied in the 1960s and 1970s. In fact, Rocardianism seemed to avoid in its discourse the possible advantages that such an embracing of republicanism might provide. This is somewhat surprising and raises questions concerning the problematic significance of republicanism's relationship to socialism.

In fact, the entry of republicanism into the mainstream of political discourse in the 1980s came not from the right of the socialist spectrum but from the left. Much of the drive towards remobilizing the idea of the Republic in French Socialist discourse came from the current on the extreme left of the party, CERES (*Centre d'Etude, de Recherche et d'Education Socialistes* which changed its name to *Socialisme et République* in 1986). *Socialisme et République*'s marginal (and throughout the 1980s declining) status within the party explains why the term was not immediately embraced by the mainstream of the party and by the government. The idea, however, was not restricted to this current, and spread, usually from the left of the party, in articles, conferences, and books, into the everyday language of socialism, to the extent that by the 1990s it began to fill the empty space left by now hollow references to socialism.

Our discussion, of course, raises the question of what exactly republicanism signifies, what kind of republic is being talked about. It is not possible within the limits of this chapter to expand on the history and intricacies of this debate.[9] We can say here, however, that there are three types of ideal republic: the untrammelled *régime d'assemblée* reminiscent of the First Republic; the representative republic of rationalized checks and balances reminiscent of the Third Republic; and the more authoritarian presidential republic quintessentially, though not exclusively, represented by de Gaulle's Fifth Republic. The fact that the revived debate on republicanism is recent means that there was little debate concerning the merits and desirability of the elements which could constitute the desired republic towards which the left might strive. Given the fact that republicanism was so undebated for decades, the PS was in uncharted, though potentially rich, doctrinal territory. Such ambiguities and confusions, however, allowed a Socialist President, government and party to adapt to changing circumstances, although not always knowingly, or in a controlled manner. Such guidance concerning the *institutions* has come almost exclusively from the President, and it was his behaviour, *in the context of republicanism's ambiguity*, which refashioned and exploited socialism's new-found republicanism. Before looking at the role of the President of the Republic in these changes, let us make a preliminary summing up. First, whether or not France may be in the 'wrong' republic, according to particular schools of thought within French socialism, the notion of the desirability of the republic was never in doubt within socialism, as it arguably was (often by default) up until 1981. Second, republicanism is not simply a centrist alternative to socialism, but has a history and mythology just as powerful as socialism, which explains why it is not an easy discourse to adopt. Indeed, republicanism's mythology is arguably more powerful, at least in the French context, than socialism itself. It may be the case that republicanism will outlast socialism to the point where the latter becomes a twentieth-century philosophical variation of republicanism itself. Third, it is true that this republicanism can be subscribed to by nearly all political currents in French life[8] and therefore accommodates various strategies in a way socialism cannot. This means that if republicanism is to develop considerably on the political left in the contemporary period, this 'catch-all' character it currently possesses will force definition and clarification. Finally, it may be that in a few years time, what for the last twenty years has been the case (that republicanism was relatively superficial, and socialism a highly complex phenomenon) will be transformed, and that republicanism will reveal a depth and complexity, and socialism appear as, arguably, inoperable in practice and superficial doctrinally.

The party

It was always the (accurate) claim of the French Communist Party that the Socialist Party was a middle-class party; this has been the case for most of its history. And in the Fifth Republic, especially since the 1970s, the social background of its members has seen an increase in its middle-class and upper middle-class composition. Indeed, by the time it was on the threshold of power in the late 1970s, its hierarchy was almost exclusively dominated by the graduates of the highly elitist *grandes écoles*, whose background and training, moreover, disposed them to the managerial solutions of the upper civil service rather than to any form of radical socialism.[9] Once the PS gained power, the influence of this element on its membership increased further as the party's impact on the political and social institutions of the Fifth Republic increased. This, coupled with the rise of the 'social democrats' in the party and in the government (in all of the post-1981 administrations), was the reality of French socialism. Republicanism, as it were, falls into a space left vacant by the rhetoric of socialism. As we have seen, however, republicanism is not a doctrine which corresponds particularly well to social democracy. It is much more volatile a doctrine than this. Republicanism, may, in part, serve the same function that radical socialism played in the pre-1981 period; and one of its functions may be internal to the party itself: republicanism is a form of political doctrine that can maintain the unity of the party by demonstrating that the policy options of Socialist governments spring from a tradition in French political culture which goes beyond a kind of managerial pragmatism. This does not mean, however, that contemporary republicanism is an alibi for technocratic social democracy, but that it offers to social democracy further development and an orientation: equality of opportunity, a strong emphasis upon education and training, social justice, the proper separation of powers, the proper functioning of the Republic's institutions, the defence of the secular against religion, and the maintenance of 'French interests' (in order that French republicanism may spread and prosper); each of these lends itself to both pragmatism and idealism; to social democracy and to republicanism. The sincerity of all of these objectives is, of course, open to doubt. What is not is that claims to them have been constant, and all have been contemporaneously or retrospectively justified in the name of republicanism. None of these objectives and ideals was appealed to more than by the President himself. Mitterrand, in fact, was the single most important factor in changes in both policy and rhetorical range. Before looking at Mitterrand's discourse and at how Socialist Party rhetoric and attitudes responded, let us briefly examine the role of the President vis-à-vis both the party and the Republic's institutions.

The President of the Republic

When Mitterrand won the presidency in 1981 he had been party leader for ten years, and had seen the party progress from the factional divisions and marginality of the 1960s[10] to the highly successful organization it had become by the late 1970s. The party's success was based partly upon its acceptance of him and his strategy of 'left union' with the Communist Party. This was a strategy which also allowed the party to flourish doctrinally and which generated a whole series of debates between the reunited strands of French socialism, many of which had been separated since the Algerian war in the mid-1950s. Nevertheless, the lively debate about socialism was possible *only because* the party knew it had in Mitterrand's leadership and strategy a recipe for success.

Upon Mitterrand's gaining the presidency, and the PS forming a government in 1981, a series of developments took place. The essence of this was that Mitterrand (in the name of his presidential office) moved away from French socialism. Paradoxically, however, French socialism both as an organisation and a discourse became more than ever dependent upon him. What is surprising is that such a development was not foreseen. However Mitterrand might wish to modify the role of the President (away, for example, from an authoritarian style), the only direction he could take it in was towards the Republic, not towards socialism, since he had become President of the French and the guardian of the Republic's institutions. As he moved away from the PS and began to deploy an alternative discourse (which we shall analyse below), the party found itself unable to continue its redefinition of socialism without him for fear of speaking in a different voice from that of the President. It was not simply, therefore, that the left's recognized leader of the 1970s, Mitterrand, was able to impose his will upon party discourse, but that the office of the presidency, once gained, obliged Mitterrand to behave in a particular way vis-à-vis both the French electorate and France's political institutions, and this in a way which altered the policies advocated before 1981 and the rhetoric which accompanied them. Moreover, the support that Mitterrand, as President, required from the party meant that it could not deploy a discourse which undermined him *or* the Republic's institutions.

Republicanism, therefore, comes at the party on two flanks, from its left in the form of the beginnings of a theorisation of republicanism in order to cope with the eclipse of virtually all the party's ideas of the 1970s, and from the President, its former leader, who through his discursive behaviour introduced another aspect of republicanism, a republicanism of practice, which would inform significantly the party's doctrinal development.

Methodological note

In order to examine the changes within French Socialist discourse in the course of the 1980s, I have limited the analysis to interviews (around thirty in all out of around sixty given in the course of the decade) by President Mitterrand to television, radio and the press. The other two possible sources were his official speeches and his press conferences (I have included two of the latter as they were of particular significance). Generally speaking, however, press conferences deal with relatively conjunctural topics, allowing little scope to the speaker to develop his ideas at any length. They are, moreover, aimed at specialist audiences; journalists (who will select only sections of the press conference to report), and the international community. Speeches are generally restricted to their various actual audiences, even though parts of the speeches will also be reported to a larger public (we might add that the President's authorship of his speeches is also only partial, their being, for the most part, the creation of his speech writers). Interviews, on the other hand, are aimed at a very wide audience (especially the TV interviews where Mitterrand says on many occasions that he is speaking not to the interviewer but to the French people), and see the interviewee able to expand in a relaxed and relatively spontaneous manner upon his ideas. Each interview lasted on average one hour.

Mitterrand's discourse

If we are searching for the development of a sophisticated discourse concerning the Republic and republicanism in the thought of François Mitterrand, we need to say straight away that his early interviews see him simply struggling to present himself as possessing a dignity and vision in

11

the face of what can only be described as a grilling from his questioners over the shortcomings or failures of the PS government's first two or three years in office, and in particular over the party's losses in the 1983 local elections.

In a typical radio interview of the period,[11] the President uses the word 'socialiste' only twice, but refers frequently to the terms 'justice' and 'justice sociale', and speaks passionately about 'redressement national', 'France', 'les Français'; as passionately as he can, that is, given that the interviewer's style and attitude allow the President little chance to develop such ideas. Only at the end of the interview is Mitterrand given the chance of a little lyricism. At the end of a relatively long closing passage, for example, he says: 'La force au dedans de moi-même et la tranquilité, elles n'ont pas changé parce que rien n'a changé en moi de ce qui est profond. J'ai comme beaucoup d'autres l'amour de mon pays. Je ne distingue pas entre les Français.....' This focusing upon the self developed throughout the decade. In the early 1980s, however, there is a clear effort by Mitterrand to overcome a sometimes belittling hostility which diminishes the President's stature and draws him back towards his status (and his treatment by journalists) before 1981. In the short quotation above, however, we can see that, given the opportunity to refer to his pre-presidential self, he makes no mention of the socialist intention which inspired him, referring rather to a deep bond between himself and France and the French. This is a clue to what is happening in the wider discursive arena: Mitterrand is not simply distancing himself from socialism but is also constructing an imagined unmediated bond between himself and the people. He nevertheless admits to being a socialist. We shall come back to this point as it takes on a curious quality which has significant effects upon the notion of the Republic itself. These tendencies are amplified considerably in a television interview in September of the same year[12] where the term 'Français' postively rains down on the interviewers and television viewers. And again there is the deliberate reference to the self: 'Tout mon effort à moi ...... mon rôle comme Président de la République Française ..... c'est de parvenir à réduire cet antagonisme pour réaliser l'union ou le rassemblement des Français pour le redressment national'. These kinds of interventions ring strangely, almost comically, given the attitude of the interviewers; nevertheless, they indicate what the speaker is trying to achieve in terms of creating a different political topography, one in which, eventually, his posited legitimacy comes solely from the people.

In the face of agressive interviewing, very early on Mitterrand develops the ability to reply at length like a finance minister as well as a head of state, arguing figures, reeling off statistics (discussion of economic issues always taking up a significant part of the interviews). This is done in part to demonstrate the speaker's mastery of detail, thus overcoming an earlier criticism (levelled frequently against him when he was the leader of the opposition) that although a good political strategist he was economically untrained. These responses to hard and unsympathetic questioning, and to issues of concern to most people (inflation, unemployment, training schemes, and so on) also have another unexpected effect, namely, the creation of a climate of plain speaking, which over the longer term facilitates a general reorientation of presidential, governmental and party discourse away from 'ideology' and towards the rational and the practical, while also allowing for the eventual development of a new republican discourse.

In the September 1983 interview two things are clear. The first is, as we have pointed out, the deliberate wish to talk of 'practical issues', which are often backed up by corrective interventions of the kind:

> J'observerai que, peut-être, vous avez compté le logement dans l'ensemble de l'investissement...

> Mais vous n'avez pas parlé autant qu'il aurait fallu de la politique industrielle.

And, as we have mentioned, this kind of intervention is consolidated by a quite startling willingness to talk in great detail about economic and financial issues. Over and above this, however, is the idea, repeated several times, that the President must speak to the French: ' J'ai besoin de parler aux Français, de leur montrer ce qu'est la vérité dans leurs affaires'; 'ce que je peux dire aux Français', are two examples among many. It is as if the speaker is trying to get across some kind of message that is being blocked by forces coming between him and the people. The three essential characteristics of these two interviews of June and September, therefore, are the willingness to talk of 'ordinary' issues, the effort to depict the interviewee as enjoying a privileged relationship with the French (this will reappear dramatically in the 1986-1988 period), and the idea of needing to transmit a message to the people. These two main characteristics of Mitterrand's interviews at this time, the attempt to 'answer the questions', and the desire to portray himself as in some kind of special relationship to the French because of the manner of his election, do not always sit comfortably together, interviewers often pulling Mitterrand towards detail and away from rally appeals. For our analysis, it is worth stressing also that Mitterrand's attempts at rally appeals do not particularly involve repeated reference to the Republic or republicanism. They do, however, involve, in the first instance, a retreat from (and, therefore, implicit denial of) French socialism.

Domestic economic crisis, therefore (and the government's record), was the President's Achilles heel, leading him reluctantly from the discussion of grand themes to more mundane matters. By contrast, international crises have the opposite effect, and provide the speaker with enormous scope to enhance his status. In the two years preceding the legislative elections of 1986, the President (although his popularity in the polls was still low) was able to create, as it were, a particular personality for himself, and most importantly for our analysis, *speak* in a particular way (and, because of the nature of the issues, often at some length). Between 1983 and 1985, the Euromissile crisis (the Soviet Union's intention to build up its stock of SS20s being countered by the US's proposed increase in the number of cruise missiles stationed in Europe); the dispute with Libya in Chad which led to French military action; the worsening situation in the Lebanon (where French soldiers had lost their lives); the civil strife between the indigenous and settler communities in France's Pacific territory of New Caledonia;[13] and a row between Prime Minister Fabius and President Mitterrand over a visit to France by the Polish military leader, General Jaruzelski: each of these issues allows Mitterrand to talk not only of grand issues and world affairs but, just as importantly, to focus attention upon himself and, even more importantly, upon the relationship between his own personality and feelings on the one hand, and his presidential function on the other. These normally coincide: it is a personal love of France, and a vision of France's future which guide his presidential undertakings (although not always; for example, he points out that his socialist sentiment must sometimes be subordinated to his non-partisan role).[14] Mitterrand's discursive depiction of external crises always involves the active depiction of his own persona in relation to events. Let us illustrate our argument with a few examples:

(on the Euromissile crisis):
> Je suis par la constitution et par le vote des Français, le garant de l'indépendance nationale et de l'intégrité du territoire, et je remplis la fonction de chef des Armées...: La pièce maîtresse de la stratégie de dissuasion en France; c'est le chef de l'Etat, c'est moi; tout dépend de sa détermination. Le reste, ce sont des matériaux inertes.[15]

(on government policy):
> Ma responsibilité...je le dis sans présomption, c'est la responsabilité de ma fonction, c'est mon devoir vis-à-vis de la France.... Je décide et je choisis, et le reste s'organise et se détermine autour de cette décision.

(on defence):
> Je dois m'exprimer, je dois dire ce que je veux faire, je dois m'expliquer, je dois éclairer ce qui peut paraître confus. Je dois engager les Français sur un chemin qui est souvent difficile, qui exige du courage, de la résolution, de l'effort. Mais la cause en vaut la peine, c'est celle de la France et c'est celle, je le crois, d'une civilisation que j'aime et que je sers.

(on peace):
> Donc ce que dit la France par ma voix compte, je le crois, dans l'évolution de l'opinion universelle.

(On Chad):
> Je suis responsable de la présence de la France dans le monde. [16]

And more generally:
> Si vous voulez bien, je me place sur un plan un peu différent aujourd'hui. Je veux dire que depuis trois ans et demi, je suis Président de la République .... j'en ai en charge la France.[17]

15

These quite dramatic focusings upon the self are clearly attempts to enhance the status of the speaker and lend him an authority by exploiting in domestic discourse the tide of international events. Such focusing, however, has another effect: conferring such *grandeur* upon the speaker and the office of the President means that he is able to begin the elaboration of a further dimension to his persona which will be exploited during the 'cohabitation' years of 1986-1988, namely, that of the keeper of a mysterious secret related to the well-being of the Republic.

It was a development, this time in domestic politics, which began this process of mystification (and which was eventually to dramatically enhance Mitterrand's popularity), namely, and paradoxically, the dawning certainty that the Socialists would lose the 1986 legislative elections, that the right would win them, and that Mitterrand would therefore have to choose a right-wing Prime Minister. This in turn would provoke a constitutional crisis which could threaten the integrity of the Republic itself. The 'cohabitation' period is an intriguing one in terms of analysis. It begins in late 1985, four months before the legislative elections themselves, when Mitterrand steps decisively into the political arena. This move took the form of a press conference on 21 November 1985 followed by three long interviews in the months preceding the elections in March 1986. At the press conference, the President attacks the right and warns it against interfering with the achievements of the Socialist years. He restates his belief in the left and praises its achievements in government. These were the telling headlines on the 8pm radio news that evening:

> La conférence de presse du Président de la République, M. François Mitterrand, défend le bilan de la politique menée depuis 1981. Il affirme sa fidélité aux valeurs de la gauche, et sans jamais prononcer cohabitation, il laisse la porte ouverte à toutes les solutions pour après 86.

Herein lies the paradox: it is at the moment that Mitterrand gets as close as he can to campaigning on behalf of the PS that he, in fact, abandons both it and, arguably, French socialism itself: by warning the incoming right-wing coalition what not to touch, he was effectively moving into negotiation with it and setting down a series of rules concerning *only the Republic's institutions* (as opposed to change within it). The break was further accentuated, and again paradoxically, by Mitterrand's praise of socialism. In such circumstances such praise functioned as a valediction. The doctrinal drama that was to engulf the party subsequently was in part due to the fact that Mitterrand's symbolic abandonment of the party (November 1985) came after he had forced it to empty itself of doctrine in support of him. The President then became free to develop his role as guardian of the Republic's integrity, and defender against all who threatened it either by design or through lack of vision and self-interest.

In each of three interviews before the 1986 election (he had given none since April 1985), the President deploys the same set of ideas: praise of the government's achievements (in the second of the three interviews a quite impassioned praise, and a reaffirmation that he is a socialist), a call to rally the French, and the laying down of the rules of 'cohabitation'. This last point is covered in the first interview on *Europe 1* [18] by his repeated emphasizing of democracy, democratic procedures, 'la loi de la République'[19] and the great loneliness of presidential decision-making. 'Cohabitation' is the result of democracy itself: 'chacun - et d'abord le chef de l'Etat - doit s'incliner devant la volonté des Français. C'est constitutionnel et c'est bien plus que ça: c'est la loi de la République', [20] 'la démocratie c'est tenir compte de la majorité du peuple', and so on. The point here is that this idea of scrupulous observance of constitutional imperatives will be carried into the 1986–88 period, and every act of resistance to and moves against the intentions and prestige of the Chirac government justified on the grounds of constitutional propriety. We can say that, particularly in retrospect, it becomes clear that strict observance of norms becomes a weapon against the political right. Nevertheless, the opposite is also true: that such observance gradually sacralizes the Republic itself to the point where only the functioning of the Republic really matters; the ideologies within it become secondary, if not sometimes irrelevant. As regards the approach of the 'cohabitation' period, it is extremely interesting to note that in his interviews, Mitterrand treats his time in office as a kind of task whose aim is to make the Republic more prosperous and caring. He also treats the approaching 'cohabitation' period as a kind of trial of the Republic whose safety and success *he* must ensure. In this way he also focuses quite specifically upon himself, his role and his task. In the same interview, in answer to the question as to what Mitterrand's *septennat* will have done, he replies: 'Nous aurions crée les

17

conditions d'une démocratie solide et saine en France'. This is a long way from the radical socialism of 1980, and, conversely, a long way down the road to a recasting of the values of republicanism in contemporary France. In the *Europe 1* interview there is a long discussion on TV privatization; Mitterrand then ends the interview by talking very personally about success in his private and public life. Once again there is a highly emotional separation (or is it rather a conflation?) of his personal life and public office:

> Il est important de réussir, comme vous dites, ou plutôt de s'accomplir dans le domaine qu'on a choisi. Cela, c'est très important, et je n'ai pas à m'en plaindre. C'est vrai. Mais tout le reste, c'est peut-être le principal, tout problème que se pose un homme devant la vie et devant sa mort, devant le chagrin, devant la joie, devant l'espérance, ses relations avec les autres, son goût de la nature, les drames qui surviennent, les catastrophes qui les abattent, tout cela, c'est aussi et c'est beaucoup plus la vie. Donc, je ne peux pas dire: j'ai réussi ma vie parce que je suis Président de la République. Disons que sur le plan de la vie politique, ce n'est pas si mal que ça. Mais ce n'est pas la fin du fin non plus, ce n'est pas une fin en soi. Ce qui est important, c'est d'être Président de la République pour hausser son pays, pour assurer son indépendance pour servir les citoyens et pour qu'en fin de compte ... le pays qu'on a dirigé soit en meilleure santé après qu'avant.

For a President who was, effectively, about to lose most of his powers, this is a strange claim to supreme authority. The psychology is intriguing: by alluding in this emotional way to the possession of some kind of supreme authority at a time when his prestige was low. Mitterrand begins to set up a kind of non-identifiable authority over the mystical destiny of France, and amplifies his highly personalized, poetic, and philosophical relation to that destiny.

A week later on television[21] he conveys the same idea of *himself as President* protecting the Republic:

> Je serai [after 16 March] le Président de la République que les Français ont élu en 1981 avec tous les pouvoirs que lui confère la Constitution. C'est aussi simple que cela.

In his final interview before the elections[22] he stresses again his respect for democracy (and suggests that none of his three predecessors was as scrupulous), and in all his answers always talks at great length in terms of protecting France and defending the Constitution (the transcript of this section lasts for twenty pages). He also answers at some length questions concerning the intricacies of the constitutionality of his posture vis-à-vis a hostile National Assembly or government. At the end of the interview he stresses that he will, of course, allow the government to govern.

At this point in our analysis we can see that it is not simply the defeat of 'socialism' which fashions the new discourse, but a series of events which cause Mitterrand to respond in a variety of ways according to his perception of himself and his role. It is clear that by March 1986 his break with 'socialism', except as an occasionally claimed personal conviction, is complete. The logic of the situation, however, raises questions of fundamental importance, given that Mitterrand's justification for establishing distance between himself and socialism was always a constitutional one (i.e. he represented France and the French people, not a party or a doctrine), and had little to do with preparing for the loss of his parliamentary majority in 1986; the point is that the break with socialism dates not from 1986 but from 1981. It is not what happened to socialism that is one of the enigmas of the 1980s but how the socialist movement could believe, or conduct itself as if it believed, that things could be any other way once Mitterrand won the presidency.

Mitterrand's own constitutional posture throughout the 1980s was more or less faultless. This too raises the question of his posture vis-à-vis socialism. It is as if the Republic obliged him to forfeit all aspirations to the kind of socialism the PS advocated in the 1970s, and from the moment he took presidential office he was transformed like Thomas A Becket into the defender of an institution whose guardian he had become. In this way (his austere observance of Fifth Republican ritual, his visit to the Panthéon in 1981 being evidence of this), Mitterrand never, in fact, needed to speak at great length of republicanism itself; it was his willing abandonment of socialism, his self-definition in relation to the institutions and norms of the

Republic, and his general behaviour that were the demonstration of his true attitudes. Let us now look at the 1986-1988 'cohabitation' period to develop this point.

Mitterrand's half-dozen interviews during the time he was President of a hostile government and parliamentary majority are those which see him beginning to employ constantly a whole series of terms including many references to the Republic itself: 'intérêts Français', 'l'Etat', 'les Français', 'la Nation', 'la République', 'la Patrie', 'la démocratie', 'les valeurs', 'la Constitution', 'la loi suprême', 'la France', 'l'indépendance nationale', 'l'intégrité du territoire'; terms such as these are used over and over again, and significantly more often than before 1986.[23]

There are two essential reasons for this shift in Mitterrand's discourse. The first is the obvious and much-commented one that mysteriously looking after France's well-being from above, and speaking always of his role according to the constitution, was all he could do given that his ability to dominate policy and governmental orientation was severely restricted, and his role confined to a near ceremonial one. The second, less obvious at the time, involves the question of his own political strategy to regain his authority. Throughout these interviews, the President continually puts forward the view that only he can see the whole picture, and indeed occasionally conveys the impression that only he is looking after the Republic:

> Finissez-en avec ces méthodes qui nuisent à la République toute entière, a chacun d'entre vous! Finissez-en! La démocratie doit susciter le respect.[24]

This rhetorical style, and the many references to the idea that France must be guided and its true interests safeguarded, will subsequently allow the President to intervene dramatically in the presidential campaign of 1988 and put himself forward as the Republic's shield against the 'cliques' and 'clans'. A part of this style were the continuing self-depictions:

> Je crois que tous les hommes aiment qu'on les aime. Et j'aimerais que la France dans 15 ans - je ne demande rien pour aujourd'hui - m'aime comme elle aime ceux qui l'ont bien servie. Y parviendra-je? Vous jugerez.[25]

It is worth pointing out that the political establishment and wider public were also beginning to centre considerably more upon the Republic itself, partly in response to the rise in popularity and political strength of the extreme right in this period. The occasionally Republican Front-type atmosphere and Mitterrand's role in it would extend into the presidential election campaign itself. The style of his candidacy in 1988, however, was present as early as 1986, and, given what we said above concerning his attitude from 1981, implicit even earlier.

We can note here that Mitterrand also begins to make reference from this time, and with a developing emphasis, to Europe, a theme which would become strongly associated with him after 1988 in his second seven-year term. Reference to Europe pitched all his discourse at a level which transcended party doctrines and evoked the idea of the need for a type of national crusade. We shall come back to this point.

The result of Mitterrand's attitude in his interviews meant that whenever the President opposed Jacques Chirac's government, he appeared to be doing so in the name of a republicanism which was more far-sighted and sacred than the government's self-interest. The accuracy of his own political analysis of the situation and subsequent strategy is testified to by the fact that during the course of 1987 his popularity in the opinion polls soared, as if he were truly the guardian of France's republican integrity during a difficult period. By the time he declared his candidacy for the Presidency of the Republic in March 1988, François Mitterrand was far and away the most popular candidate, and this largely because of his behaviour vis-à-vis the Republic's institutions. He had also distanced himself irrevocably from the Socialist Party which was floundering in factional squabbles as it searched for a new identity and role. (And it is worth pointing out that if the PS were to win the presidency again under another Socialist leader, the PS's role in French politics might be as subservient to the President as it had been in the 1980s; the imperatives of the Republic were, therefore, reaching to the very roots of socialism's raison d'être).[26] This near arrogation of republican virtue by the President of the Republic, which had been developing for at least the previous two years, was deployed vigorously throughout the campaign of 1988. At the personal level, Mitterrand declared his candidacy long after all the other candidates, and only six weeks before the first round of voting on 24 April. In his declaration of candidacy he attacked the 'cliques' and 'clans', thus

21

projecting himself as a shield against threats to the Republic. This kind of stance has, we should note, a long pedigree in French history (and is not, in fact, restricted to republicanism). In his first interview as candidate[27] Mitterrand's dramatization of the situation facing the regime is quite startling:

> Ce que je crains, c'est que si au mois de mai les Français font le choix de dirigeants des partis qui sont les partis intolérants, les partis sectaires, les partis qui veulent tout - je le répète: du pouvoir et de toutes façons - je crains que peu à peu, ne monte dans l'avenir, une sorte de colère sociale ou de refus, que les divisions ne s'accroissent, que l'injustice gagne. Je le crains, alors je le dis.

All the elements are here: the republican virtue (and insightfulness) of the speaker; the clamouring power seekers (there is an implication in Mitterrand's thought that political parties per se are guilty of this); the threat to social harmony; the need to speak out; and the eventual collapse of the Republic if action is not taken. The point we need to make here is that Mitterrand could only behave in this way if there existed to a significant extent a shared set of beliefs about the Republic and the notion of threats to it in the wider political culture.[28] A further point to make here is that Mitterrand's popularity during this period must have been largely based upon a dominant view within French society that the role of President should be of the kind he was fulfilling; he certainly was not successful in the presidential election because he asked the people for a mandate for the kind of presidency his predecessors and he himself in 1981 had offered. Nor did he win because of his behaviour after 1981; but essentially because of his behaviour after 1986: accepting a limited role, allowing the government to govern, intervening here and there to demonstrate a watchfulness concerning the intricate equilibrium in the system as engineered by the constitution, looking after France's interests abroad; in a word, conducting himself according to some *near-ineffable* set of principles, principles that he, in his declarations, maintained at the level of great generality, and therefore ambiguity.[29]

In these campaign interviews, the terms republican (as both adjective and noun) and Republic are legion. Paradoxically, socialism is referred to several times as a personal conviction although not a party allegiance (this

22

of course was not the case in his speeches at the time to PS rallies). The effect of the references to his own socialism is paradoxical; they enhance the persona of Mitterrand because they are like honest admissions (e.g. 'En verité, quel est le Français qui ignore que je suis socialiste?') while neutralizing the accusation that he is partisan. We shall come back to this point in our conclusion. At this time, a great deal of reference is also made to the candidate's own political programme, a highly personalized document in which Mitterrand's ideas concerning the Republic are elaborated.[30] A point worth making here is that one of the major methods used by the speaker to enhance his image as the defender of republicanism, is the creation of the illusion that his role was not a *cause* of change but an *agency* through which change occurred without upheaval. In his second campaign interview[31] he argues that it was his presiding over political *alternance* in *both* 1981 and 1986 which meant that 'la France n'a pas souffert', and 'les Français ne se sont pas divisés outre mesure': 'chaque fois que la menace a été là, moi aussi j'étais là et j'ai veillé. Les Français le savent'.

A further interesting feature in Mitterrand's *Questions à domicile* interview of 31 March 1988 is his admission that his earlier attitude to the presidency had been mistaken in many respects (he had made this point on and off throughout the 1980s); that is mistaken *before* he became President in 1981 (on the idea, for example, of using the presidential elections as a means of proposing a governmental programme). Implicitly, what is being suggested is that *only* he is fit to be President because experience is the essential requirement. In 1988, Mitterrand was the only candidate who a) had been President, and b) was not putting forward governmental proposals as part of his campaign.[32]

From our analysis it is clear that by 1988, the notion of the Republic was once more, after nearly thirty years of relative lack of interest, at the forefront of French political life, and this in great part because of the way Mitterrand had behaved vis-à-vis the consititution, vis-à-vis the political parties, and vis-à-vis the French 'people'. After Mitterrand's resounding victory in the 1988 presidential elections and the PS's ensuing failure to win an outright majority, the notion of a more consensual Republic involving a kind of 'all men of goodwill' attitude emerged quite decisively. It was as if the pendulum had swung dramatically to the left in 1981, equally dramatically back again in 1986, and in 1988 Mitterrand was still there to ensure a transition to a more peaceable, consensual France that would tackle the overriding issues: social justice in France, and French economic effectiveness in the 'Europe of 1992'.

In contrast to this new, pragmatic, more down-to-earth French politics, the mysterious guardian role ascribed to Mitterrand was accentuated in that he withdrew, not from public life, but from the kind of high public profile he had enjoyed throughout the 1980s. It was as if he had a further and even more ineffable chivalric task to perform, the establishment of France's role in Europe, now that he had brought the country through the political storms of the 1980s. After winning his second seven-year term Mitterrand was able to pitch his interviews at a high level of generality, stressing Europe and the need for a united France, while dwelling on international issues more generally. He referred often to 'grandes ambitions' for France, referring always in a detached and now self-effacing way to his own position, even his own succession. And as with the 'external events' and their role in the 1981–86 period mentioned earlier, history itself intervened in 1989, in the shape of the bi-centennial of the French Revolution, to crown Mitterrand's public appraisal of the Republic and republicanism, and his role within it. Two long interviews in particular in 1989 illustrate this change.[33] It is worth going into some detail on these as they are highly revealing of the evolution of Mitterrand's political thought on the eve of the 1990s.

The two interviews, the traditional 14 July interview and an interview with *L'Express* for its 14 July edition, offer us a great deal of information about the kind of Republic Mitterrand envisioned for France. Let us make two contextual points. The first is that Mitterrand (and not, say, a right-winger) was President during the bicentennial year. This allows him to talk in such a way as to equate a general kind of humanist leftist sentiment with republicanism. In this way, the *République sociale* and the *République (tout court)* coincide, at least implicitly in his discourse. With Mitterrand as President, and the ideologically much-travelled Socialists back in power in 1988 with a relative majority, the left (and its 'progressive' allies) can be treated in Mitterrand's discourse as if they are the Republic. There is, therefore, no need for the speaker to go into a detailed argument concerning the relationship between a republican and a socialist view of the Republic itself (as was always formerly the case in left-wing thought). In a malicious reference to the political right (who had boycotted some of the July 14 celebrations) Mitterrand remarks with understated relish:

> Alors, bien entendu, il y a des gens qui ne seront pas d'accord. Ils n'étaient déjà pas d'accord en 1789. Je ne dis pas que ce sont les mêmes, bien entendu, mais enfin il y a des traditions.[34]

The second contextual point is simply that 1989 and the bicentennial allow the speaker to wax lyrical about republicanism; allow him, therefore, not only to substitute it for socialism, and to put forward a particular kind of republicanism, but also to discursively impose, in the late twentieth century, a view that to talk of the Republic and of republicanism is relevant and inspirational, even via the agency of conversation with the world-weary elite of France's TV, radio and press journalists; his enthusiasm sometimes contrasts strongly with their cynicism. But now, with hindsight, the contrast is not between the journalists' realism and Mitterrand's wish to substitute lyricism for it, but between their bemused acquiescence and his effortless control of the interviews and ability to define his views:

> Je sens, j'éprouve profondément l'anniversaire du Bicentenaire de la Révolution. Pour moi, c'est une date majeure, c'est la naissance de la République, c'est la naissance des temps modernes, c'est l'avènement de la démocratie et c'est la France qui incarne cette bataille pour la libération de l'homme.

These ideals are vague but, we might add, no more so than those of any political ideal or ideology, and to them are added the notions of a) the institutions and their proper functioning and b) the role and vision of the leader:

> Les institutions sont totalement respectées. Le governement légifère plus qu'il ne l'a jamais fait. Les débats sont très libres, très ouverts, on le sait bien. Il n'y a jamais eu de procès de presse entre le governement et les journaux, de la presse écrite ou de la presse audiovisuelle.

It is clear from this that Mitterrand is implying that it is only now, since 1988, that 'the Republic' is functioning properly at last; that is, is not simply the Fifth Republic but an approximation to an ideal Republic. We say approximation for two reasons. First, because, as Mitterrand points out in many of his interviews, the Fifth Republic's constitution is not his constitution, and does concentrate too much power in the executive and allows individuals to abuse somewhat the power conferred upon them. The second reason is that nothing is carved in stone. Everything involves the vision, courage, commitment of individuals whose task it is to make the institutions work correctly. The Republic (for Mitterrand and, to an even greater extent, de Gaulle) is fundamentally about people, not institutions. And his own 'vertu' is always underlined (often in contrast to other individuals: de Gaulle, for example:)

> Que l'on me cite un seul cas, au cours de ces huit dernières anneés, où il y aurait eu abus de droit .... Concentration, exercice des pouvoirs .... Il a fallu que je m'en défasse. C'était installé là depuis 1958 dans des proportions qui me choquaient, moi, en tant que républicain.

Mitterrand's Republic is clearly more reverential of institutions and constitutional propriety than was de Gaulle's. Nevertheless, it is a question of degree, and the emphasis upon will and human action and intervention is there, and justifies Mitterrand's many references to himself. On the perfecting of the Republic's institutions:

> Eh bien, je m'efforcerai de bien entendre la voix populaire, d'ajuster exactement les choses comme il faut le faire en République.

Mitterrand's Republic resembles de Gaulle's, moreover, in that the President's authority surpasses all others because of his mystical relationship with the people:

> Il est normal que le Président de la République, Chef de l'Etat, dispose d'une grande autorité .... je pense que j'ai de grands devoirs, mais en même temps j'éprouve une sorte de, comment

dirai-je, de force en moi-même qui m'est donné par le peuple français.

This is, therefore, a Republic maintained not only by institutions but by individuals of vision and courage and their mystical bond with the people. This is a Republic far closer to de Gaulle's than to traditional socialism's. Such a Republic renders elaborate political doctrines such as socialism not only apparently unnecessary but, in fact, dangerous inasmuch as 'republicanism' underpins, creates even, the institutions; republicanism is therefore normative. To a certain extent republicanism here is the functioning of the institutions and the strengthening of republican citizenship, nothing more, nothing less. Socialism on the other hand (like all doctrines which are not the very essence upon which the Republic's institutions are built) destabilizes because it proposes change to what is not only normative but also in a very delicate equilibrium between forces and institutions. Of the two aspects of the Republic in the French context, what we might call the revolutionary and the institutional, it is the latter, the quiet, just, and rational (though beloved) Republic, which is preferred over the insurrectionary.[35]

The President's other big interview of 1989 repeats many of the points regarding both the Revolution and the Republic made in his traditional 14 July interview.[36] Two further points are of interest which bring what we might call Mitterrand's 'new Republic' into closer relationship to de Gaulle's: first, there is the mythification of the people (more generous, in fact, than de Gaulle's) and reference to a host of examples which demonstrate the people's thirst for liberty past and present (most of the interview is on the meaning and relevance of 'liberté'); second, is the notion, often deployed by de Gaulle, that what is at issue in France is an identity and a 'réalité nationale' (as Mitterrand calls it in this interview) which date not from 1789, but go back ten centuries, and of which the Revolution is but one, although perhaps the most important, expression. As with Mitterrand's repeated insistence upon the Republic's institutions, this is in the tradition which perhaps de Gaulle epitomised more than any previous leader in French history: the reconciliation of the republican and the pre-republican. This is in the tradition of Montesquieu rather than Rousseau: 'la liberté n'existe pas à l'état naturelle'; 'Pour préserver la liberté, des institutions sont nécessaires qui arbitrent entre les intérêts et les passions'. Everything in France's history is cherished and everything is dependent upon care and insight and the will to build and preserve.

It is clear that with a discursive climate such as this, socialism could never return to its style of the 1970s. Virtually excluded from the debate, even its role as complementing the Republic was being usurped. The scope left to socialism by the end of the decade seemed very little. Mitterrand's admissions to being a socialist illustrate the point. In many of his interviews the President admits, often as if proudly or else stating a simple fact, that he remains a socialist. The effect of this, curiously, is to domesticate socialism within the Republic. It is reminiscent of the common knowledge that de Gaulle, the Republic's first President, was a practising Catholic. Such professions of faith reinforce the Republic because they restrict themselves to private affairs. The Republic will contain Catholics, it will contain socialists, given the experience of the 1980s it may even tolerate fascists. None, however, will threaten the Republic or call into question its existence or adequacy as a form of regime suited to France's history. Attempts may be made to improve its institutions and bring them closer to an ideal Republic, but whereas before socialism saw itself as somehow going beyond the Republic, by the end of Mitterrand's first ten years in office, it was the Republic which had become the untranscendable spiritual, historical and political entity in French political culture.

Notes

1. Gaffney, J. (1990), 'The Socialist Party' in A. Cole (ed.) *French Political Parties in Transition*, Dartmouth, Aldershot, pp. 61-9.
2. See Bell, D. S. and Criddle, B. (1988), *The French Socialist Party*, Clarendon Press, Oxford, especially chapters 6 and 8.
3. Ibid., p. 152.
4. Even the nationalisations which were widely seen as the evidence of the government's true socialist intentions simply streamlined the industries involved so that by the time they were returned to the private sector by the Chirac government (1986–88), many of them were leaner, fitter, and making a profit.
5. Gaffney, J. (1989), *The French Left and the Fifth Republic*, Macmillan, London, especially chapter 1.

6. Ibid., chapter 7.
7. For a discussion of this complexity, see Nicolet, C. (1982), *L'idée républicaine en France*, Gallimard, Paris; see also Gaffney, J. (1991), 'French Political Culture and Republicanism' in Gaffney, J. and Kolinsky, E. (eds), *Political Culture in France and Germany*, Routledge, London, pp. 13-33.
8. Even the extreme right National Front adapted its discourse in the course of the 1980s to accommodate Republicanism.
9. See Gaffney, J. (1991), 'Political Think Tanks in the UK and Ministerial Cabinets in France', *West European Politics*, vol.14, no. 1, pp. 1-17.
10. In the 1969 presidential elections, the Socialists' candidate, Gaston Defferre, gained a mere 5 per cent of votes cast.
11. *Europe 1*, 26 June 1983.
12. *TFI*, 15 September 1983.
13. Mitterrand avoided as much as possible any reference to the Rainbow Warrior affair in which a civilian died when the French secret service blew up a Greenpeace ship in 1985.
14. Interestingly, in his interview on the 10 May 1984 to *Libération*, a newspaper read widely in socialist circles, Mitterrand uses the terms 'socialist' and 'socialism' many times, this in complete contrast to his omission of the terms in his other interviews given at the time.
15. This and the following quotations are transcriptions from the interview given on the television station *Antenne 2*, 16 November 1983.
16. *TF1*, 12 February 1984.
17. *Antenne 2*, 16 January 1985.
18. A 2 hour interview on *Europe 1*, 9 December 1985.
19. In this interview, Mitterrand further illustrates the authority of presidential office by several references to the dispute with his Prime Minister, Laurent Fabius, over the visit of the Polish military leader, General Jaruselski.
20. *Europe 1*, 9 December 1985.
21. *TF1*, 15 November 1985.
22. *TF1*, 2 March 1986.

23. *Europe 1*, 9 December 1986; *7 sur 7*, 29 March 1989; *RTL*, 16 November 1987; *TF1*, 17 September 1987. To cite but a few examples.

24. *RTL*, 16 November 1987.

25. *Europe 1*, 9 December 1986.

26. On factionalism in the PS at this time see Gaffney, J. (1988), 'French Socialism and the Fifth Republic', *West European Politics*, vol. 11, no. 3, , pp. 42-56. For a general analysis of the presidential election, Gaffney, J. (ed.) (1989), *The French Presidential Elections of 1988*, Gower, Aldershot.

27. *Europe 1*, 25 March 1988. It is interesting to note that on this *Découvertes* programme, the previous interviews had taken place at the Elysée. Here, as a candidate, Mitterrand chose to be interviewed in the studio.

28. Gaffney, 'French Political Culture and Republicanism'.

29. This is often done by use of verbs which have great connotative and little denotative power, e.g. 'gérer la République', 'voir', 'veiller', 'assumer le fonctionnement de la République'.

30. For an analysis of Mitterrand's *Lettre à tous les Français* see Gaffney, J. (1993), 'The Language of Politics' in Sanders, C. (ed.), *France Today: A Socio-linguistics of French*, Cambridge University Press, Cambridge, pp. 185-98.

31. *Questions à Domicile, TF1*, 31 March 1988.

32. The irony here was he could not make more specific proposals because he did not know which parliamentary majority he would be working with. Paradoxically, however, under all the rhetoric of the *Lettre à tous les Français*, approximately seventy proposals can be identified.

33. *A2 & TF1*, 14 July 1989, and in an interview entitled 'Liberté', in *l'Express*, 14 July 1989.

34. This and the following quotations are from the interview on *A2 & TF1* on 14 July 1889.

35. The revolutionary heritage from the 1789–99 period was much debated in the press throughout 1988–89, although not without a certain discomfort within the PS itself.

36. The following quotations are from the interview given to *L'Express* on 14 July 1989.

Bibliography

Bell, D.S. and Criddle, B. (1988), *The French Socialist Party*, Clarendon Press, Oxford.

Cole, A. (ed.) (1990), *French Political Parties in Transition*, Dartmouth, Aldershot.

Cole, A. (1994), *François Mitterrand: A Study in Political Leadership*, Routledge, London.

Cotteret, J-M. et. al, (1976), *54,774 mots pour convaincre*, Presses Universitaires de France, Paris.

Cotteret, J-M. and Moreau, R. (1969), *Recherches sur le vocabulaire du Général de Gaulle : analyse statistique des allocutions radiodiffusées 1958-1965*, Colin, Paris.

Decaumont, F. (1991), *Le Discours de Bayeux, hier et aujourd'hui*, Economica, Paris.

Delahaye, Y. (1979), *L'Europe sous les mots*, Payot, Paris.

Gaffney, J. (1989), *The French Left and the Fifth Republic: The Discourses of Socialism and Communism in Contemporary France*, Macmillan, London.

Gaffney, J.(ed.) (1989), *The French Presidential Elections of 1988*, Dartmouth, Aldershot.

Gaffney, J. (1988), 'French Socialism and the Fifth Republic', *West European Politics*, vol. 11, no. 3.

Gaffney, J. (1991), 'Political Think Tanks in the U.K. and Ministerial Cabinets in France', *West European Politics*, vol. 14, no. 1.

Gaffney, J. and Kolinsky, E. (eds) (1991), *Political Culture in France and Germany*, Routledge, London.

Labbé, D. (1990), *Le Vocabulaire de François Mitterrand*, FNSP, Paris.

Mitterrand, F. (1969), *Ma part de vérité*, Fayard, Paris.

Mitterand, F. (1975), *La paille et le grain*, Paris, Flammarion.

Mitterrand, F. (1977, 1983), *Politique*, 2 vols, Fayard, Paris.

Roche, J. (1971), *Le style des candidats à la présidence de la République*, Privat, Toulouse.

Sanders, C. (ed.) (1993), *A Sociolinguistics of French*, Cambridge: Cambridge University Press.

2 François Mitterrand, France and European Integration

HELEN DRAKE

Introduction

This chapter will examine the path travelled by François Mitterrand during the period between 1981 and 1993 in relation to European integration.[1] It will consider the factors which defined this path, and its likely trajectory into the mid-1990s. In order to do so, we will examine the European legacy inherited in 1981 by Mitterrand, and remind ourselves of the electoral positions he and the Socialist Party (PS) had adopted before coming to power in 1981. We shall then record the unfolding of the Socialists' European choices during the period under review, revealing the nature of the role played by François Mitterrand in interpreting and shaping France's European policy and discourse during those ten years. What we shall see is that as domestic and international contexts evolved, so too did Mitterrand's overt commitment to, and resourcefulness in European affairs, although by the early 1990s, the likelihood that the President would continue to react so flexibly and resourcefully had been called into question, not least by the French themselves.

The legacy

One of the contexts to which François Mitterrand had to respond on coming to power was the European legacy of his predecessors. Valéry Giscard d'Estaing had formalized the regular meetings of Community Heads of State and Government (the European Council) in 1974, contributed to the launching of the European Monetary System (EMS) four years later and to the holding of direct elections to the European Parliament a year after that. He had also maintained close and friendly relations with Germany's leaders. In many respects, Giscard's policy was a continuation of that of his predecessors, Georges Pompidou (1969–74) and Charles de Gaulle (1958–69). The European Council, for example, is considered by some observers as the coming to fruition of de Gaulle's earlier, thwarted plans for a European Community (EC) run by conclaves of national leaders acting outside the formal Treaty framework.[2]

Giscard's emphasis on a strong Franco-German relationship within the EC also echoed de Gaulle's insistence on reconciling France and Germany for the satisfaction and protection of France's interests within the Community and beyond. In other respects, both Pompidou and Giscard had reached beyond de Gaulle's immediate legacy: Pompidou to allow the UK finally to enter the EC in 1973; Giscard to accept that the members of the European Parliament could be directly elected by EC citizens (a development previously blocked by de Gaulle[3]) and to declare that unanimous voting in the EC's Council of Ministers could be relaxed on small issues.[4] The Presidents of the French Fifth Republic between 1958 and 1981 each therefore furthered European integration, and this despite the fact that none of them had in fact embraced the term 'integration' (and even less, 'supranational') into his discourse concerning the EC, and that all had pursued in Europe a policy designed to satisfy short and long-term French interests. The Europe of Jean Monnet, in which supranational institutions would progressively organize the integration of previously national activities, had been seriously challenged since de Gaulle; nevertheless, Europe under de Gaulle and his successors had continued to evolve into a European Community and by 1981, France, with Germany, remained centrally involved in the process.

François Mitterrand, before coming to power, gave no indication that he wished to reverse or impede this process. On the contrary, he clearly believed in France's centrality to Europe, and of the necessity for European integration, and had stressed his own consistently favourable approach to the building of Europe between 1951 and 1981.[5] As First Secretary of the French Socialist Party (PS) from 1971 onwards, Mitterrand had typically represented the pro-integration tendencies of the party and was generally successful in ensuring that compromises between extremes of views within the party were achieved in favour of continued European integration.[6] He portrayed himself as critical of certain of the EC's characteristics, particularly its economic liberalism, but convinced that change could be effected. He held broadly similar views to Giscard, Pompidou and de Gaulle concerning the balance of power between the EC's institutions, and between the EC and its member states, preferring an arrangement tipped in favour of national decision-making and international cooperation. Certain of his proposals for the EC bore the hallmarks and the ambiguities of French socialism in the 1970s. Let us look at these in more detail.

French Socialism and European Integration in 1981

François Mitterrand's 1981 election campaign was fought on the basis of the *110 propositions pour la France,* in essence a mix of declarations of principle and demands for the improvement of France's society, economy and relations with the world. The proposals were derived from the PS's own manifesto for the electoral campaign which had been adopted by the party's executive in January 1981; both contained some references to the EC. In its manifesto the PS called (under a first heading: *paix*) for the full implementation of the Treaty of Rome in order to ensure the Community's solidarity (*cohésion*): EC countries had to close ranks in the face of world bipolarity and Japanese economic competition. There then followed two lengthy sections, headed *l'emploi* and *la liberté*, in which Europe was not mentioned. It re-emerged under the final section of the text (*la France*) where the document stated that the Community should protect France's legitimate interests and allow the French to play a world role, thus guaranteeing France's security.

The same four headings (*la paix, l'emploi, la liberté, la France*) were used to organize François Mitterrand's *110 propositions*. In order for

34

France to be strong within an independent Europe, Mitterrand called in *proposition* 8 for negotiations on European security; in *propositions* 11, 12 and 13, he appealed for the provisions of the Treaty of Rome to be applied more rigorously, specifically in order to make the institutions of the EC more democratic, and to implement the Treaty's social provisions. The EC was to act to protect European jobs and employees' rights; to reform the Common Agricultural Policy (CAP) and the Community's regional policies; and to subject Spain and Portugal's entry to the EC to various preconditions (covering agricultural, industrial, regional and fishing interests). Mitterrand returned to Europe only twice more in his 110 proposals; first, to reiterate France's desire to reform the CAP in order, above all, to ensure fair pay for agricultural workers across the EC; second, to call for greater European solidarity (*cohésion accrue*) within the Atlantic Alliance.

The idea of Europe clearly existed within these documents. However, in comparison to domestic issues *(l'emploi* and *la liberté*) Europe did not stand out. On the contrary, integration was treated as background to the prime domestic concern, unemployment. Moreover, these references to Europe were inserted into texts which were radical in their emphasis on national solutions to France's perceived ills. The reasons for the radical tone of the 1981 Socialist election campaign have been dealt with elsewhere;[7] here we can conclude that the perspective on European integration in the Socialists' and Mitterrand's electoral campaign was one of qualified acceptance.

On coming to power, François Mitterrand did not neglect European affairs. Although the President himself appeared content with minimal personal involvement in European affairs, he invested others with the means to manage European policy. Claude Cheysson was appointed as Head of the Foreign Office (now known as the Ministry for External Relations – *Ministère des Relations extérieures*). Cheysson was a career diplomat with previous experience of European politics; he could therefore be expected to deal competently with European affairs. André Chandernagor was made junior minister (*ministre délégué*) within Cheysson's ministry specifically for European affairs. Other politicians experienced in European matters were also placed by Mitterrand in Pierre Mauroy's governments (Jacques Delors and Maurice Faure for example).[8] Mitterrand's new European team was therefore credible and reasonably experienced, despite the PS having spent the previous twenty-three years in opposition.[9] Nevertheless, the President's judgement (that Europe could be dealt with satisfactorily without his direct intervention, and that Europe would be responsive to Socialist France's proposals for European integration) was to prove misplaced.

The first initiatives

The European Council meeting of Heads of State and Government held in Luxemburg on the 29 and 30 June 1981 provided François Mitterrand with a first opportunity to present his government's programme for Europe. He proposed a series of concrete measures for, essentially, launching the Community into a new phase of integration via the establishment of a 'social European space' (*espace social européen*, a term first used by the Commission of the EC as early as 1968). The term denoted a framework within which increased industrial investment by the EC, and the Europeanization of certain major industrial sectors such as information technology, would safeguard the jobs of Europe's industrial workers; it also implied the acceleration of studies into working practices throughout the Community. These proposals echoed those of Mitterrand's and the PS' election manifestos.

In the formal record of the summit's proceedings published by the *Elysée's* press service, the overall indifference with which these proposals were received is clear; even if, as has been suggested, certain of France's EC partners welcomed them in theory, the Ten together could not agree on concrete measures to implement them.[10] In response to each of Mitterrand's proposals, the European Council had agreed only to look further into the matter; in the language of diplomacy, and in the history of the EC in particular, many ideas couched in such terms have generally not resurfaced.[11] Mitterrand's ideas were nevertheless echoed by Pierre Mauroy, Prime Minister between 1981 and 1984, in his speech outlining governmental policy to the French National Assembly in early July 1981. He included in this address mention of an *espace social européen*, situating this firmly in the context of the EC as the most propitious environment for the resolution of France's own domestic problems. Compared to Mitterrand's Luxemburg paper, however, Mauroy's talk of the need to solve outstanding problems before embarking on new tasks for the Community did indicate a slight shift in the French position towards a realization that concessions, particularly on institutional reform, might be necessary in order to achieve any of the French government's aims in Europe.

This was a thread taken up a month later by André Chandernagor, the junior Minister for European Affairs, when, in an interview given to *le Monde* on 11 August 1981, the Minister explained how France's leaders would consider a more dynamic Commission, and a less systematic use of the national veto in the Council of Ministers, should this facilitate the formulation and adoption of common social policies (aimed primarily at increasing worker participation in company decisions and combatting unemployment). Chandernagor also pointed to the French government's readiness to link its ideas for a relaunch of European integration with negotiations, particularly with the UK, on the much-needed *restructuration* of the EC's budget.[12] Chandernagor's subsequent text, in which he outlined government policy on Europe (the so-called Chandernagor memorandum of October 1981) contained similar ideas.

François Mitterrand and the French Government appeared, then, within months of their arrival in power, to have realized that their approach to EC politics needed revising. Divergences within the PS concerning European integration may be one explanation for the more pragmatic tone of Chandgernagor's memorandum compared to Mitterrand's presentation at the June 1981 Luxemburg summit.[13] Both the French President and government ministers had also been exposed to the type of deals and negotiations which characterized EC politics. More generally, and importantly, François Mitterrand had had a taste of the harsh world of international politics. At the Ottawa G7 summit of industrialized nations in July 1981, for example, Mitterrand had been made to feel uncomfortable due to both his inability to speak English, and the manifest inappropriateness of his calls for a more sympathetic American response to his ideas for international economic reflation.[14] France alone, it appeared, could not achieve all it wanted; with European backing, would it be more successful?

Neither Mitterrand's nor his government's initial initiatives for European integration inspired France's EC partners to visible action. In many respects the lack of positive reaction was inevitable: Europe in 1981 had entered a difficult phase where it was more preoccupied with resolving existing problems than with embarking on new projects. British Prime Minister Margaret Thatcher's liberal market economics were clearly at odds with France's proposals for a more protectionist and interventionist Community policy in the social and industrial fields, this compounded by the United Kingdom's conviction, reinforced after Thatcher's arrival, that not only was the UK contributing too much to the EC's budget, but that that budget itself should not under any circumstances be increased. In addition, Germany was unlikely to wish to participate in action which could threaten its own policy of containing inflation. These were circumstances to which the French Socialists would have to adapt within only two years of forming their administration.

Priorities change

The PS had come to power in June 1981 promising solutions to France's rising unemployment, and a better deal in general for its workers; European integration was of interest insofar as it furthered these specific goals. By 1982, France had on two occasions been obliged to devalue the franc within the EMS, and the government had also had to resort to severe measures to protect the franc against further damage (the most visible of these were wage and price freezes; limits imposed on foreign currency purchase, and obligatory government loans). In addition, the Socialists were losing public support, as measured by regular opinion polls: their plans for reform at home had evidently run into trouble.

 After much internal party debate and presidential deliberation, Mitterrand confirmed his country's commitment to the EMS at the Brussels European Council meeting of Heads of State and Government in March 1983, before publicizing his decision in June of that year via a televised address. This was a decision which acknowledged the extent of France's international economic interdependence, and which would force the French government to pursue economic policies more in line with those of its powerful neighbour, Germany, in order to prevent a further decline of France's competitiveness and trade balance.[15] By personally intervening in government policy-making, and choosing the EC as the essential framework for France's economic policy-making, Mitterrand indicated that integration itself now had to be made to work in France's favour.[16]

Mitterrand's approach implied, correctly, that he would henceforth be paying closer attention to the technicalities of European affairs (generally dealt with by governmental and prime ministerial machinery); he had effectively defined and delimited future governmental action. In particular, Mitterrand's step overtly lent backing to those in the government who had proposed the decision he finally favoured. Foremost amongst them was Jacques Delors, then Minister of Finance and the Economy, who was well known for his pro-integration views. Henceforth, Delors' was the line the government would be obliged to follow, and those in the party in favour of other policy orientations were forced to fall in with this line.[17]

Observers have remarked, nevertheless, that François Mitterrand's increasing focus on European affairs from 1983 onwards was not simply the result of a worsening domestic economic situation, but the continuing effects of his learning curve: in international policy as at home, France was simply not an adequate instrument to bring about desired goals. Thus the areas in which Mitterrand had originally intended to concentrate his efforts (France's relations with the Third World and the superpowers, for example) had proved more problematic than anticipated.[18] Consequently, Mitterrand's intervention in early 1983 in what had previously been mainly governmental decision-making marked the start of a virtually continuous presidential presence and influence in France's policy vis-à-vis European integration, a process which was henceforth openly acknowledged as vital to France's economic survival. Europe would now begin to dominate the presidential agenda, and provide scope for the French President to change the European context within which France was forced to function. Let us consider a number of decisions and texts which illustrate the argument.

1983 was a year in which François Mitterrand and his ministers made a number of key interventions concerning Europe to signal Mitterrand's increasingly close interest in European integration, and to spell out his priorities. In a much analysed, and highly personalized speech delivered to the German *Bundestag* on 20 January 1983, Mitterrand had already set out to convince the new Kohl administration in Germany that Soviet SS20 installations had to be matched with US-sponsored Cruise and Pershing missiles in Europe, and, more generally, of the necessity of Franco-German cooperation within Europe. We shall return later to the role of the

Paris-Bonn relationship in Mitterrand's unfolding European policy;[19] what we can say here is that Mitterrand's approach to the issue of defence signalled an appreciation of one of the realities of European integration: the need to make the Franco-German relationship work.

On another level, that of the EC budget, Mitterrand demonstrated his growing commitment to taking the routine and grind of EC affairs seriously by agreeing to enter into negotiations on the subject. We saw earlier how the President had used the European Council meeting in Brussels of March 1983 to announce to his EC counterparts that France would be remaining within the EMS, despite the domestic economic difficulties that this decision would entail. On the same occasion, he had also indicated his willingness to negotiate on the thorny EC budget issue. He insisted that any long-term resolution of the UK budgetary dispute, overall budgetary reform, or an increase in the EC's resources would have to be matched by a commitment, by the Ten, to new common policies (we should remember that Mitterrand, prior to and following his election as President, had always called for more Community action in the fields of social, industrial and regional policy). One way to advance, he suggested, might be for interested states alone to develop new projects which could be financed outside the Community's budget; a Europe *à géométrie variable* (whereby multiple forms and levels of integration could co-exist).[20]

Mitterrand left it to his ministers to spell out in more detail such revised priorities for Europe. On 12 September 1983, André Chandernagor outlined the government's key priorities for European integration in a memorandum that was similar in form to the one he had issued two years previously. The emphasis in the document, as in 1981, was on the need for the EC to move to a new stage of integration. Unlike its predecessor, this text focused explicitly on the need for common policies in the areas of industry and research. The EC was to undertake more joint industrial projects; work on the harmonization of industrial standards and the protection of new industries; make better use of the EC's lending facilities; work towards the development of the EC's infrastructure, and consider the creation of new, specialized European 'agencies' for the development of projects between EC members who wished to take part and, possibly, non-EC states (this was how *géométrie variable* would operate in practice). As in 1981, Chandernagor's October 1983 memorandum had very little to say concerning institutional reform of the EC and in fact reaffirmed that for

France, common action towards shared goals was to precede discussion or reform of the EC's institutional arrangements; unlike in 1981, it reflected that the French government was now primarily concerned with the modernization and competitiveness of its economy, within the framework of the EC.

Pierre Mauroy's address to the National Assembly of 6 October 1983 on the subject of foreign policy was further evidence of governmental loyalty to the President's attitude towards Europe (he emphasized France's correct and positive behaviour in the EC since 1981 and the importance of the new ideas it had introduced) and, with Chandernagor's memorandum, completed the picture: one from which Mitterrand emerged as the key decider and shaper of France's European policy, once policy in this area was revealed as essential to France's economic health and international credibility. A second dimension to this picture was the governmental reshuffle made by Mitterrand, the most important change of post being the replacement of Pierre Mauroy as Prime Minister by Laurent Fabius in July 1984. The appointment symbolized the beginning of a period in which the modernization of France's economy, and its capacity to compete economically, particularly within the EC, would be stressed. Changes were also made in the personnel concerned directly with European affairs; these reflected Mitterrand's intention to take a far greater personal role in European affairs than had previously been the case. In December 1983, André Chandernagor was replaced at European Affairs by Roland Dumas who, within a year, had become Foreign Minister (*Ministre des Relations extérieures*) in place of Claude Cheysson. Dumas was well known to be a close associate and friend of François Mitterrand; he could therefore be expected to sympathize with subsequent presidential initiatives concerning Europe and, from a position of authority, guide their implementation.

Publicly announcing revised priorities for Europe, and shuffling key post-holders were both signs that the domestic economic difficulties experienced by the Socialist administration during its first two years, combined with François Mitterrand's own instinctive concern for European matters, had brought about a shift in European policy. The state of European integration itself was to provide a convenient platform for these revised priorities.

Towards a new phase of European integration?

We have already said that European integration by the early 1980s had slowed down in the face of innumerable problems, of which the overstretched EC budget, disputes over financing this budget, and the strains of enlargement were the most serious. By the end of 1983, very little significant progress had been made in any of these areas. A minimalist agreement on the UK's budgetary contributions had been reached at the European Council held in Brussels in March 1982, and on farm prices at the end of April in the same year yet, despite the Solemn Declaration of the ten EC Heads of State and Government signed in Stuttgart in June 1983 by which Europe's leaders acknowledged the need for a distinct European identity, the European Council meeting hosted by Greece in December 1983 was generally recognized as a failure, since no concrete breakthrough on any issue was made.

Given France's revised priorities for Europe, and the state of European integration in 1983, it was to prove a fortunate coincidence that France would be taking over the presidency of the EC's Council of Ministers and European Council between January and June 1984. Chairing the Council of Ministers allows a country's ministers to propose initiatives and, to a degree, set the agenda for European integration within a six-month period, whilst chairing the European Council provides a country's Head of State or Government with the opportunity to make personal interventions on the state of integration and, in general, to assume a high public profile, Europe-wide. 1984 would indeed see Mitterrand and his ministers make considerable use of France's turn at the presidency of the EC's institutions.

Mitterrand, in final preparation for the French EC presidency when leaving the Athens gathering of EC Heads of State and Government on 6 December 1983, made a declaration on the state of European integration, depicting himself as a heroic character who, in the name of France and by virtue of his own reputation as a pro-European, was poised to sweep into Europe's institutions where, with vision and determination, he would resolve the Community's outstanding and long-standing difficulties. France, he suggested, would be prepared to make concessions, sacrifices even, in the name of the common European good; all EC members, he suggested, must no longer shy away from discussions of national interest (for example concerning Spain and Portugal's application to the EC); nor should they allow these interests to block progress towards new horizons. As Mitterrand reiterated in his televised New Year wishes for 1984 to the French nation, France's imminent presidency of the EC was an opportunity for Europe to overcome its crisis and relaunch its vocation. The main purpose of the highly rhetorical address after the Athens summit was to convince his EC partners of this. What then were the main events, and the factors most relevant to the outcomes achieved during the six months of the French presidency of the EC's decision-making institutions?

The French presidency of the EC's decision-making institutions, January–June 1984

During the six months of the 1984 French presidency, a number of solutions to long-standing problems were indeed found, and new initiatives launched. The most urgent problems were, to recapitulate: first, the severe strain placed on the EC budget over the previous years which was threatening to bankrupt the Community unless new resources were found; second, the specific British request to find both a long-term arrangement ensuring it would no longer contribute more to the EC's budget than it thought it should, and a method of reimbursing in the short-term the surplus contributions it had already made; third, the question of enlarging the Community to include Spain and Portugal. Other difficulties also existed: for example, the Common Agricultural Policy was in need of serious and long-term reform.

By the end of the French presidency in June 1984, the following decisions had been reached: first, national VAT contributions to the EC budget were to be increased from 1 per cent to 1.4 per cent of VAT revenue from 1986, with the possibility of a further increase to 1.6 per cent from 1988; this would, for a short time at least, increase the overall size of the EC budget. Second, the previously taboo notion of *juste retour* (meaning that any EC member state could expect a rough balance between what it put into the EC's finances and what it received in return) was invoked to regulate the British compensatory problem and became, effectively, standard practice. Third, a decision was made to conclude negotiations on Spanish and Portuguese entry to the EC by the end of September 1984 and, in addition, to increase EC spending in its Mediterranean regions in general. Fourth, new initiatives were launched, in particular via the setting up of two working parties, one to research proposals for a People's Europe (the Adonnino Committee); the other to examine possibilities for reforming the EC's institutions and to review the EC's goals; this Committee was headed by the Irish Senator James Dooge and would eventually lead to the advent of the Single European Act (SEA).[21] The collaborative technological research programme known as ESPRIT was also launched, in February 1984.

On several accounts, therefore, the French presidency was a fruitful one. We have already suggested the principal reason why this was so: François Mitterrand had clearly committed his country to European integration during the most difficult economic times of 1983; now he wished to shape integration as favourably as possible for France. Mitterrand consequently made concessions during the French presidency on behalf of France: having previously maintained a negative attitude towards Spanish entry to the Community, he agreed not only to let Spain in but to hasten the negotiations to do so. He also agreed to accept that the idea of *juste retour*, previously in his eyes an affront to the spirit of the Treaty of Rome, could apply not just to the British budgetary dispute but to any further suitable cases even if, as in this case, the solution cost France money. In return for such concessions, overall spending on the EC's southern and poorest regions would be increased: this would help absorb the impact on French farmers of the entry of Spain to the Community, and of France's increasing contribution to the CAP; furthermore, by making concessions to overcome the obstacles which had halted the progress of integration, the chances of subsequent French-designed initiatives being adopted and financed would be higher.

In order to make such progress, Mitterrand employed to the full the resources and potential of the machinery of the EC presidency. As President of the European Council, he attempted to ensure that the Council only dealt with those matters which needed consideration by all ten Heads of State and Government; other matters were dealt with either on a bilateral basis between national leaders or by lower-level Ministers and their officials. Roland Dumas, for example, then Minister for European Affairs, but effectively Mitterrand's personal envoy, undertook many visits to European capitals prior to the June Fontainebleau summit of Heads of State and Government (at which the majority of the decisions outlined above were reached). Thus certain key issues, such as France's agreement to Spanish EC membership, were dealt with quietly and speedily during the six months. François Mitterrand also used the opportunity provided by the EC presidency to address the European Parliament in May 1984: his speech on that occasion, although it was in many respects ambiguous, was considered to confirm his personal, as well as political commitment to European integration, including institutional reform. The speech certainly signalled Mitterrand's desire to demonstrate the coincidence of French and European interests, and so convince members of the European Parliament of France's unfailing commitment to integration.[22]

European integration relaunched

Following the French presidency, much of what Mitterrand had initiated in the previous six months gained in momentum: above all, the Dooge committee's final report led to the establishment of an Intergovernmental Conference entrusted with drafting a new treaty to incorporate institutional and other changes; this draft treaty, by 1986, had become the Single European Act (SEA). Furthermore, the newly-appointed Commission of the EC in 1985 under the leadership of Jacques Delors published the Commission's White Paper on the Completion of the Single Market which came to be linked, for its successful implementation, to the provisions for institutional reform contained in the SEA. The nature of European integration itself, therefore, was changing more rapidly than for many years, and Mitterrand responded in 1985 with a number of projects bearing his own stamp.

The EC, for example, was to be equipped to play a role in ensuring Europe's (and thereby France's) competitiveness as an industrial and technological power, particularly in the face of growing US and Japanese expertise in these fields. Roland Dumas, in April 1985, spoke of François Mitterrand's ideas for a Europe of technology which would transform Europe into the leading continent of the twenty-first century;[23] these ideas were, moreover, complementary to those which the President had aired during the speech delivered in the Hague in the early stages of the French presidency in 1984 when he called for a Europe capable of launching a manned space station into orbit, as part of Europe's overall defence capability. Mitterrand's specific initiative, designed to make a technological Europe possible, became known as EUREKA: a programme for co-operation in technology amongst EC and other nations outside the framework of the EC's institutions. EUREKA was adopted by the Community in 1985 and, alongside the EC's own programmes for technological research and development (such as RACE and BRITE), was given formal status within the Single European Act.[24]

European integration itself then had indeed entered a new phase during 1985 and 1986; by the end of 1986, the SEA had been signed and ratified by all twelve EC member states (the debate in the National Assembly took place in France in November 1986, ratification in December of that year: 498 votes for, 35 against). France's domestic situation also entered a new phase in 1986.

La cohabitation

Public support for the French Socialists had been on the wane throughout 1985, and in 1986, the PS lost support to the parties of the French right in the legislative elections. As a result, President François Mitterrand, with two years of his first seven-year mandate left to run, found himself faced with a hostile National Assembly, and was forced to choose a Prime Minister from the Rally for the Repubic (*Rassemblement pour la République*), the chief opposition party. This was the situation that became known as *la cohabitation*. One of the most significant consequences of *cohabitation* was that it drove Mitterrand to adopt, in domestic politics, a revised attitude towards his role as President of the French Republic. The impact of *cohabitation* on the relations between the President and the Socialist party on the one hand, and the President and the government on the other has been dealt with in detail elsewhere.[25] Here we should note that Mitterrand's essentially non-partisan role during *cohabitation* also affected his behaviour in European affairs.

François Mitterrand stated on a later occasion that of all the areas where he feared *cohabitation* would be detrimental to French policy-making, Europe was the one which had concerned him most, but that, in fact, the matter had been handled well. Referring in 1988 in his electoral *Lettre à tous les Français* to the 1986–88 period, he wrote that relations had been well managed where, for example, measures designed to implement the Single Market of 1993 were concerned. In terms of the French constitution, François Mitterrand as French President should have continued to act as sole guarantor of France's treaty obligations (and so of the aims of the Treaty of Rome and the Single European Act) and of France's military security, while delegating much of the detailed work of European integration to the government. The reality of *cohabitation* in these institutional terms is not quite as clear-cut: during this time, Mitterrand did lose a good deal of power and access to information where foreign policy, including European affairs, was concerned, and his ability to take initiatives was impàired.[26] Paradoxically, this loss of power led to specific gains for Mitterrand in international relations during this period. Mitterrand's reponse to the constraints of *cohabitation* on his foreign policy activities was to focus on the most symbolic functions of the French President as the legitimate representative of French sovereignty and nationhood and the incarnation of the country's security and destiny. Mitterrand continued, for example, to represent France at the most visible and prestigious international events, such as the G7 summit of industrialized nations in Tokyo in March 1986 and the EC European Council meetings. Such an approach ensured that Mitterrand's standing emerged enhanced, rather than diminished, from the effects of *cohabitation*.

The second *septennat*, 1988

Mitterrand's re-election as French President in 1988 was evidence that *cohabitation* had been positive for him overall. He was re-elected, however, under considerably different circumstances to his initial victory in 1981: as the President of all the French and not of a primarily socialist electorate. But the plans for Europe which he had presented to the French in his electoral document (*Lettre à tous les Français*) largely represented a continuation of what European policy had in fact become, under Mitterrand, during the 1983–88 period. This *Lettre* conveniently provided the President with the opportunity to reveal the extent of France's contribution to European integration during that period, and therefore of the significance of a continued commitment in that direction. There was an overall thrust to Mitterrand's text which was similar to his discourse of the 1984–88 period: Europe was France's chance to modernize and maintain its competitiveness; the prospect of the single European market simply reinforced his point. Continuity with pre-1988 statements was also ensured via Mitterrand's emphasis upon himself, if re-elected President, as the sole legitimate representative of France's EC policy.

Following his re-election as President of the Republic in May 1988, Mitterrand's revitalized commitment to Europe, as spelt out in his *Lettre à tous les Français,* gave rise to concrete initiatives. First, Michel Rocard as Prime Minister and Edith Cresson in charge of European Affairs had a clear brief to prepare France for 1993. Cresson's subsequent appointment as Prime Minister in May 1991 was also made explicitly with this aim in mind. Second, Mitterrand's re-election coincided fortuitously with France's second turn since 1981 at holding the French presidency of the EC's Council of Ministers and European Council (from July to December 1989); as in 1984, François Mitterrand used the opportunity to launch policy initiatives; as in 1984, European elections were scheduled for the same year (although in 1989 they were held just before and not during the six-month presidency) and this time saw the French Socialist Party making great display of its loyalty to presidential choices, especially those concerning Europe.

Mitterrand set his priorities for the 1989 EC presidency in the first press conference of his second seven-year presidential term on 18 May 1989: progress on Economic and Monetary Union (EMU); introduction of the Social Charter (for the protection of workers' rights); developments in EC cultural, audiovisual and environmental policy, and a citizens' Europe. Some progress was made in several of these areas: the Social Charter was adopted by eleven of the twelve Heads of State and Government in December 1989 (the UK refusing to join its partners); a European Environmental Agency was to be created in 1990; *assises* on audiovisual policy were held, and agreement on a broadcasting directive assured. Moreover, a compromise was reached on EMU which was also adopted (by all member states with the exception of the UK) at the European Council summit in Strasbourg, held on 8-9 December 1989 to conclude the French presidency. Furthermore, Mitterrand gained agreement from his partners for the convening, in 1991, of an Intergovernmental Conference on EMU.

Against the background of a relatively calm domestic and international situation between the re-election of François Mitterrand as French President in May 1988 and the mid-term of the French EC presidency in autumn 1989, France's European policy did indeed progress along the continuum begun in the mid-1980s: Mitterrand took policy initiatives subsequently elaborated by the French Socialist Party and government; the President was backed up by openly pro-European government ministers; the Single Market of 1993 was steadfastly portrayed as an opportunity both for France and was thus seriously pursued (although it was invariably referred to as being in need of a constant rebalancing in favour of its social and cultural provisions). Many of France's specific priorities had been tackled (Economic and Monetary Union; collaboration in research and development; the drafting of a Social Charter); France's general call, in the mid-1980s, for a relaunch of European integration had also taken effect. Unforseen changes, however, both internal and external to the EC and its projects for 'ever closer union',[27] began to occur in the autumn and winter of 1989, and were considerably to affect Mitterrand's ability to influence European policy from then on.

Europe transformed

We have said that shaping circumstances themselves was a strong point of Mitterrand's, for example in 1984 during the French presidency of the EC's Council of Ministers and European Council. But when circumstances were less susceptible to manipulation, because unexpected or, effectively, beyond French control, Mitterrand's stance towards European integration was to become markedly less confident.

We saw that France's second period of chairing Europe's decision-making institutions came to an end at the Strasbourg summit of EC Heads of State and Government in December 1989. At the top of the agenda at this European Council gathering was discussion of the events which had taken place in Central and Eastern Europe, namely the fall of the Berlin Wall, and the revolutions in certain of the European Soviet satellite states. This was the occasion for François Mitterrand to conjecture on the future nature of the EC and European integration following such momentous political change.

In November 1989, François Mitterrand had already indicated that he believed the prospect of German unification to be distant; in December, he stated that the nations of Eastern and Central Europe would be best dealt with by a 'confederation' of European states. On both counts, the French President's view was subsequently contested: in the case of Germany, by events themselves; in that of the newly-democratizing European nations, by their own interpretation of Mitterrand's 'confederation': an attempt to hold them at arms' length from Community membership for several years.

Mitterrand had always paid considerable attention to the Franco-German relationship and was fully aware, as we have seen, of the need for good and strong ties between the two partners within the Community. The relationship had not been without tension but, overall, had been constructive thanks in part to the bi-annual summits of French President and German Chancellor, and the upgrading of the 1963 Franco-German Friendship Treaty throughout the 1980s. Nevertheless, several observers noted that German unification was the first development within Europe since 1981 on which Mitterrand failed to display the skills of adaptability to which we referred above.[28] Much of France's activity in the EC following the winter of 1989 appeared to centre on a single objective; ensuring that Germany's commitment to European integration did not wane as its commitment to German unification grew. But this activity did not constitute a firm, confident policy. Joint Franco-German plans for accelerating European political union were, for example, overshadowed by differences between the two leaders concerning the balance between the EC's institutions in such a Union, how to deal with the Yugoslavian civil war, and what the link should be between the countries of East and Central Europe and the Community.[29]

Whereas the eight years leading up to 1989 saw Mitterrand reacting to shifting circumstances by taking definite action within Europe, the two years from 1989 to 1991 were different. Indeed, after 1989, and particularly during 1991, Mitterrand's legitimacy to deal with circumstances in this way was called into question at home. This partly coincided with a generalized political dissatisfaction in France directed towards a government, party and President who, many felt, had finally been emptied of their drive and direction as the result of having spent too long in power, and this without having overcome the seemingly insoluble domestic problem of unemployment. Despite a nationally popular response to the Gulf War, the shock of German unification and Mitterrand's perceived impotence vis-à-vis his German counterpart over the issue (as well as the unpopular appointment of Edith Cresson as Prime Minister to replace Michel Rocard in May 1991, and an ill-considered response to the Soviet coup in August of that year) damaged Mitterrand's credibility, certainly in the eyes of the French, in European as well as domestic affairs.

Mitterrand attempted on several occasions during the second half of 1991 to regain the initiative in European policy, and to win back the confidence of the French. He gave a press conference in September 1991 in which he explained the most recent of his foreign policy choices (particularly concerning the Soviet Union). In October 1991, he announced, with German Chancellor Kohl, joint Franco-German plans for the beginnings of a common defence policy. In October and November 1991, the French President gave a series of radio interviews in which he responded in familiar terms to questions concerning Europe: Mitterrand's own past ensured his unswerving commitment to European integration; the Franco-German friendship was unaffected by events, and in fact was closer than ever before; France needed Europe and Europe needed France.[30]

The Maastricht European Council summit of 9-10 December 1991 led to Mitterrand's appearing on television, on 15 December 1991, on the programme *7 sur 7* in order to reinforce what he considered to be a successful outcome to that European Council: an irreversible commitment by eleven of the twelve EC members to implement a single currency by 1999 at the latest (the UK having negotiated an opt-out); and an agreement, again by the Eleven, to finally enforce many of the provisions set out throughout the 1980s by François Mitterrand and his ministers for better working conditions for employees throughout the Community. In fact, much that was decided at Maastricht did indicate that at the end of 1991, France had gained satisfaction on many issues, including defence and EMU, for example.[31]

Despite these real successes, and Mitterrand's attempts to reimpose himself in European affairs, opinion polls during late 1991 showed consistently low support for the President amongst the French. It appeared that Mitterrand, by early 1992, was wounded by events to the extent that he would not be able to make sufficient political capital out of Maastricht, or of the fact that France largely represented the majority of EC states concerning the future of European integration. It was certainly the case that in the months following the signature of the Maastricht Treaty, the first real signs of concern, if not dissent, relating to the Treaty's implications for France as a sovereign nation, began to appear.

These were aired in an unprecedented fashion in May 1992 in the context of the parliamentary procedures deemed necessary for constitutional reform prior to the ratification of the Treaty, although they were particularly harmful to the opposition parties, between and within which fundamental differences concerning European integration were made painfully public. Then on 2 June the Danish people, voting by referendum, unexpectedly declined to ratify the Treaty. Mitterrand's reponse was to proceed to ratification in France nevertheless, but by referendum, rather than via parliament. Henceforth the debate in France was to intensify, as the process of European integration looked set once more to put traditional patterns of French politics to the test. Mitterrand's success in forcing the pace of European integration, and in maintaining a consistently high political profile for it in France was, paradoxically, to create one of the most significant trials of his own legitimacy during his long presidency.

Conclusions

To some extent, Mitterrand's declining popularity, and the way in which this spilled over into the results of the French referendum on the ratification of the Maastricht Treaty (only the narrowest of majorities voted in favour of Maastricht),[32] were representative of a more generalized shift in the political climate throughout the EC. Public opinion, unsettled by economic recession and the political uncertainties of Eastern and Central Europe, began to question the benefits of European integration, and so too their leaders' positions towards integration; in this respect, France was no different from its neighbours.

More specific to France, however, was the fact that Mitterrand, having associated himself so closely with the fortunes of Europe during his two presidential mandates, was bound to suffer once European integration itself got into difficulty. In this respect, the outcome of the French referendum demonstrates how closely the fortunes of a political leader and a policy choice may be bound. Furthermore, Mitterrand's image had by the early

1990s become discredited in public opinion along with that of his Socialist administration, for a number of reasons (continuing high unemployment and political scandals amongst others), and the Socialists' defeat in the legislative elections of March 1993 was in this context no surprise. Arguably, it occurred in spite of, rather than because of, the Socialists' and Mitterrand's positions on Europe.

The referendum revealed that the French public and political class alike were divided over Europe, and that these divisions cut across traditional party lines. Such a situation implied that Edouard Balladur's government, formed in April 1993 of ministers drawn from the majority of the parties of the right in the National Assembly (and which ushered in a second period of *cohabitation* for François Mitterrand), was unlikely to embark upon an entirely new, partisan path regarding European integration. By the same token, the *présidentiables* (the contenders for the presidential elections of 1995) would have little room for manoeuvre when outlining their European policy proposals.

Continuity in France's role in European integration also seemed likely in terms of France's continued political leadership role within the Community. By mid-1993, Germany had still not settled into a position from which it could convincingly, or legitimately, claim to be leading the Community; Great Britain had still not ratified the Maastricht Treaty, and many EC countries were undergoing serious domestic political turbulence (such was the case of Italy and Spain, for example), which precluded them from offering an immediately acceptable model for European political leadership. In this context, we shall conclude with two remarks concerning the factors of continuity underlying Mitterrand's European position, and the consequences of these for the *après-Mitterrand* era.

First, we have seen throughout this chapter how the institutional organization of the French Fifth Republic was instrumental in shaping France's role in European integration during the period 1981-1991. François Mitterrand came to lean heavily on the office of President of the Republic in representing European policy, and in particular on its symbolic function as the legitimate voice of France's sovereignty; this was evident during the period of *cohabitation* between 1986 and 1988, as well as during the months (in 1984 and 1989) when France chaired the EC's principal decision-making institutions. But the presidency not only allowed Mitterrand symbolically to represent France in Europe; it also meant that he could decisively and visibly intervene in French policy-making on occasions where policy decisions had to be taken. Publicly opting in 1983 for economic policies which respected the constraints of European integration is the obvious example of such intervention.

Second, it was a fortunate coincidence that in many respects the EC's decision-making system itself corresponded closely to the presidential characteristics of France: the role of the European Council and the notion of the EC presidency in particular provided Mitterrand, as Head of State, with the opportunity to champion France's European preferences within the EC, and to a certain degree ensure that EC policy closely resembled French policy choices. These prevailing institutional arrangements for the EC (where national leaders preside and decide) were consistently favoured, not only by François Mitterrand between 1981 and 1993, but by his predecessors de Gaulle, Pompidou and Giscard d'Estaing, as well as by France's major political parties.[33] All resisted moves to reform the Community's institutions in ways which would allow for more supranational decision-making. François Mitterrand made his own views clear on several occasions during the 1981 to 1991 period, for example during an interview he gave to the radio station *Europe 1* on 10 November 1991. In this interview, Mitterrand stated that the role of the European Council was to represent Europe's citizens, because only national leaders were directly in touch with respective national opinion. On other occasions he had explained how in his view the Commission's role, in comparison to that of the European Council, was to provide technical and specialist expertise, and that of the European Parliament to control the Commission.[34]

Mitterrand was nevertheless, as we have seen, instrumental in bringing about the Single European Act, which dictated that more decisions could be taken by majority vote in the Council of Ministers, thus removing a measure of national sovereignty from each EC member state and allowing the Commission a greater role in arbitrating between the various national positions in order to reach a decision. It was also while Mitterrand was French President (at the EC Maastricht summit in December 1991) that agreement was reached by the twelve to increase the powers of the European Parliament in the EC's legislative process. Nonetheless, part of Mitterrand's strategy in these cases was to exact concessions, in the form of progress on concrete projects, in return for agreeing to such developments. It was also, paradoxically, partly due to Mitterrand's success in setting new goals for integration during the 1980s that both the developments cited above (increased majority voting and a greater legislative role for the EP) became inevitable.

François Mitterrand perceived himself as being a European, and on many occasions during the 1980s pointed to his presence at the earliest post-war gatherings of Europeans,[35] and to his consistently pro-European stance vis-à-vis the milestones of European integration as proof of his deep understanding of the necessity for European integration, and as an explanation of his possessing a vision of how Europe should look. As a rhetorical tool, such references to his past clearly marked Mitterrand off from virtually all other European leaders: only he could claim such involvement in the history of the EC. By 1991 he was also the longest-serving national leader within the EC and so able to draw on considerable experience and expertise. This, according to some observers, bred confidence in the French President as it gave him an influence that no other European leader enjoyed: a near-certainty that he would have the time to see his proposals through to fruition.[36] We will limit ourselves to the observation that the combination of institutional arrangments (a strong French presidency constitutionally committed to a strong say in European policy), Mitterrand's understanding of these arrangements to build himself a prestigious image, and his own sense of first-hand experience of European affairs, allowed him credibly to represent France's European positions and initiatives throughout the decade, to the extent where much literature on European integration concurs in attributing much of the momentum surrounding the Single Market initiative to the French President and his success in using the Single Market and 1992 as a "mobilizing myth" to win the support of his party, the political opposition and the French public.[37]

Mitterrand's successors to the presidency may not share Mitterrand's personal history of involvement with the creation of a more united Europe. But they will inherit a political culture which has shaped France's position towards European integration throughout the Fifth Republic, including during Mitterrand's presidency, and enabled it to influence the course of integration. Subsequent French presidents will be engaged in EC institutions and policy-making which have thus been shaped, at least partially, by François Mitterrand as President of France. These factors will guarantee a minimum of continuity in France's future role in European integration.

Notes

1. By 'integration' is meant the process, begun in 1951 with the establishment of the European Steel and Coal Community, by which an increasing number of West European countries legally committed themselves to decide jointly on common action in defined areas via the creation of institutions complementary to those of the national political systems. It is a process which has largely defied attempts at normalization and which is marked by its unique character when compared to existing models of political organization. It is a term in fact rarely used by French leaders, and François Mitterrand was no exception, due to its connotations of loss of national sovereignty in policy and decision-making. It is used in this chapter as a convenient shorthand term for the process by which the EC has progressively become a polity of increasingly interdependent member states.

2. See, for example, Formesyn, R. (1984), 'Europeanisation and the Pursuit of National Interests' in Wright, V. (ed.), *Continuity and Change in France*, George Allen and Unwin, London, p. 234. Formesyn suggests that Giscard d'Estaing successfully established much of what de Gaulle had hoped for when masterminding the Fouchet Plans of 1961 and 1962.

3. It should be added here that Giscard played down the significance of this particular development as simply a new means of designating the members of the EP whose powers were, in any case, limited by the Treaty of Rome. See Formesyn, 'Europeanisation', p.227.

4. See Giscard d'Estaing's press conference of 24 October 1974.

5. See Mitterrand, F. (1980), *Ici et maintenant*, Fayard, Paris, pp. 253-4.

6. See Bell, D.S. and Criddle, B. (1988), *The French Socialist Party: the Emergence of a Party of Government*, 2nd edition, Clarendon Press, Oxford, pp. 69-70.

7. See Cole, A. (1989), 'François Mitterrand: From Republican Contender to President of all the French' in Gaffney, J. (ed.), *The*

French Presidential Elections of 1988: Ideology and Leadership in Contemporary France, Dartmouth, Aldershot, pp. 40 and 44. The author explains the electoral strategy behind François Mitterrand's *110 Propositions*, in particular the need to ensure Communist electoral support on the first ballot; that of centrist supporters on the second.

8.   Jacques Delors was Chair of the European Parliament's Economic and Monetary Affairs committee at the time of his appointment to Mauroy's government; Maurice Faure was a co-signatory (with Christian Pineau) of the Treaty of Rome.

9.   Of note is the fact that, in keeping with the President's intention to concentrate European policy-making within the *Quai d'Orsay*, the General Secretariat of the Interministerial Committee on European Questions *(Secrétariat général du Comité interministériel - SGCI)* was moved from Prime ministerial to External Relations ministry control. This was considered by those working for the SGCI to have been a mistake. See Grosser, A. (1989), *Les Affaires extérieures. La politique de la France 1944-1989*, Flammarion, Paris, p. 307.

10.   See Formesyn, 'Europeanisation', p.238. The author states that although the smaller of the Community states, along with Italy, were sympathetic to Mitterrand's 'new French topics for reflection', Chancellor Schmidt of Germany and British Prime Minister Thatcher were sceptical.

11.   See *Résumé des travaux du Conseil européen, Luxembourg 29 et 30 juin 1981*, Présidence de la République Française, Service de Presse. See also (1982), *L'Année politique, économique et sociale en France 1981*, Editions du Moniteur, Paris, p. 244.

12.   *Le Monde*, 11 August 1981.

13.   See *L'Année politique 1981*, p.244. Ministers such as Delors began campaigning very soon after May 1981 for a more conciliatory and realistic approach to the EC.

14.   Giesbert, F-O. (1990), *Le Président*, Editions du Seuil, Paris, p. 364; Favier, P. and Martin-Roland, M. (1990), *La décennie Mitterrand 1: les Ruptures (1981-1984)*, Seuil, Paris, p. 242-9, point to the lack of common ground between the American and French leaders over economic policy, despite the relatively good personal relationship established between Presidents Mitterrand and Reagan.

15. It was also a decision which ensured that Mitterrand would not find himself at the mercy of the left wing of his party. See Keohane, R. and Hoffmann, S. (1990), 'Conclusions: Community politics and institutional change' in Wallace, W. (ed.), *The Dynamics of European Integration*, Pinter, London, p. 288.

16. Of interest is the perspective of Moreau Defarges, P. (1985), '..."J'ai fait un rêve...". Le président François Mitterrand, artisan de l'union européenne', *Politique étrangère*, vol. 2, p. 365. He suggests that ever since the 1930s, France has continually had to make choices about Europe. See also Duhamel, O. (1991), *De Gaulle - Mitterrand: La Marque et la Trace*, Flammarion, Paris, p. 108; Giesbert, p. 197, who both interpret Mitterrand's intervention in 1983 as a sign that the President had in fact made a decisive break with socialism.

17. They favoured the "(...) defence of purchasing power, higher investment, and - to protect the balance of payments - a withdrawal from the EMS, aid to exports and the introduction of import controls." Bell and Criddle, p. 255.

18. See Levy, D.A.L. (1987), 'Foreign Policy: Business as Usual?' in Mazey, S. and M. Newman, (eds), *Mitterrand's France*, Croom Helm, London, pp. 183-6.

19 See Moreau Defarges, 'J'ai fait un rêve', p. 366-7; Grosser, *Affaires extérieures*, p.303 for a discussion of this speech and its significance.

20. Taylor, P. (1989) in his chapter 'The New Dynamics of EC integration in the 1980s' in Lodge, J. (ed.), *The European Community and the Challenge of the Future*, Pinter, London, has suggested this was a tactic to persuade others, notably the UK, to negotiate, particularly as Mitterrand in fact also employed the term *à deux vitesses* (a two-tiered Europe) to describe a possible way forward: this carries the connotation of less enthusiastic member states (Britain for example) being left behind.

21. François Mitterrand had appointed his own personal representative to this committee, Maurice Faure, a politician highly experienced in and favourable to European integration rather than a government envoy, as was the case with France's partners.

22. The speech itself is reproduced in Mitterrand, F. (1986), *Réflexions sur la politique étrangère de la France. Introduction à vingt-cinq discours*, Fayard, Paris, pp. 280-97; for commentary see *Agence*

Europe, 30 May 1984, editorial p.1; Burgess, M. (1989), *Federalism and Political Union: Political Ideas, Influences and Strategies in the European Community 1972-1987*, Routledge, London, pp. 183-6. It is also worth noting that the second direct elections to the European Parliament were to be held during the French presidency in June 1984. In that the election campaigns in France led to much inter- (and intra) party conflict, the fact that he held the Presidency of the EC allowed Mitterrand to be seen by the French to rise above these conflicts and represent France as a whole within Europe's institutions. This was a stance which was to be beneficial later during the so-called *cohabitation* period between 1986 and 1988 and to which we shall return. In terms of providing a measure of the prevailing support, or lack of it, for Mitterrand and the Socialist government, the elections were also significant, and provide some explanation for the positive tone of Mitterrand's speech to MEPs in May 1984. See Saint-Ouen, F. (1986), 'Les partis politiques français et l'Europe: système politique et fonctionnement du discours', *Revue française de science politique*, vol. 36, no. 2, pp. 205-26.

23. *L'Annee politique 1983*, p.208.
24. This was a practical case of Mitterrand's suggestions for a *géométrie variable* form of integration, and was to a large extent a direct response to the USA's Strategic Defense Initiative (Star Wars) launched by Ronald Reagan around this time and in which other EC member states, notably Germany, had expressed interest.
25. Cole, 'François Mitterrand'.
26. Cohen, S. (1991), 'François le Gaullien et Mitterrand l'Européen', *Histoire*, April (*Les Années Mitterrand*), p. 21; Wells, S.F. (1988), 'Les Politiques étrangères de Mitterrand. Bilan d'un premier septennat', *Commentaire*, vol. 11, p. 665.
27. The term employed in the preamble of the Treaty of Rome to describe the EEC's ultimate goal.
28. Much has been written on this period (November 1989 to late 1991) and Mitterrand's reaction to German unification, in the context of European integration. See in particular Fabra, Paul, 'Mitterrand-Metternich' in *Le Monde*, 3 July 1991; Audibert, Dominique, 'Mitterrand en marge de l'histoire' in *Le Point*, no. 991, 14 September 1991; Duhamel, A., *de Gaulle-Mitterrand*, pp. 91-115;

Cohen, 'François le Gaullien', p. 31; Giesbert, *Le Président*, p. 378-9; Drake, H. (1991), *L'unification des deux Allemagne* in ACTIF , Birmingham AMLC, p. 2.

29. See *L'Année Politique 1990*, pp. 221, 224-5 for an outline of the joint initiatives taken by Mitterrand and Kohl during 1990 in the field of political union, foreign and defence policy.

30. Interviews with *France Inter*, 22 October 1981 and *Europe 1* radio stations, 10 November 1991.

31. *Lettre de Matignon*, no. 363, 17 December 1991.

32. The results: 'Yes' votes: 51.04 per cent of votes cast; 'No' votes: 48.95 per cent of votes cast.

33. In the case of France's political parties, see Saint-Ouen, F. (1990), *Les Partis Politiques et l'Europe: une approche comparative*, Presses Universitaires Françaises, Paris, p. 102.

34. For example, see Mitterrand's interview with *Le Monde* on 20 June 1990.

35. See for example Mitterrand's speech delivered in The Hague on 7 February 1984 in Mitterrand, *Réflexions*, p. 267.

36. See Formesyn, 'Europeanisation', p. 238; Hayne, M. (1989), 'The Quai d'Orsay and the Formation of French Foreign Policy' in Aldrich, R. and Connell, J. (eds), *France in World Politics*, Routledge, London, p. 198.

37. See Hayward, J. (1990), 'Ideological Change', in Hall, P.A., Hayward, J. and Machin, H. (eds.), *Developments in French Politics*, Macmillan, Basingstoke, p. 29 for a discussion of this 'mobilizing myth'.

Bibliography

L'Année Politique, économique et sociale en France, Editions du moniteur, Paris, all years 1981-1991.

Aldrich, R., and Connell, J. (1989), *France in World Politics*, Routledge, London.

Bell, D.S., and Criddle, B. (1988), *The French Socialist Party: The Emergence of a Party of Government,* Clarendon Press, Oxford.

Burgess, M. (1989), *Federalism and Political Ideas. Influences and Strategies in the European Community 1972-1987,* Routledge, London.

Chapsal, J. (1990), *La Vie Politique en France de 1940 à 1958,* Presses Universitaires de France, Paris.

Chapsal, J. (1990), *La Vie politique Sous la Ve République 1: 1958-1974,* Presses Universitaires de France, Paris.

Chapsal, J. (1990), *La Vie Politique sous la Ve République 2: 1974-1987,* Presses Universitaires de France, Paris.

Cohen, S. (1991), 'Entretien avec Samy Cohen: François le Gaullien et Mitterrand l'Européen', *L'Histoire,* April (Les années Mitterrand 1981-1991).

de l'Ecotais, Y. (1990), *Naissance d'une nation,* Bernard Grasset, Paris.

de Ruyt, J. (1989), *L'Acte unique européen,* Editions de l'Université de Bruxelles, Brussels.

Delors, J, and Clisthène (1988), *La France par l'Europe,* Bernard Grasset, Paris.

Drake H. (1991), 'L'unification des deux Allemagne: quelle signification pour la politique communautaire de la France?', *ACTIF,* Aston Modern Languages Club, February.

Drake, H. (1991), 'Political Parties and European Integration', *ASM&CF Review,* no 47, October.

Duhamel, A. (1991), *De Gaulle-Mitterrand: La marque et la Trace,* Flammarion, Paris.

Duhamel, O., and Jaffré, J. (1987), *Le Nouveau Président,* Seuil, Paris.

Favier, P., and Martin-Roland, M. (1990), *La décennie Mitterrand I. Les Ruptures (1981-1984),* Seuil, Paris.

Featherstone, K. (1988), *Socialist Parties and European Integration. A Comparative history,* Manchester University Press, Manchester.

Formesyn, R. (1984), 'Europeanisation and the Pursuit of National Interests' in Wright, V., (ed.), *Continuity and Change in France,* George Allen and Unwin, London.

Gaffney, J., (ed.) (1989), *The French Presidential Elections of 1988. Ideology and Leadership in Contemporary France,* Dartmouth, Aldershot.

Giesbert, F-O. (1990), *Le Président,* Editions du Seuil, Paris.

Grosser, A. (1989), *Affaires extérieures. La Politique de la France 1944-1989,* Flammarion, Paris.

61

Hall, P.A., Hayward, J., and Machin, H., (eds) (1990), *Developments in French Politics,* Macmillan, London.

Keohane, R. and Hoffmann, S. (1990), 'Conclusions: Community politics and institutional change', in Wallace, W. (ed.), *The Dynamics of European Integration*, Pinter, London.

Lemaire-Prosche, G. (1990), *Le PS et l'Europe,* Editions Universitaires, Paris.

Lodge, J. (ed.) (1989), *The European Community and the Challenge of the Future*, Pinter, London.

Ludlow, P. (1989), *Beyond 1992: Europe and its Western Partners*, Centre for European Policy Studies, Belgium.

Mazey, S. and Newman, M. (eds) (1987), *Mitterrand's France,* Croom Helm, London.

Mitterrand, F. (1980), *Ici et Maintenant,* Fayard, Paris.

Mitterrand, F. (1986), *Réflexions sur la politique extérieure de la France. Introduction à vingt-cinq discours (1981-1985),* Fayard, Paris.

Moravcsik, A. (1991), 'Negotiating the Single European Act: National interests and conventional statecraft in the European Community', *International Organization,* Winter, Vol. 45, no. 1.

Moreau Defarges, P. (1985), 'J'ai fait un rêve... Le Président François Mitterrand, artisan de l'union européenne', *Politique étrangère,* vol. 2.

Pinder, J. (1991), *European Community: The Building of a Union*, Oxford University Press, Oxford.

Pryce, R. (ed.) (1987), *The Dynamics of European Union*, Croom Helm, London.

Robin, G. (1985), *La Diplomatie de Mitterrand ou le triomphe des apparences 1981-1985,* Editions de la Bièvre, Paris.

Saint-Ouen, F. (1990), *Les Partis Politiques et l'Europe: Une approche comparative,* Presses Universitaires de France, Paris.

Saint-Ouen, F. (1986), 'Les Partis politiques français et l'Europe: système politique et fonctionnement du discours', *Revue française de science politique,* Vol. 36, no. 2.

Sandholtz, W. and Zysman, J. (1989), '1992: Recasting the European bargain', *World Politics,* part 42, October.

Sloot, T. and Verschuren, P. (1990), 'Decision-making Speed in the European Community', *Journal of Common Market Studies,* Vol XXIX, no.1, September.

Wallace, H., Morgan, R. and Bray, C. (1986), *Partners and Rivals in Western Europe: Britain, France and Germany,* Tower, London.

Wells, S.F. (1988), 'Les politiques étrangères de Mitterrand. Bilan d'un premier septennat', *Commentaire,* no. 11.

Zorgibe, C. (1986), *Le Chef de l'Etat en question. Scénarios de cohabitation ou de séparation,* Editions Atlas Economica, Paris.

3 A House Divided: Socialism *à la française*

ALISTAIR COLE

Introduction

François Mitterrand's conquest, mastery and subjugation of the French Socialist Party was one the major political feats of the 1970s. Mitterrand had finally taken control of the rebaptised Socialist Party (*Parti socialiste*) at the Congress of Epinay in June 1971, a momentous event which reflected his status as de facto leader of the left since the presidential election of 1965. His initially tenuous control over the leadership was consolidated partly because of the party's early successes, partly because he was its only plausible presidential candidate, and partly because of the absence of any serious alternative.

Even the most ardent advocate of the great man theory of history could not pretend that Mitterrand himself had created the social movement or philosophical trends he was to articulate as leader of the Socialist Party from 1971-81. The rise of the Socialists during the 1970s was explicable only in relation to a number of closely interconnected spheres, which surpassed the personality of François Mitterrand: these included political opportunity, sociological change and ideological evolution.

Political resurgence

The revival of the PS during the 1970s under Mitterrand's leadership was remarkable, as illustrated by the statistical summary of its electoral performance below.

The Restoration of Socialist Electoral Fortunes[1]

Year	%
1958 (SFIO)	15.40
1962 (SFIO)	12.50
1967 (FGDS)	18.70
1968 (FGDS)	16.50
1973 (PS/MRG)	20.70
1978 (PS/MRG)	24.97
1981 (PS/MRG)	37.77
1986 (PS/MRG)	36.61
1988 (PS/Allies)	37.55
1993 (PS/Allies)	20.27

Quite apart from the upturn in its electoral fortunes, the party's new vitality was certified by the number of new party members who flocked into the PS, including many enthusiastic activists influenced by the ideas of May 1968. The infusion of such activists led to a definite transformation away from the rather stagnant SFIO, whose activists were in a minority in most federations by 1975. The rallying of Michel Rocard and a minority of the Unified Socialist Party (PSU) to the PS in 1974 removed the party's most ostentatious rival for the inheritance of May 1968, only to relocate the ideological conflict between the 'two cultures' of the French left within the Socialist party itself.

During the 1970s Mitterrand's PS was a party well-attuned to the institutional, social and political imperatives of the political regime of the Fifth Republic and the social structures of French society. Unlike the Communist Party (PCF), the PS was a party which, on an institutional level, could credibly contend to win the presidency, the supreme political prize of the Fifth Republic. His presidential stature had been of considerable importance in explaining why François Mitterrand, de

Gaulle's challenger in 1965, had been able to capture the leadership of the Socialist Party in 1971: there was no future for a party, such as the old SFIO, which refused to respect the new political rules of the Fifth Republic, centered upon victory in the decisive presidential election. Mitterrand understood this.

In terms of political strategy, Mitterrand's PS adopted a complex approach which the old SFIO would have proved incapable of undertaking. The party attempted to appear as 'all things to all men'. Thus, Mitterrand signed the PS-PCF common programme of 1972: this was intended to wean PCF voters away from their party to support the PS, which was presented as a more credible, but still left-wing party. The PS was remarkably successful in this respect: by 1981, one-quarter of 1978 PCF voters had switched over to the PS. But the PS also appealed to many hesitant, centrist voters, for whom the party represented the only prospect of political change. In spite of the radicalism of PS programmes during the 1970s, Mitterrand used every occasion to reassure hesitant voters that he would moderate the left's programme if elected. The Socialist Party thus attempted simultaneously (and paradoxically) to attract support beyond the left as a 'catch-all' party; to appeal to the traditional left-wing electorate attracted by orthodox marxism (the culture represented by the French Communist party); and to articulate the concerns of new social movements and themes given expression in May 1968.

On a sociological level, the new French Socialist Party appeared in the 1970s to be a genuinely interclassist party, repeating a feat achieved previously only by the Gaullists in the 1960s. This was in marked contrast with the old Socialist party (SFIO) in the Fourth and early Fifth Republics: the SFIO had become reduced to being an institutional expression of lower civil servants, and public sector workers, penetrating neither the ranks of the industrial working class, nor the new emerging social groups. Mitterrand's PS, by contrast, attracted support from many of the new social groups produced by post-war socio-economic and demographic change: new tertiary sector workers (especially in the public sector), the new and expanded professions (teaching, social work), as well as a high proportion of the cadres, the managerial strata whose ranks had increased dramatically in the post-war period.[2] In addition to these dynamic, expanding groups within French society, the party proved remarkably successful at attracting the support of older, more traditionally left-wing constituencies, such as industrial workers, and low status office and shopworkers (*employés*), over which the Communist Party had traditionally exercised a strong influence.[3] The development of the PS during the 1970s and early 1980s under Mitterrand's leadership thus saw the party transformed into a virtual microcosm of French society as a whole.

In contrast to the 'interclassist' basis of the Socialist electorate, various studies into the sociological composition of party activists and office-holders converged in their conclusions: the new Socialist Party was 'a party of intellectuals', peopled predominantly by secondary schoolteachers, university lecturers and those involved in the intellectual professions.[4] There was an overwhelming shortfall of workers, so much so that one authority concluded that, 'in reality, the PS is an exclusion zone for industrial workers'.[5] Moreover, the higher up the party heirarchy one went, the greater preponderance there was of an intellectual elite exercising real power. The prevalence of intellectuals within the party's ranks undoubtedly helped explain why it could simultaneously elaborate detailed utopias of future socialist society, and highly specialized policy proposals in preparation for government in the party's burgeoning policy commissions.

The progression of the Socialist Party was replete with contradictions, not least that the party proved capable of appealing for the support of the crucial swing groups in the electorate, while at the same time radicalizing its political discourse and programme. For François Mitterrand, the party's formal radicalism was the necessary price to be paid for realizing the objective of alliance with the Communists, an alliance consolidated in the Common programme in June 1972. This committed the party to radical reform which prefigured the measures eventually adopted by the Socialists (in a watered-down form) in the early reformist period known as the state of grace (1981–82). Moreover, although the formal alliance between the PS and PCF did not last for long (in September 1977 the parties failed to agree on an 'updated' programme), it had become politically impossible, according to Mitterrand, for the PS to abandon the key proposals of the 1972 programme; this would only provide ammunition for the Communists. Subsequently, the party's *Projet socialiste* of 1980, and even Mitterrand's *110 Propositions*, the 1981 presidential platform, essentially reiterated many of the main demands of the 1972 programme.

François Mitterrand's personal contribution to the rejuvenation of the French Socialist Party in the 1970s was undoubtedly considerable: most observers concur that the balance of flexibility and strategic vision offered by Mitterrand served the party well. Ultimately, however, the party's revival stemmed from more immutable structural factors than the personality of its leader, in particular from far-reaching changes in French society and in the ideological climate which were always likely to favour the PS at the expense of the PCF. The electoral victories of 1981 finally proved that, under the intelligent leadership of François Mitterrand, the left, dominated by an (ecumenical) Socialist Party, was at last a viable political alternative to the mainstream right. In the ensuing sections of this chapter we shall consider firstly the ideological transformation of French socialism during the Mitterrand decade; secondly, the diminished role performed by the Socialist Party as an autonomous institution during this period; and finally the continuing importance of factionalism as an indispensable ingredient of the political culture of the French Socialist Party.

The ideological transformation of French Socialism 1981-91

Elected in 1981 when committed to a 'break with capitalism', Mitterrand was re-elected in 1988 preaching the imperatives of national unity and social consensus. In the intervening years the French Socialist Party moved away from being the 'European exception' into the mainstream of European social-reformist movements. Carried to power on a wave of left-wing enthusiasm in May 1981, Mitterrand supported a radical programme of social and economic change presided over by his first Prime Minister, Pierre Mauroy, who headed a Socialist-led government with Communist ministers for the first time since 1947. During the 'state of grace' (May 1981-June 1982), the reforms carried out by the left stemmed directly from Mitterrand's presidential platform, the *110 Propositions*. Mitterrand shared the belief (previously imposed upon the Socialist leader of the Popular Front government, Léon Blum, in 1936) that after such a long absence from power, it would have been politically impossible for the left not to have gone ahead with an ambitious reform programme.

The measures enacted during the 'state of grace' comprised a classic left-wing programme, conceived predominantly in the mainstream centralizing tradition of the French left: large sections of French industry and the entire banking system were nationalized; new powers were decentralized to the regions and local government; labour relations were reformed; important redistributive social and fiscal reforms were enacted (notably through increased welfare benefits, and the introduction of a wealth tax), and significant progress was effected in the field of civil rights. In fact, this was a model of socialism which (apart from the decentralization legislation) reflected the enormous faith placed in the State as an agent of social transformation; it was the embodiment of the *première gauche*, of centralized jacobinism, and of the indirect influence of the Communist Party.

It was no real exaggeration to assert that, upon achieving office, the left did not have a well-thought out economic policy: the primacy of ideological and political considerations had ensured that the economy was largely overlooked. This was to the considerable distaste of 'realists' such as Michel Rocard, Mitterrand's challenger for the party's nomination in 1978-80. Once in government, the left relied upon Keynesian-style reflationary policies as the key to growth and to fighting unemployment, declared to be the government's number one priority. The Socialists' decision to reflate the French economy, by a massive public expenditure programme designed to stimulate growth by relaunching domestic consumption, failed unambiguously. There was a substantial increase in short-term consumer spending, which the economy could ill-afford. The Socialists had believed this would signal a new era of prosperity for French industry, but in fact it mainly boosted the economies of France's chief industrial rivals, especially that of West Germany. The resulting trade and budget deficits forced the Socialists into an embarrassing economic u-turn. The old taunts that the left was synonymous with economic profligacy reappeared.

The left's economic U turn took place in two stages: in June 1982 and in March 1983, despite Mitterrand's early reservations. In June 1982, President Mitterrand succumbed to the pressure exerted by Prime Minister Mauroy and his Finance Minister Jacques Delors and agreed to a temporary wage and price freeze, accompanied by a second devaluation of the franc (after an initial devaluation in October 1981 had failed to produce its desired effects). At this stage, neither Mitterrand, nor Mauroy were willing to admit publicly that the left had changed course. The crucial turning point in Mitterand's first *septennat* occurred in March 1983, when the President was called upon to arbitrate between two opposing economic policies in a move which set the course for the rest of his presidency.[6] The choice lay between whether to remain within the European Monetary System (EMS), devalue the franc for the third time and accept a deflationary economic package (the choice adopted); or else to withdraw from the EMS, adopt protectionist measures for French industry and continue on the reflationary path traced since May 1981. After much hesitation, Mitterrand chose the former course of action, confirming thereby that France could neither isolate itself through protectionism, nor indefinitely pursue radically different economic policies from those of its main trading partners, especially those within the EEC. The great paradox of the Socialist administration of 1981–86 was that once they had failed to make what they perceived to be Socialist policies work, Mitterrand's governments proved highly competent at administering capitalism. This was of great significance, since the Socialists gained considerably in terms of economic credibility: by the time they left office in 1986, Socialist ministers had become competent, experienced administrators, respectable personalities to be entrusted with the burden of governing the country at some future date.

In the midst of this tumultuous conversion, the party itself was largely absent, at least after the early reformist phase. It was indicative of the relationship which existed between the different partners of the Socialist power structure (president - government - party) that the Socialist Party's ideological *aggiornamento* followed, rather than preceded the government's practical apprenticeship of the contraints involved in governing the country. This point can be illustrated by a brief panoramic overview of Socialist Party congresses during the period from 1981-86. At the congress of Valence in October 1981, leading socialist orators created a highly detrimental effect by calling upon the government to radicalize its programme and by threatening reprisals against those hindering its application. This made Mitterrand determined to limit the party's autonomous means of expression in the future. Subsequently, the PS was rarely involved in crucial policy debates.

The party was disoriented by the magnitude of the economic u-turn of 1982-83, and initially sought solace in the belief that the change in economic policy would only prove to be a temporary affair. Once it became apparent that the *politique de rigueur* was henceforth to be a permanent feature of government policy, the party leadership reluctantly adjusted its political message. In his speech to the 1983 congress, party leader Lionel Jospin affirmed that the party's attitude towards economic and social policy was one of resolute support for the action of the government, within the framework of the orientations fixed by the President of the Republic. This was in marked contrast to the tone of the Valence congress two years earlier. In private, party leaders were far less sanguine: indeed, economic policy provided an enduring source of intra-party division which cut across the boundaries of the party's official *courants*. The stagnation of internal party life became steadily more apparent after the economic u-turn of 1982–83: there was no real open debate within the party (or the Socialist group) over economic policy, the departure of the Communist ministers in 1984, or the reform of the electoral system in 1985.

In July 1984, the old-style socialist Pierre Mauroy was replaced by Laurent Fabius, the youngest Prime Minister this century (thirty-seven), a man carefully nurtured by Mitterrand since the early 1970s. Fabius headed an homogeneous Socialist government bereft of Communist ministers. Analysis of Fabius's programme between 1984–86 lies outside of the present study, but we should note that the 'ideology' underpinning the Fabius administration was that of modernisation, which was variously interpreted as a euphemism for the left abandoning its left-oriented reformist programme of 1981–82, and an intellectual alibi to enable the Socialists to shed their former ideology. Once Fabius had become Prime Minister, his full-scale modernisation programme arguably contributed to the slow death of old-style socialism in France. In a whole range of policy areas, the left's shibboleths were quietly called into question in the name of economic efficiency: nationalizations, economic planning, welfare policy, employment policy, attitudes towards the private sector, fiscal policy, and industrial policy. At an Extraordinary Convention in December 1984, the PS adopted a charter entitled *Modernisation et progrès social*, which provided a conceptual justification for the activities of the Fabius government; once again, the party fell into line with ulterior policy developments which it had not foreseen in advance and which party activists misunderstood.[7]

In October 1983, at the congress of Bourg, the PS had somewhat grudgingly declared its solidarity with the new economic direction taken by François Mitterrand in March 1983; in October 1985, at the congress of Toulouse, the Socialist Party proclaimed itself to be a party within the European social-democratic tradition. The congress of Toulouse represented a major landmark in the party's history; drawing on the difficult experience of over four years of government, the party declared itself in theory what it had become in practice, a party committed to gradualist, social-democratic reform, rather than a rapid break with capitalism. This represented a break with the traditionally endemic conflict between a 'radical' political discourse aimed at party activists, and a 'realistic' governmental practice (a divergence initially inherited from the SFIO).

In the course of the 1981–86 governments, the 'culture of government' had replaced the union of the left as the fundamental reference point for the party leadership. With this a number of neo-marxist concepts inherited from the period in opposition were unceremoniously abandoned: for example the *front de classe* (the marxist-inspired formulation of the party's alliance strategy); and the messianic call for a 'break with capitalism'. Likewise references to the two cultures of the French left, which had re-emerged regularly at PS congresses since 1977, became less common. In a remarkable speech to the 1977 congress, Michel Rocard had diagnosed the existence of two cultures within the French left: a centralizing Jacobin culture which placed its faith in the transformative capacities of the state; and a decentralizing culture, inherently suspicious of excessive state interventionism.[8] Rocard's reference was taken up by his enemies within the Socialist Party, most especially by Mitterrand, who, at the PS congress of Metz in 1979, condemned Rocard for embodying a 'revisionist tendency' alien to the traditions of the left.

The 1985 congress represented the triumph of *rocardisme sans Rocard*: that is, an incorporation of the principal ideas expressed by Michel Rocard in the 1970s, against the prevailing trends of the *Projet socialiste* of 1980, or of Mitterrand's *110 propositions* of 1981. Many of Rocard's ideas, especially in relation to the need for rigorous economic management or restraints on state economic interventionism, were now widely accepted by the party leadership, not least by Laurent Fabius, whose premiership bore far greater similarity with the later one of Michel Rocard than with the one of his immediate predecessor Pierre Mauroy. The party fought the campaign for the 1986 legislative election as a party of government, which concentrated on defending its record of the previous five years.

Once Mitterrand was re-elected in May 1988, after the two year parenthesis of cohabitation, he named his old adversary Michel Rocard as Prime Minister.[9] Rocard's premiership continued with the consensual brand of social-democracy practised by Fabius. This could best be characterized as unspectacular, cautious reformism, accompanied by a rigorous economic policy, with the latter taking increasing precedence over the former. The main reforms enacted during the Rocard government (May 1988–May 1991) were all contained in Mitterrand's 1988 Letter to the French People: the reintroduction of a moderated wealth tax, the introduction of a guaranteed minimum income, and a major investment in education. As Prime Minister, Rocard adopted an overtly consensual style, consistent with his own pragmatic approach towards the resolution of conflicts. This style worked with dramatic results early on, notably with the resolution of the conflict in New Caledonia. But it was, arguably, a style ill-adapted to the resolution of harsh disputes and hard political choices. In spite of its early successes, the three years of the Rocard government were marked by increasingly bitter disputes within French society, to the extent that some commentators began evoking a break-down of confidence in the political system of the Fifth Republic and the social fabric of French society. For left-wing critics (especially but not only within the Communist Party) the economic perspective appeared so dominant that the Socialist Party had lost its *raison d'etre* and had become indistinguishable from governments of the centre-right. Rocard was replaced in May 1991 by Edith Cresson, Mitterrand's fifth Prime Minister, who was in turn succeeded by Pierre Bérégovoy in April 1992.

François Mitterrand and the Socialist Party: *Un Parti de godillots?*

The emergence of the presidential party has been one of the most striking features of the Fifth Republic, perhaps the most important indirect legacy

73

of Charles de Gaulle. Until 1986, the presidential party depended upon the authority of the (directly-elected) President for its privileged position, and upon the electorate's unfailing tendency from 1962-86 to re-elect the party, or the coalition supporting the President, to a majority in the National Assembly. The expression *Parti de godillots* (party of bootlickers) signified the subordination of the presidential party to the will of the directly elected President and his government. It was first employed by the satirical journal *Le Canard Enchaîné* to deride the subservient Gaullist Union for the New Republic (UNR).

By the time of Mitterrand's election in 1981, the *Parti de godillots* had become an established, if somewhat uneven, feature of the Fifth Republic: the presidential party existed in a largely subordinate relationship to the President of the Republic, since its fortunes depended to a great extent upon the latter's own good fortune.[10] The pattern of presidential supremacy was re-established in 1981: once Mitterrand had been elected President, he dissolved the Assembly designated in 1978; the absolute Socialist majority returned in June 1981 thus owed its existence largely to François Mitterrand. This, combined with the established primacy of the French President, was sufficient to ensure the dependence of the party upon presidential instructions.

By 1981, after a decade of skilful manoeuvring and considerable success, the PS had been firmly subordinated to Mitterrand's leadership. In certain important senses, the relationship between the Socialist Party and President Mitterrand corresponded to the model of the *Parti de godillots* first developed during the period of Gaullist ascendancy (1958–74): as the dominant party from 1981–86, the PS occupied a similar institutional position to that of the Gaullist UNR during the earlier period. Nonetheless, there were a number of novel departures, due to the nature of the PS as a different style of party from the UNR; notably, a self-proclaimed mass party, rather than merely a personal appendage of a providential leader. Mitterrand's eventual mastery over the Socialist Party was achieved only after a hard-fought campaign during which he earned his spurs as a party leader of the type that the General professed to despise.

From the beginning of his mandate, Mitterrand insisted that the party had an important, but essentially limited function within the new regime. In his first message to Socialist deputies, the new President insisted that the *110 propositions* were 'the charter of the government's activity, and therefore of your legislative programme'.[11] Furthermore, Mitterrand made it clear that he would accept 'no open criticism' on the part of the Socialist group, and that there could be no question of 'going beyond my campaign commitments'. This principle was constantly reiterated by Mitterrand in his messages to PS congresses throughout the 1980s: the function of the party was essentially based on subordination to the President and his governments, although the President initially acknowledged the need for an element of 'feedback', whereby the party would act as a channel to express (in private) the prevalent preoccupations of the left-wing electorate. Even this limited feedback function was played down after the early reformist period.

The party's subordination to the President warranted several explanations. First, François Mitterrand's early actions clearly reasserted the pattern of presidential supremacy that had characterized the Fifth Republic under previous presidents: quite simply, the party owed its majority to Mitterrand. Second, the governmental system was largely dominated by Mitterrandistes, who increasingly permeated all levels of government. In theory, and to some extent in practice, this minimized conflict between the different layers of the Socialist power structure (presidency, government, parliamentary party and PS executive) and facilitated the subordination of the party to presidential directives. As indicated above, Lionel Jospin had been coopted as party leader by Mitterrand in January 1981; Mitterrand's trusted allies controlled the parliamentary party (Pierre Joxe, and then André Billardon) and the presidency of the National Assembly (Louis Mermaz, 1981–86), as well as the important parliamentary committees. The replacement of Pierre Mauroy by Laurent Fabius as Prime Minister in July 1984 completed the domination of the Mitterrandistes.

By a judicious use of political appointments, Mitterrand (as his predecessors before him) was able to ensure that loyal presidential appointees occupied the key positions within government, the administration and the party. Presidential patronage thus ensured that faithful Mitterrandistes were appointed not just to the key posts in government, but also in the universities, the diplomatic service, amongst the prefectorial corps and so on. It has been contended that during the period 1981–86 political appointments under Mitterrand reached further than under any other President. The extent of changes in personnel in 1981 led to accusations of a French spoils system being operated, or the beginnings of *L'Etat-PS*. It would have been more accurate to label this as *l'Etat Mitterrand*: the common feature of the new elite in the positions of real power, far beyond any common technocratic background or even party allegiance, was the degree of proximity to François Mitterrand himself.

In spite of the initial profusion of party activists in ministerial cabinets, it was difficult to consider the party as an autonomous entity.[12] There existed a virtual osmosis between party and government, the former being largely subordinated to the latter: this was further illustrated by the fact that prominent government ministers had the right to sit on the party's executive organs; that the composition of the party leadership was (until 1988) heavily influenced by the Elysée; and that there was direct presidential involvement in the selection of PS candidates for parliamentary elections.[13]

In the aftermath of Mitterrand's election, official party spokesmen continued to refute any suggestion that the PS would be a *Parti de godillots*; rather, it was a party of government in government. Various conceptions of the party's role existed, all of which determined to avoid the fate of the *godillot*. The notion of the avant garde party was favourite with the left of the Socialist Party: as the CERES motion for the 1983 congress insisted, the Socialist Party's task was less to follow the government than to lead the way, in order to clarify its route. The Socialist Party had a triple function to perform: as representative of the interests of the left-wing electorate; as the guardian of socialist doctrine, and as a party guide, defining the parameters of future governmental activity.

At early congresses after Mitterrand's victory (i.e. 1981 and 1983), the official motions paid lip-service to the idea that the role of the party was not merely to rally support for government policies; it was also to reflect upon future policies. Thus, the majority motion for the 1983 congress of Bourg-en-Bresse stipulated that the mission of the party was to articulate the correct balance between short-term policy and medium-term reflection. The aspiration to discover a positive function for the party within the restrictions of the Fifth Republic remained a powerful one.

But the crucial working definition of the correct role of the Socialist Party was given by its leader Lionel Jospin at the 1983 congress, when the PS had at last come to terms with the constraints imposed by the political regime: 'It is not possible to oppose government policy (which is necessarily that of the President of the Republic) and to belong to the party leadership'. Henceforth, this standard guaranteed that the Socialist Party too would become a 'dominant but dominated party'. In private Jospin's attitude was considerably less passive: in a confidential report presented to the party's *Comité Directeur* in July 1985, at the height of the conflict over whether he, or Laurent Fabius (the incumbent prime minister) should lead the 1986 election campaign, Jospin complained: 'We have known for a long time that the PS cannot live with the institutions of the Fifth Republic in the same way the UDR or the UDF used to. We are a different sort of party, a democratic Socialist party. As far as possible, we have attempted to ensure that the institutions function in a different manner.'[14]

Jospin resented the claim put forward by Fabius that, as Prime Minister, he should lead the party's campaign for the 1986 legislative election. A sharp conflict arose between the culture of the Socialist Party which, despite everything, retained a strong belief in the party's autonomy and self-sufficiency; and the prevalent logic of the Fifth Republic, whereby the governing party, an instrument of the President of the Republic, should be led by his chief political agent, the Prime Minister. In the event, the 1986 campaign was distinguished by the active, partisan engagement of François Mitterrand himself and lesser roles for both Fabius and Jospin.

In the legislative election of March 1986, the right-wing RPR-UDF electoral alliance won a narrow majority of seats; the PS, the presidential party, was thus forced to return to opposition; and at one stroke, the political basis for the executive President, the existence of a supportive parliamentary majority, was removed. In place of the executive-President, Mitterrand reverted to the de Gaullian posture of the arbiter-President of all the French, above the particular concerns of all political parties and interests, including his own. This had serious implications for the PS, the presidential party in opposition. The extent of Mitterrand's continuing domination of the presidential party (even when in opposition) was striking: the party continued to be subordinated to a President who, for the first time in the Fifth Republic, had lost the essential prerogatives of his power. The strength of the Mitterrandiste connection, in conjunction with a fear of the alternative (the candidacy of Michel Rocard in 1988 and probable defeat) combined to ensure the continuing subordination of the PS to its historic leader. During the period of *cohabitation*, the PS was no longer a party of government, nor was it a genuine party of opposition, given that its President remained in the Elysée. It could best be depicted as a party of government in opposition, paralyzed by the institutional context of cohabitation, by Mitterrand's positioning for the 1988 presidential election, and by the legacy of its five years in government, which precluded any return to a pre-1981 oppositional stance. The strains imposed by this continuing subservience to a providential leader, but without the rewards of office, in conjunction with the intolerable pressures developing within the Mitterrandiste faction, augured ill for the party's future cohesion, even in the event of a presidential victory.

The model of the dominant but dominated presidential party outlined by Jean Charlot corresponded only imperfectly to the case of the Socialists during Mitterrand's second term.[15] Relations between the directly elected President and his parliamentary supporters are always likely to be problematic, notwithstanding the clear subordination of the latter to the former established under all four Presidents of the Fifth Republic. In part this reflects the natural tensions caused in relations between the executive and its parliamentary supporters in all unitary political systems. The specificity of the French case rests upon its status as a semi-presidential system; the fact that the President is directly elected by a majority of voters on the vital second round of a presidential election confers an authority upon the French president which surpasses that of most other 'chief executives' in western Europe. Once elected to the Elysée, the presidential candidate becomes Head of State, with a constitutional duty to represent all French people. From the inception of the Fifth Republic, this has induced Presidents to distance themselves publicly from their parliamentary supporters.

Different Presidents have, of course, sustained rather different relationships with their parliamentary majorities. The pattern established by the first three Presidents of the Fifth Republic was to maintain a public aloofness in relation to their parliamentary supporters, but to move closer towards their supportive party organizations throughout the course of their presidential terms in office, especially in order to appeal for support during legislative election campaigns. In the case of François Mitterrand and the Socialists a reverse pattern appeared to occur: initially very close to his party, the fourth President gradually distanced himself from the PS. This process, which began in earnest under *cohabitation*, accelerated after

Mitterrand's re-election in May 1988, and stemmed in part from the conditions of his re-election.[16]

Once re-elected, Mitterrand reaffirmed that the principle of presidential initiative remained intact, and that his Letter to the French People, his 1988 campaign manifesto, constituted the new framework of government policy. Presidential supremacy in policy orientation was reaffirmed after the parenthesis of cohabitation: but for most of the Rocard government, Mitterrand immersed himself in the traditional presidential domain of foreign policy, European affairs and defence, leaving the Prime Minister in charge of coordinating domestic policy. And presidential supremacy was recalled with force in May 1991, when Mitterrand obliged Michel Rocard to resign and nominated a new Prime minister, Edith Cresson, a close personal friend since the period of the *Convention des Institutions Républicaines* (the movement led by Mitterrand from 1964–71). That the party itself was not consulted over Rocard's replacement by Cresson (soon to become Mitterrand's most unpopular Prime Minister) provoked considerable bitterness amongst party leaders, including hitherto loyal Mitterrandistes such as Laurent Fabius.[17]

After his re-election in May 1988, Mitterrand's capacity to dominate the presidential party greatly diminished, leaving the President unable or unwilling to prevent the re-emergence of policy and personality-based factionalism.

The resurgence of factionalism

From its origins, French socialism has been characterized by its factional nature.[18] Indeed, the resurrection of the PS during the 1970s was intricately linked to its accommodation of a variety of pre-existing political groups who fused into a single party. As with other such parties the existence of factions reflected in part the continuing reference point provided by separate historical origins.[19]

During the decade of renewal (1971–81), the Socialist Party was composed of four main factions (*courants*), each articulating a specific strand of the French socialist tradition. The central Mitterrandiste faction proved to be by far the most fruitful for aspiring politicians, since it occupied the centre of party gravity, it deployed more patronage than any other, and it was led by the party's historic leader François Mitterrand. There were, in addition, three other main *courants*: the left-wing CERES group led by J.-P. Chevènement, which most closely approximated to a tightly organized parallel faction; the group led by Michel Rocard, which represented a curious synthesis of May-68 inspired new left ideals and the economic prudence of the left's Fourth Republic statesman Pierre Mendès-France; and the group led by Pierre Mauroy, who articulated the political and organizational interests of the old SFIO within the new party.

While it would be a gross exaggeration to assert that the Socialist Party was no more than a collection of factions, in the mould of the Italian Christian Democrats (DCI) or the Japanese Libral Democrats (LDP), it was nonetheless a party which comprised a variety of organized political opinions. Indeed, this was a logical counterpart to its attempt to become an electoral catch-all party: the party's message was fundamentally (and purposely) ambiguous; its wide array of *courants* contributed to the party's 'ubiquitous' appeal. The relative novelty of the party, and the contrast such internal diversity afforded with the old, stagnant, SFIO meant that its internal diversity was probably a bonus for the PS: it testified to the fact that genuine life had been restored to the moribund body of French socialism.

The historical legacy of factionalism was a central feature of the party as the left returned to office in 1981. The participation of all factions within the government throughout the first five-year administration led to a marked lessening of overt factional activity. Even when this participation was symbolic, there were intense pressures to respect a principle of solidarity and restraint and not to challenge the direction of government policy. The dynamic of division of the party in opposition thus gave way to a laboured unanimity, whereby all factions were automatically represented within the party leadership, parallel to their participation in government (even when the latter was symbolic, as on occasion with CERES or the *Rocardiens*). This was in order to present a united front to public opinion; but it had the consequence of stultifying internal party debate, and of demobilizing party activists and cadres: in many respects the party ceased to exist outside of election campaigns.

There were occasional resurgences of the bitter factional disputes which had characterized the PS before 1981: notably by Chevènement's *Socialisme et Republique* (ex-CERES) from 1983–84 to protest against the new economic policy; and by Michel Rocard's supporters after he resigned from the Fabius government in April 1985. But these were timid indeed, in comparison with past antics. The party's factions closed ranks as the government's unpopularity deepened. Moreover, for as long as Mitterrand continued as President, there was little prospect of a serious challenge to his leadership in the 1988 presidential election: Michel Rocard's half-hearted bid for the PS nomination was made conditional on Mitterrand not standing again. In fact, on each of the major contentious issues upon which the party pronounced itself during the Mitterrand decade, the official *courants* were likely to provide only a rough guide as to the real divisions existing within the party; this strongly suggested that the ideological divisions inherited from the party of opposition had become meaningless, outdated by new concerns for which the old *courants* could not provide ideologically compact responses. This has been the case especially for *Socialisme et république* (who split in 1991 over the Gulf War); and the Mitterrandistes, whose cohesion was brusquely called into question after May 1988.

In the period following Mitterrand's re-election, intra-party disputes greatly contributed to the image of the Socialists as a divided ruling clique. The re-emergence of factionalism, artificially suppressed during the first presidential term, was inescapable at the PS congress of Rennes in March 1990, scene of a public relations disaster unrivalled since the congress of Valence in October 1981. At the Rennes congress, the party split into two main coalitions (Fabius-Chevènement against Jospin-Mauroy-Rocard), divided far more in relation to personality and rival organizational imperatives than anything else: that Fabius and Rocard found themselves in opposing camps was more than adequate testament to this. The congress of Rennes was remarkable for the animosity dividing hitherto loyal Mitterrandistes; it was also remarkable for Mitterrand's refusal to allow Rocard and Jospin to create a new governing majority coalition within the party which would have isolated Fabius in the minority. Such presidential intervention reaffirmed the indirect control Mitterrand could still exercise over the outcome of party conferences; but it created an additional source of tension within the party, as well as with his Prime Minister Rocard, who was forced to bow to the presidential will.

The nomination of Edith Cresson as Prime Minister in May 1991, which *Le Monde* journalist J.-M. Colombani portrayed as Mitterrand's 'present to himself as a celebration of ten years of rule', was greeted with dismay by the Socialist party leadership (notwithstanding the growing opposition there had been to Rocard). It soon became clear that Mitterrand's presidential whim had burdened the party with an intolerable weight in advance of the 1993 legislative elections. The collapse of public confidence in the Prime Minister in the course of 1991 was dramatic: minus 23 percentage points in the six months following Cresson's nomination. This beat all records for the Fifth Republic, including those established by Barre and Mauroy.[20] Quite apart from ignoring Socialist Party considerations when naming Cresson, François Mitterrand gave other indications that his interest no longer necessarily converged with that of the party he had led: conscious of the strong feeling of rejection towards political parties by the electorate, Mitterrand had attempted to distance himself further from the PS by encouraging the creation of rival pro-presidential groups and personalities, such as Brice Lalonde's *Génération Ecologie* (which directly threatened the Socialist Party's electoral fortunes).

Mitterrand's protégé Laurent Fabius finally took over the party leadership in January 1992, with the consent of former leader Pierre Mauroy in a show of unity prior to the regional elections of March 1992, and, crucially, in the run up to the legislative elections of 1993. By this stage, it was far from clear whether Fabius could still be considered primarily as a Mitterrand loyalist, or whether his actions were those of a politician coolly assessing his own interests in the cold light of political realism. The Fabius succession might, paradoxically, be considered as one further indication of the post-Mitterrand sentiment sweeping the party.[21] This was suggested by the fact that Fabius was supported in his bid for the leadership by Michel Rocard, on condition that the latter was recognized as the party's 'virtual' presidential candidate; as well as by Mitterrand's scarcely concealed preference for Jacques Delors as Socialist candidate in the forthcoming presidential election as opposed to Rocard. The Fabius succession, although satisfactory from the President's point of view, illustrated, amongst other things, that Mitterrand had little control over who his successor was to be. This revealed the ultimate weakness of incumbent Presidents in the French semi-presidential system: no President has been able to designate his successor. This has acted as an ultimate limitation on presidential control over the party.

Conclusion

It is difficult to avoid the conclusion that the Socialist Party experienced the Socialist decade as an observer, rather than as a major participant. Not only did the party *stricto sensu* remain absent from the main centres of decision making and influence (after an initially elevated importance), but throughout the first *septennat* at least, it was constrained to provide ideological justifications for policies it had neither initiated nor approved.

It is clear that during his second mandate, President Mitterrand was unable (or unwilling) to prevent the resurgence of policy and personality-based factionalism within the PS, of the type largely suppressed during the first seven-year term. This was in itself testament to the distance henceforth separating François Mitterrand (an increasingly lameduck President) and the Socialist Party. The PS remained a highly factionalized party, bringing together variegated strands of political opinion ranging from extreme-left to centre-left. It was, moreover, a party searching desperately for an identity and a role, after the political and ideological u-turns of the Mitterrand decade which definitively buried the 'lyrical illusions' upon which the PS built its revival in the 1970s. In the aftermath of its humiliating electoral defeat in March 1993, and the capture of the party leadership by Mitterrand's historic rival Rocard in the following month, it appeared probable that Mitterrand's *Parti socialiste*, painfully reconstructed since the congress of Epinay in 1971, would metamorphose into something else, the form of which remained unclear at the time of writing.

In spite of itself, the PS was a presidential party, with the strengths and weaknesses this implies. Throughout the first *septennat* subordination to its President tended to preclude any substantive internal party debate; the counterpart to this was an initially unprecendented degree of access for party leaders to the Elysée. The proximity of party leaders to the real centres of power diminished steadily after 1982; in the course of the subsequent decade, the relationship between party and president deteriorated slowly but steadily, to the point where the President often seemed to act against the interests of the Party. There was clear evidence during Mitterrand's second term that the party was reluctant to follow its providential leader unconditionally. Rocard's capture of the party leadership in April 1993 represented the final humiliation for Mitterrand.

The other sense in which presidentialism has had an enormous impact upon the PS lies in the proven worth of the party as a vehicle for ambitious contenders for the Elysée. Even in the depths if its unpopularity in 1993, it is likely that the PS-backed candidate will again be present at the second round in the presidential election scheduled for 1995. The near-certainty that Mitterrand will never again stand for the presidency has liberated the presidential appetites of a range of more or less plausible contenders for his succession (led by Rocard, and Delors).

The breakthrough of powerful new forces such as the Greens, in conjunction with widespread evidence of a new depth of distrust in politicians and their Parisian manoeuvrings, suggest not only that the Socialists in government were unable to provide responses for 'new' issues such as immigration or the environment, but that the party had lost the capacity to generate new ideas; its greatest originality during the decade of revival of the 1970s. Assessment of the underlying reasons for the PS's electoral debacle in 1993 lie beyond the parameters of the present chapter. They stemmed in part from the nature of Mitterrand's political leadership, widely perceived as Machaivellian and self-serving.[23] And yet the Socialist's defeat ought not to be reduced primarily to the failures of Mitterrand's leadership. There were more profound structural reasons, notably the perceived failure of Socialist economic management, the corrosive consequences of a decade in power, the desire for political alternation, and the impact of political corruption. The reasons underpinning Mitterrand's aloofness from the PS were themselves linked to the pervasive image of political corruption and scandal that the Socialists conveyed during the 1988–93 period. The Socialists only had themselves to blame for the instances of corruption within their midst. The widespread perception of the Socialists as a corrupt and self-serving clique had a debilitating effect on the party's electoral fortunes in 1993. It was symbolic in this respect that even premier Bérégovoy succumbed to the suspicion of malpractice, in spite of his pledge to root out corruption.[24] The tragic aftermath of Bérégovoy's suicide in May 1993 closed the final chapter on the left in power in an atmosphere of recrimination, melancholy and finality.

Notes

1. For further explanation see Cole, A. and Campbell, P. (1989), *French Electoral Systems and Elections since 1789*, Gower, Aldershot, pp. 116-31.

2. Schweisguth, E. (1983), 'Les couches moyennes salariées sont-elles socialistes?', *Intervention*, no. 5-6, pp. 58-66.

3. See Hardouin, P. (1978), 'Les caractéristiques sociologiques du parti socialiste', *Revue française de science politique*, April, pp. 220-56; Hardouin, P. (1983) 'Le PS: un parti d'intellectuels?', *Intervention*, no. 5-6, pp. 66-76; Rey, H. and Subileau, F. (1986), 'Les militants socialistes en 1985', *Projet*, no. 198, pp. 19-34.

4. Hardouin, 'Le PS: un parti d'intellectuels?', p. 68. This was in spite of the fact that the new party created workplace sections (*sections d'entreprises*), and loudly proclaimed its attachment to the working-class.

5. Ibid. The parties of the right, by contrast, were largely dominated by a business and professional elite.

6. Thus, by 1986 inflation had declined to under 5 per cent from its 1982 peak of over 20 per cent, the balance of payments deficit had considerably narrowed and the economy was beginning to expand modestly. Only on unemployment, the key economic policy in the 1981 manifestos, was the record disappointing.

7. *Modernisation et progrès social*, text presented to the party's National Convention held at Ivry, 15-16 December 1984. *Le poing et la rose*, no. 111, 1984.

8. Rocard's speech is reprinted in the *Nouvelle Revue Socialiste*, no. 27, 1977, pp. 69-76.

9. See Dupin, E., 'Mitterrand/Rocard: Portrait d'un couple politique contre nature', *Libération*, 16 May 1991.

10. The concept of the *parti de godillots* was, however, rather ill-suited to evaluate the Giscard presidency, since the President's own avowed party supporters (regrouped in the UDF in 1978) never comprised more than a minority of the minority. That Giscard's governments survived regardless illustrated the strength of the position accorded to the Executive in the 1958 constitution.

11. Cited in Charlot, J. (1983), 'Le Président et le parti majoritaire: du gaullisme au socialisme', *Revue Politique et Parlementaire*, no. 905, pp. 27-40.

12. On the proliferation of Socialist Party activists in the ministerial *cabinets* after May 1981, see Dagnaud, M. and Mehl, D. (1983) 'Portraits d'hommes dans les coulisses du pouvoir', *Intervention*, no. 5-6, pp. 78-84.

13. Quermonne, J.-L. (1987), 'La présidence de la République et le système de partis', *Pouvoirs*, no. 41, p. 99.

14. Report presented by Jospin to the *Comité directeur*, 7 May 1985. PS archives, Lille.

15. Charlot, 'Le Président et le parti majoritaire'.

16. In 1988, the PS had been totally excluded from the election campaign, with the incumbent President preferring to rely on presidential support committees. Moreover, Mitterrand had been re-elected with crucial second-round centre-right support on the basis of a theme, *l'ouverture*, which appeared designed to minimize the influence of the Socialists. See Cole, A. (1989), '*La France unie*: François Mitterrand', in Gaffney, J. (ed.), *The French Presidential Election of 1988*, Dartmouth, Aldershot, pp. 81-100.

17. See J.-M. Colombani, 'Le Président contre le PS', *Le Monde*, 8 October 1991.

18. For a detailed analysis, see Cole, A. (1989), 'Factionalism, The French Socialist Party and the Fifth Republic: an explanation of intra-party divisions', *European Journal of Political Research*, vol. 17, no. 1, pp. 77-96; Hanley, D. (1984), *Keeping Left? CERES and the French Socialist Party*, Manchester University Press, Manchester, especially chapters one and two.

19. Hine, D. (1982), 'Factionalism in the West European Party System: A Framework for Analysis, *West European Politics*, vol. 5, no. 1, pp. 39-52.

20. See Jaffré, J., 'Socialistes et l'opinion: le divorce', *Le Monde*, 23 January 1992.

21. See Jarreau, P., 'Le fait accompli', *Le Monde*, 8 January 1992; Colombani, J.-M., 'Changer, jusqu'où?', *Le Monde*, 10 January 1992.

22. For a thorough analysis, see Gaffney, J. (1990), 'The Emergence of a Presidential Party: the Socialists', in Cole, A. (ed.), *French Political Parties in Transition*, Dartmouth, Aldershot, pp. 61-90.
23. See Cole, A. (1994), *François Mitterrand: a Study in Political Leadership*, Routledge, London, chapter four for an appreciation of Mitterrand's leadership.
24. In February 1993 the satirical journal *Le Canard enchaîné* revealed that Bérégovoy had obtained an interest-free loan of 1,000,000 francs from Patrice Pelat, a close Mitterrand aide hopelessly compromised over the scandal involving the French company Péchiney. While not strictly illegal, this increased public cynicism with regard to the ruling Socialists.

Bibliography

Bell, D.S. and Criddle, B. (1988), *The French Socialist Party*, Clarendon, Oxford.

Beller, D. C. and Belloni, D. (1978), *Faction Politics*, Clio Press, Santa Barbara.

Capdeveille, J. (1981), *France de gauche, vote à droite*, Presses de la FNSP, Paris.

Charlot, J. (1983), 'Le Président et le parti majoritaire: du gaullisme au socialisme', *Revue Politique et Parlementaire*, no. 905.

Cole, A. and Campbell, P. (1989), *French Electoral Systems and Elections since 1789*, Gower, Aldershot.

Cole, A. (1989), 'Factionalism, The French Socialist Party and the Fifth Republic: an explanation of intra-party divisions', *European Journal of Political Research*, vol. 17, no. 1.

Cole, A. (ed.) (1990), *French Political Parties in Transition*, Dartmouth, Aldershot.

Cole, A. (1994), *François Mitterrand: a Study in Political Leadership*, Routledge, London.

Colombani, J.-M., 'Le Président et le parti', *Le Monde*, 17 March 1990.

Colombani, J.-M., 'Changer, jusqu'où?', *Le Monde*, 10 January 1992.

Dagnaud, M. and Mehl, D. (1982), *L'Elite rose*, Ramsay, Paris.

Dagnaud, M. and Mehl, D. (1983), 'Portraits d'hommes dans les coulisses du pouvoir', *Intervention*, no. 5-6.

Dupin, E., 'Mitterrand/Rocard: portrait d'un couple politique contre nature', *Libération*, 16 May 1991.

Fauvet-Mycia, C., 'Elysée: Maison des fidèles, puis machine présidentielle', *Libération*, 6 May 1991.

Gaffney, J. (1989), *The French Left and the Fifth Republic*, Macmillan, London.

Gaffney, J. (ed.) (1988), *France and Modernisation*, Gower, Aldershot.

Gaffney, J. (ed.) (1989), *The French Presidential Election of 1988*, Dartmouth, Aldershot.

Hanley, D. (1984), *Keeping Left? CERES and the French Socialist Party*, Manchester University Press, Manchester.

Hardouin, P. (1978), 'Les caractéristiques sociologiques du parti socialiste', *Revue française de science politique*, April.

Hardouin, P. (1983), 'Le PS: un parti d'intellectuels', *Intervention*, no. 5-6.

Hine, D. (1982), 'Factionalism in the West European Party System: A Framework for Analysis', *West European Politics*, vol. 5, no. 1.

Jaffré, J., 'Socialistes et l'opinion: le divorce', *Le Monde*, 23 January 1992.

Jarreau, P., 'Le fait accompli', *Le Monde*, 8 January 1992.

Jarreau, P., 'Trois courants pour un parti', *Le Monde*, 12 December 1991.

Johnson, R.W. (1981), *The Long March of the French Left*, Macmillan, London.

Jospin, L. (1985), report presented to the *Comité directeur*, PS archives, Lille.

July, S. (1986), *Les années Mitterrand*, Grasset, Paris.

Machin, H. and Wright, V. (eds.) (1985), *Economic Policy and Policy-Making under the Mitterrand Presidency: 1981–84*, Pinter, London.

Mazey, S. and Newman, M. (1987), *Mitterrand's France*, Croom Helm, London.

Nouvelle Revue Socialiste (1977), no. 27.

Nugent, N. and Lowe, D. (1982), *The Left in France*, Macmillan, London.

Pfister, T. (1985), *La vie quotidienne à Matignon au temps de l'union de la gauche*, Hachette, Paris.

'Spécial responsables' (1983), *Le poing et la rose*, no. 158, March.

'Modernisation et progrès social' (1984), *Le poing et la rose*, no. 111, November.

Quermonne, J.-L. (1987), 'La présidence de la République et le système des partis', *Pouvoirs*, no. 41.

Rey, H. and Subileau, F. (1986), 'Les militants socialistes en 1985', *Projet*, no. 198.

Ross, G., Hoffman, S. and Malzacher, S. (1987), *The Mitterrand Experiment*, Polity Press, Cambridge.

Schifres, M. & Sarazin, M. (1985), *L'Elysée de Mitterrand*, Alain Moreau, Paris.

Schweisguth, E. (1983), 'Les couches moyennes salariées sont-elles socialistes', *Intervention*, no. 5-6.

4 The Decline of the Established Parties

GINO RAYMOND

'French socialism is not my bible'.
François Mitterrand.

Introduction

The declaration quoted above, made by François Mitterrand during a speech at Figeac on 27 September 1982, set the tone for a decade during which the French head of state would circumvent the most stubborn political obstacles by public and ostensible rejections of political expediency, and at the end of which the electorate over whom he presided would repeatedly signal their disenchantment with politics.

The winning strategy of Mitterrand the politician and Mitterrand the President may be described as one of 'redemption by elimination':[1] redeeming the socialist cause by discarding its ideological justification; redeeming the middle ground electorally from the mainstream right by portraying himself as the embodiment of order and legitimacy; redeeming the declining credibility of political discourse by framing his utterances in a way that reflected on his own function as the republican persona above all partisan interests and considerations. The ritual consecration of his triumph in 1981, when he visited the Pantheon to honour the memory of great heroes of the Republic, marked the transformation of the erstwhile socialist tribune into a figure whose charisma would appeal to an electorate that was to become increasingly unresponsive to what in their eyes would seem the jaded discourse of party politics. Mitterrand's success and eventual fall from favour in the opinion polls reflect a period when the pattern of apparent political preferences belied the increasing volatility and disenchantment of the French electorate.

As has been cogently argued elsewhere, given the manner in which the charismatic authority of the President has been institutionalized under the Fifth Republic, what is elicited from the French electorate at the end of a campaign for the presidency is not their verdict on the candidates' political credibility, but on the credibility of the charisma they deploy as *présidentiables*.[2] Mitterrand's charisma quotient in 1988 greatly eclipsed that of his rivals, and his ultimate victory on May 8 with 54 per cent of the vote marked a resounding victory for a candidate who had made an indifference to partisan politics one of his major assets, and whose discourse, as John Gaffney illustrates in his chapter, systematically distanced him from the socialist cause.

The central importance of presidential charisma in determining the outcome of the elections was in fact suggested by the various polls taken in the lead up to the first round on April 24, and which indicated the existence of a significant disjunction between the way French voters viewed the campaign in political terms and their ultimate voting intentions. Polled regarding their strictly social and political concerns, the respondents underlined the following: unemployment, training, purchasing power, social justice and law and order. When asked to judge the presidential campaign in the light of these concerns, the general view was that it was uninteresting and lacking in real debate.[3] Clearly, the level of political conviction of the French voter could not be judged fully by the outcome of the presidential contest and had yet to be deduced from the voting patterns, often paradoxical, of the succeeding elections. This chapter will endeavour to analyse the evidence, which began accumulating in the ballot-boxes during the latter half of the 1980s, suggesting a general disenchantment with the entire political class in France, and then probe the difficulties encountered by that class, to the left and right of the Socialists, as parts of it attempted to respond to that challenge.

Paradoxical voting patterns

Hard on the heels of the presidential contest came the legislative elections of June 1988. Notwithstanding the element of indifference that might have been provoked by calling on the electorate to return to the ballot-box again in so short a space of time, the outcome of the first round of voting on 5 June was nonetheless notable for a level of abstentionism running at 34 per cent; a record for legislative elections during the life of the Third and Fourth, as well as the Fifth Republic. Implicit in this level of non-participation was the suggestion that the electorate was less indifferent to the idea of universal suffrage than to the constraints that governed the exercise of their political choices. The incipient feeling that the majority voting system designed to ensure the stability of executive authority had also forged alliances and dependent political postures that seemed increasingly anachronistic to the electorate, was something which surfaced more clearly in the aftermath of the second round of voting on 12 June.

Paradoxically and uniquely in the life of the Fifth Republic, the party of the President had neither an absolute majority in the National Assembly, nor was it sure of forging an alliance that would enable it to constitute a majority. Conversely, the President and the PS (*Parti socialiste*) were able to benefit from one of the features that characterize parliamentary politics under the Fifth Republic: the difficulty faced by the opposition should it attempt to constitute a negative majority capable of censuring the government. The verdict passed by the electorate in June 1988 made this highly unlikely since the way their preferences had been translated by the voting system had weakened the Gaullist right, represented by the RPR (*Rassemblement pour la République*) and pulled the PCF (*Parti communiste français*) back from the brink of catastrophe. Unless facing an active coalition comprising such opposites as the two foregoing parties, the government was unlikely to be threatened. However, of more profound significance to the entire political class was a greater long-term lesson that could be adduced from the changes in government brought about in 1981, 1986 and the following period of cohabitation: on the one hand, public opinion did not exclude the prospect of any of the major parties acceding to governmental power, but by the same token did not believe in any single party as possessing the secret of good government.[4] Traditional allegiances and voting habits that had hitherto sustained the bond between the electorate and the political elite purporting to advance their interests were showing distinct signs of fatigue. The voters were showing themselves less inclined to be guided by the established political parties and less susceptible to their political discourse.

On the one hand, an analysis of second round voting in the legislative election of 1988 indicated a return to the classic French pattern. The penetration of support for the Socialist candidate in the fiefdoms of the mainstream right like the departments of the Bas-Rhin, Moselle, Haute-Loire, and Manche, that had occurred in April and May 1988, receded. Equally, the progress made by the FN (*Front National*) as represented by Jean-Marie Le Pen in places like Haute-Loire in April, was reversed in June. Whereas in the presidential elections he had polled almost 15 per cent of the vote, in the legislative elections his party and diverse elements of the far right polled 10 per cent, thus returning to the same level of support they enjoyed in the legislative elections of 1986. In keeping with tradition, grassroots organization and the loyalty to local notables played a preponderant role in determining the choices of the electorate. On the other hand, however, this could not entirely erase the evolution signalled by the voting patterns of the previous election, or the scale of it.

The depth of the defeat suffered by the mainstream right in the first round of the presidential elections on 24 April 1988 was illustrated by the fact that its two candidates gathered only 36 per cent of the votes cast. The decline of its popularity among bedrock voters like the retired and the self-employed may be partly explained by the competition from the far right, and the legitimist vote cast for the presidential incumbent which characterizes this type of contest. A closer scrutiny of the failures of the two challengers from the mainstream right, however, suggests the influence of more long-term factors. The failure of Raymond Barre of the UDF (*Union pour la démocratie française*) to mobilize the traditional bases of support which, in addition to those already mentioned, include the agricultural constituency, skilled trades and practising Catholics, was more marked than Valéry Giscard d'Estaing's had been in 1981. Similarly, Jacques Chirac of the RPR only succeeded in gathering 24 per cent of the votes in the 15 departments which had proved to be most loyal to his party in 1981. The tactical errors of Barre's campaign notwithstanding, and taking into account the attractions of Le Pen to certain sections of the RPR, the fortunes of the candidates of the mainstream right could nonetheless be viewed as evidence of the fact that there had been a noteworthy loosening in the structures of partisan voting.[5]

The resurgent influence of traditional loyalties in the legislative elections that followed were nuanced in an untraditional way by the expectations and behaviour of the electorate. The opinion polls carried out at the end of May 1988 confirmed that, in stark contrast to 1981, the presidential victor had been chosen on the grounds of his personal qualities rather than political considerations based on his programme. By the same token, it was both paradoxical and not entirely surprising that 47 per cent of the cross-section of voters polled would have preferred to see the implementation of liberal conservative policies rather than the socialist ones desired by 38 per cent of voters sampled, and that 25 per cent of those who had voted for Mitterrand were in favour of liberal conservative policies. In contrast also to 1981, what was clear at the end of May 1988 was that the triumph of the Socialist candidate had not unleashed a wave of enthusiasm for his party and a concomitant surge in membership. Only 26 per cent of French voters questioned believed that the outcome of the election would have a positive effect on their everyday lives, as opposed to 44 per cent in 1981. The decline in expectations was spectacular among those sections of the electorate which one might have assumed would be buoyed by the result of 8 May 1988. In contrast to 1981, the percentage of 18-24 year-olds expecting a positive impact on their lives declined from 54 per cent to 27 per cent; among skilled workers the decline was from 59 per cent to 32 per cent; among Socialist sympathisers the fall was from 72 per cent to 49 per cent.[6]

The electorate, therefore, had decided not to provide the party of the President with the period of grace which it had been granted in 1981, and deprived the legislative elections which followed of the dynamic which would have allowed the victory of 8 May to be complemented by a clear presidential majority in the legislative contest in June. What may be judged as a return to a more classical Fifth Republic pattern of voting in June has to be attenuated by the fact that for the left, and in particular for the 41 per cent of the Socialist voters sampled on 6 and 7 June, presidential and prime ministerial warnings about the dangers of a majority not emerging for the PS after the second round did not constitute a terrifying prospect. The level of abstentionism remained at a record level of 30 per cent, only four points less than in the first round of voting. The successful mobilization of the mainstream right must be qualified by the fact that this contained a significant disparity. The ability of the Socialists to squeeze home with a relative majority was, to a crucial degree, attributable to the failure of one of the partners in the URC (*l'Union du rassemblement et du centre*), the RPR, to regain lost ground. Of the 81 marginal constituencies where the right had obtained between 48 per cent and 52 per cent in the first round, the success rate for the RPR candidate going forward to the second round under the URC banner was 15 per cent, whereas for the UDF candidates in the same position the success rate was 44 per cent. In view of the fact that the transfer of votes from the far right to the mainstream right had operated with reasonable smoothness, the influence of the FN could not in this instance be regarded as a factor mitigating the failure of the RPR. It could therefore be deduced that the brand of Gaullist right-wing politics purveyed by Chirac and the RPR was not keeping pace with the changing tastes of the voters. The classic confrontation of left and right in general was no longer as securely underpinned by predictable partisan voting on the part of the electorate.

The abstentionist phenomenon and the major parties

The municipal and European elections which took place in the spring of 1989 confirmed the tendencies symptomatic of change in France's political culture. The exceptional degree of abstentionism was undeniably due, in part, to an overloaded electoral calendar, but it also expressed a certain degree of scepticism on the part of the electorate as a whole. One of the major paradoxes to emerge from the municipal elections of March 1989 was that the PS more than recovered from the reversals it had suffered in March 1983 in order to secure its highest ever level of penetration at local level, while at the same time recording less support in large towns than it had done in 1983 (down 1-2 points), and 1977 (down 8 points). Overall, 38 per cent of voters in communes of 30,000 inhabitants or more chose not to vote (compared to 30 per cent in 1983), and in Paris 43 per cent of registered voters deserted the ballot-box, leading to another record level of abstentionism since 1945 of 27 per cent.[7] This phenomenon needs to be allied with the fact, however, that abstentionism occurred selectively during the late 1980s, according to the nature of the election and also social and demographic distinctions. Certainly, compared to the level of abstentionism which characterized the cantonal elections of September 1988 (60 per cent) and the referendum on New Caledonia in the following November (62 per cent), March 1989 could be seen as a kind of upturn. But what made the general picture less sanguine for the future was the pronounced level of non-participation revealed by polls conducted between the two rounds, among women, blue-collar workers, salaried staff and 18-24 year-olds. The key factor in the success of the Socialists was that the republican discipline of the left operated more effectively than the alliances on the right.

There was, in fact, a significant weakening of the bi-polar conditions determining who should go through to the second round on 19 March, largely to the detriment of the right. The resulting 58 three-way contests and 17 four-way contests in the second round were first and foremost due to the determination of the FN to 'punish' the mainstream right, and the reluctance of the ecologists to choose between right and left. Conversely, and in spite of some appearances to the contrary, the PS and PCF exploited their alliance more fruitfully within the context of the bi-polar coalition in which they had to operate. The PS was therefore able to claim victory at the outcome of the municipal elections, but this was obtained within a broader context notable for the following features: the rising indifference to politics; inter-party relations beginning to strain within the confines of the bi-polar coalitions that had developed since the 1960s; the growing rootedness of alternative poles of attraction represented by the FN for the right, and the ecologists for the left.

An analysis of the results of the European elections of 18 June 1989 in the light of the conclusions drawn from the results of the municipal contest that had preceded it three months earlier, needs to be qualified by the consideration that given the absence of a second round, a focus on the right versus left nature of the contest is necessarily attenuated. Furthermore, since its inception the European election has come at the bottom of the list in terms of voter participation: a 39 per cent abstention rate in 1979, 43 per cent in 1984 and 50 per cent in 1989. By the same token, however, these considerations allow for a more general look at the phenomenon of abstentionism and the standing of the major parties, as intimated by the European election.

Compared to 1984, the argument that the failure of the European election to mobilize the voters was due to its overriding appeal to the more advantaged social classes enamoured of the possibilities offered by Europe, lost some of its cogency in 1989. The gap between the abstentionists with a higher education and those without, for example, had narrowed in comparison with 1984. The post-electoral soundings carried out by the polling organisation SOFRES showed, as expected, that on the left and the right, voter participation was greatest among the better-educated, business and professional classes. More surprising, however, was the discovery that the differential advantage, in terms of participation, accruing to the right, was not due to the greater mobilization of the socio-economic categories mentioned above, but the enduring instinct to participate among some sections of the retired, small traders, those in agriculture and low incomes. One explanation for this may lay in the hypothesis that these groups represent an electoral fringe which has preserved a political culture where a fundamental expression of fidelity to civic duty remains the obligation to vote. The general tendency revealed by the SOFRES findings, however, indicated quite the opposite. The culture defining the political behaviour of the mass of French voters was undeniably changing, altering in a profound way the perception of civic duty. In the definition offered to a representative cross-section of the electorate of what constituted a good citizen, the characteristic of being a 'regular voter' had, in 1976, been cited by 51 per cent of the respondents, in 1983 this figure had dropped to 43 per cent, and in 1989 it was down to 38 per cent.[8] The depth and frequency of abstentionism was undeniably linked to the voters' declining faith in politics, and in particular, in the three great parties of government representing the political establishment.

One of the striking results of the European elections was the fact that the three major parties combined elicited the support of barely a quarter of registered voters (excluding the centrist list put forward by Simone Weil) and obtained half of the votes cast. This was not something specific to the European elections, but confirmed a trend that could be traced through all of the electoral contests since the first round of the presidential election of 1988. This decline was matched by the presence of increasingly well-entrenched alternatives to the right and the left of the PS-RPR-UDF political establishment. The fact that the score of the FN in the European election of 1989 (12 per cent) was barely more than it had been in 1984 (11 per cent) was not an accurate reflection of its growing strength at grassroots level, underlined by the party's success in the by-elections at the end of 1989 and the cantonal by-elections in November 1989 and July 1990. This success was undoubtedly linked to the FN's ability to capitalize on the changing concerns of the electorate by appropriating the narrow band of themes causing the greatest alarm to the voters. Whereas in September 1989 immigration came seventh in the order of concerns identified by the French, in February 1990 this had risen to the second slot, behind unemployment. This transition was signalled in the *SOFRES/Nouvel Observateur* poll of November 1989, which showed that more RPR voters were inclined to trust the FN's Jean-Marie Le Pen on the immigration issue than their own Jacques Chirac, and that Le Pen's credibility on this matter among UDF voters was second only to that of their leader, Valéry Giscard d'Estaing.

The rise of the ecological vote in 1989 (11 per cent) was in marked contrast to 1984 (4 per cent), and its greatest successes were recorded among those under 35, the middle classes and those voters with a higher education. The ecologists progressed across the board politically but had their best results among the voters who considered themselves centrist or left-wing. This, however, did not mean that the ecologists constituted a left alternative for disaffected PS voters. In addition to its stand on the environment, disarmament and social action, the ecological cause was a rallying point for voters disillusioned with the established parties and its success was directly linked with the disenchantment of a section of the electorate with the system produced by partisan voting. Paradoxically therefore, though in their challenge to the status quo on certain key issues they stood to the left of the PS, the appeal of the ecologists to left-wing voters did not lay in their potential as a new, more effective vehicle for left-leaning ambitions, but in the broader and apolitical vision they offered. It is fair to conclude that one of the lessons to be drawn from the succession of elections that brought the 1980s to a close in France was that the major parties were losing their ability to convince.

One of the developments which wrongfooted many pollsters and commentators in the regional and cantonal elections of March 1992 was the turnout. At less than 29 per cent, the level of abstentionism was far lower than expected and reversed the trend established by previous elections. On this occasion the rejection of politics much commented on beforehand was not expressed by voter apathy. What participation did express, however, was a complex patchwork of anxieties and perplexities rather than a purposive affirmation of political allegiance.[9] In essence, the French electorate had turned out to confirm in an emphatic manner its disaffection vis-à-vis the established parties.[10]

In one sense, the willingness of the electorate to vote was more notable, compared with the preceding pattern of abstentionism, in view of the technical innovation represented by the simultaneous operation of two elections using different voting systems: a one-round proportional system for the regional elections and a two-round majority system for the cantonals. The results of both elections nonetheless merited their characterization as 'élections sanction', a barometer of disapproval for all the major parties of government. For the PS, the score of 18.30 per cent in the regional elections and 19 per cent in the first round of the cantonal elections marked a regression to the low levels of support it had to endure in the immediate aftermath of its foundation in 1971. Yet the RPR and the UDF in alliance as the UPF (l'Union pour la France) polled only 33 per cent of the vote in the regional elections and neither party polled more than 15 per cent in the first round of the cantonal elections, thereby underlining their inability at that stage to capitalize on the failures of the Socialist government and restore their own image in the eyes of the electorate as a credible alternative.[11]

To the left of the Socialist government, its generally tacit but sometimes resentful parliamentary ally, the PCF continued its historic decline by polling only 8 per cent of the votes in the regional elections, compared to 10.20 per cent in the same contest in 1986. This was translated in terms of regional representation by a loss of 33 seats, down from 149 to 116, and in the cantonal elections the number of Communist-controlled cantons shrank from 120 to 98.[12] The only parties whose standing was enhanced by the elections were the notable outsiders vis-à-vis the political establishment: the FN and the ecologists. Although it failed to capture any of the regions or to rival the RPR or UDF in the cantons, the 14.10 per cent polled in the regional contest and the 12.31 per cent scored in the first round of the cantonal contest marked a clear advance for the FN. Unquestionably, however, the greatest success was gained by the ecologists: 7.10 per cent for Brice Lalonde's Génération Ecologie and 6.80 per cent for Antoine Waechter's Verts in the regional contest, and a 10 per cent share for the ecology platform in the cantonal elections. As important as the quantitative support was the growing breadth of support for the ecology platform, especially among women, young people, and the professional classes.

If one thing was clear after a decade of Socialist power in France it was that the electorate would obey first and foremost its own dictates rather than fulfil the expectations of the political establishment, as was amply demonstrated by the landslide in the legislative elections of March 1993 which swept the Socialists out of government.[13] When this landslide is viewed in the longer perspective provided by the entire period of the Socialist years, certain underlying tendencies are confirmed and superficial assumptions dispelled. The 31.10 per cent abstention rate in the first round on 21 March signalled that far from confirming a new-found enthusiasm for the exercise of their prerogatives by the French electorate, the landslide actually obscured the rising tendency to abandon the conventional expressions of political preference; a conclusion further supported by the large number of blank or spoiled voting slips, which at 5.20 per cent was considerably higher than the 2 per cent rate in 1988. Although the RPR and UDF won 84 per cent of the seats, opinion polls between the two rounds clearly indicated that they would benefit from the punitive intentions of the electorate vis-à-vis the PS rather than a renewal of support for themselves. In global terms, although the right scored 5 points more than in 1988 by scooping 57 per cent of the votes cast, this was still 3.5 points down on 1986.[14]

The argument that the victory of the mainstream right was won by default explains the apparent contradiction contained in the fact that the UDF-RPR came to occupy four-fifths of the seats in the new Assembly, while scoring less than they did in the legislative elections at the beginning of the Socialist years: 39.60 per cent in the first round in 1993 as opposed to 41.20 per cent in 1981. The reason lay clearly in the collapse of the third great party of the political establishment, the PS, which together with its diverse left allies could gather barely more than 19 per cent of the vote in the first round; its lowest level of support since 1973.[15]

The declining appeal of the established political parties which became apparent as the 1980s drew to a close, cannot nonetheless be attributed to the total failure of those parties to perceive the need for organizational change and ideological repositioning in order to regain the trust of the electorate. On the right and on the left, voices were raised expressing a need for the established parties to change in order to catch up with the changing priorities and attitudes of the electorate: calls for renovation that often elicited divisive expressions of reaction.

Renovation and reaction, left and right

As Alistair Cole illustrates in his chapter on the PS, although during Mitterrand's first term as President the PS was largely confined to observer status and obliged to provide justifications for policies it had not produced, during Mitterrand's second term there was a resurgence of factionalism, based on policy and personality, as different strands within the party promoted their proposals for what they regarded as the painful but inevitable process of ideological redefinition. In contrast to the PS, however, movements in its senior and erstwhile dominant sister party on the left, the PCF, called into question the fundamental identity of the party in the quest for renovation, and elicited splits and reactions that were to emerge dramatically in the public eye.

Challenges to the leadership, its management, and its interpretation of the role of the PCF were carried into the 1980s by the 'contestataires', the name given to the members of the PCF university branch at Aix, and were worked into the debates animated by Communist intellectuals like Louis Althusser and Jean Elleinstein.[16] By the middle of the 1980s, however, a fundamental transformation had occurred in the demands for change within the party. Senior figures in the hierarchy began to articulate a desire to revise not only the means of achieving party policy, but the very essence of that policy. The first and most unequivocal call for renewal rather than reform was articulated by the central committee member Pierre Juquin, in a speech in Limoges in June 1984 which challenged the organizing principle of the party: democratic centralism. This is the principle which places a strait-jacket on the membership by allowing party directives to be discussed and passed down the party structure in a vertical manner, but which inhibits discussion along a horizontal plane at the base of the party structure, among the cells, and which might promote an ambition among the cells to exert an influence on the leadership taking decisions on their behalf, or what could be negatively interpreted by the leadership as 'factionalism'.

Juquin's watershed speech came in February 1985, at the party's 25th congress, when he made an overt call for a 'PC rénové', a modernized Communist party in which the concept of democratic centralism would be radically expanded to accommodate the will to self-management. Thus identified as the leading light of a growing 'rénovateur' movement, Juquin developed more openly his ideas concerning the need for the PCF to develop the pluralism that would enable it to respond and appeal to an increasingly pluralistic French society. The response of the leadership, especially after the PCF's poor performance in the legislative elections of 1986 when it obtained only 9.80 per cent of the votes cast, was one of harsh reaction. In a speech on the television channel *Antenne 2*, on 14 January 1987, the PCF's general secretary, Georges Marchais, accused the 'rénovateurs' of being in reality the 'liquidateurs' of the party, thus leaving little room for reconciliation between the leadership and the dissenting element within the party. Frustrated in his ambition to transform the party from within and below, in June 1987 Pierre Juquin resigned his position on the central committee and on 12 October he made the move which would precipitate the most dramatic and public split in the PCF's history, by announcing his decision to stand as a candidate in the presidential elections scheduled for the spring of 1988.

By the end of October 1987 the Communist 'rénovateurs' had rallied to Juquin and formed a co-ordinating committee. As a consequence the PCF found itself entering the prelude to the second presidential campaign of the decade facing a challenge that only a few months beforehand would have been wholly inconceivable: in addition to its traditional rivals, the officially selected PCF candidate, André Lajoinie, would be faced with a former high-ranking member of the party hierarchy supported by an organization of former high-profile PCF members. The platforms adopted by the rival Communist candidates clearly illustrated the impetus for renovation on the one hand, and the reaction it elicited on the other. Whereas Juquin elaborated ideas that would draw communism out of a mentality of 'massification' and reconcile it with the French electorate by placing it on the path to a greater accommodation with 'différence',[17] Lajoinie and Marchais focused their campaign on the egalitarianism and collectivism of the communist movement, leaving Lajoinie in the ironical position of being a presidential candidate campaigning against what he portrayed as the anti-democratic prerogatives of the office to which he aspired.[18]

Pierre Juquin's failure in the first round of the election with only 2.10 per cent of the votes cast brought little cheer to the PCF, for whom Lajoinie's 6.76 per cent share of the vote represented a historic low. Moreover, Juquin's failed attempt at renovation had not discouraged other highly placed members from attempting to reform the party from within. In October 1989 Charles Fiterman, a former Minister in the Socialist government led by Pierre Mauroy and a close associate of Georges Marchais, sent a written exposition to the central committee of the reforms he believed the party should undertake in order to move away from negative sectarian politics and towards 'universal values'.[19] The reaction of the leadership was to accuse Fiterman and his followers (a group christened the 'refondateurs', and not to be confused with the more radically breakaway 'reconstructeurs'), of wishing to take a 'step backwards' in their desire to alter fundamentally the nature of the party.[20] The enduring failure of the PCF to reconcile the elements within its ranks arguing for the ideological emancipation of the party and its redefinition vis-à-vis the electorate was illustrated by the fact that in the regional and cantonal elections of 1992, the official candidates promoted by the party were obliged, on a number of occasions, to compete against 'reconstructeur' candidates put forward on 'dissident' lists such as those of the *Alternative Démocratie Socialisme*, and endure being beaten by them, most notably in the departments of Sarthe, Haute-Vienne, Aisne, Drôme and Doubs.[21]

In contrast to the left as a whole, the PCF might, at first sight, have been able to congratulate itself on a soft landing after the legislative elections of March 1993. Whereas the left in total saw its numbers fall from 309 prior to the elections to 91 in the new Assembly, and the presidential majority saw its numbers fall from 282 to 67, the PCF endured only a mild erosion in its representation from 27 to 23 Deputies. Yet as analysis of this outcome shows, support for the PCF had come to rest on an even narrower base in national terms with, for example, over half of the PCF Deputies being returned by constituencies in the former 'red belt' around Paris. Dissenting voices could not fall silent faced with the fact that the party's support among registered voters had fallen to 6 per cent; lower even than the 6.80 per cent recorded in 1932.[22]

The political establishment of the mainstream right, as represented by the RPR and the UDF, was also to enter the 1980s with barely concealed divisions, especially among the leading personalities of these parties.[23] The defeat of the right in the 1981 presidential elections may be partly explained by the internal divisions between the RPR and the UDF, and on a personal level between Jacques Chirac and the presidential incumbent, Valéry Giscard d'Estaing, who had effectively forced Chirac out of his prime ministerial post in 1976 by reducing his role in the policy-making process. Chirac's notably lukewarm endorsement of Giscard d'Estaing in the presidential elections of 1981 was no less damaging for its transparent motivation.[24]

The underlying ambition of the 'rénovateurs' of the right was to become more apparent as the years of opposition were to lengthen: to find a way of uniting the right and the centre, the RPR and the UDF, into a more effective alliance capable of securing the majority represented by their individual constituencies and thereby be capable of taking power. The depth of the challenge this posed is easy to underestimate from an Anglo-American perspective, given the largely homogeneous nature of these forms of conservatism. For the mainstream right in France to come to power, however, the distinct tendencies within the RPR had to ally with the UDF, which itself was a federation of forces.[25]

The links between the ambitious young men from both the RPR and the UDF, like Michel Noir, Philippe Séguin, Charles Millon and François d'Aubert and who were later to be tagged as the 'quadragénaires rénovateurs', went back in some cases to 1982 to the study group called *le Cercle*, set up to elaborate ideas that reconciled the Gaullist convictions of the RPR with the more centrist notions identifiable with Raymond Barre, Giscard d'Estaing's former Prime Minister who was to occupy the centre ground of French politics with increasing intellectual authority as the 1980s progressed. In contrast to the 'quadragénaires', the behaviour of their political 'elders' on the centre-right was to convey a costly proclivity for internecine conflict.

The attempts of the Socialists at damage limitation in the face of the legislative elections of March 1986 suggested a strong presentiment on their part of impending defeat. The victory for the right, however, was attenuated by the fact that although Chirac's RPR emerged as the biggest party, it still needed the UDF and Chirac faced a figure in Raymond Barre who was perceived by the electorate as more presidential than himself, and who opposed the accommodation which would lead to the 'cohabitation' of a conservative Prime Minister and Cabinet with a Socialist President. Mindful of his ultimate ambition to be the presidential contender of the mainstream right, Chirac therefore adopted the invitation to form a government with the concomitant high-risk strategy for preserving his prospects as a 'présidentiable': the simultaneous attempt to undermine the Socialist president, as well as Raymond Barre and his supporters in the UDF.

The effect of Chirac's strategy with regard to relations among the parties of the mainstream right was to produce a mounting tension between his party and the centrists; a problem compounded by a tactical error on his part which led to dissenting opinions being voiced by the 'rénovateurs' in his own ranks. With the growing outline of the presidential elections on the horizon, Chirac chose to consolidate his position on the right, in view of the increasingly powerful and rival pole of attraction represented by the FN for those constituents, to the detriment of his support from the centre.

The drift to the right was sufficiently alarming for Michel Noir, then Chirac's Minister with responsibility for Foreign Trade, to declare in May 1987 that it was better to lose an election than to lose one's soul. Noir's warning, however, was not heeded and resulted in his growing isolation vis-à-vis the party hierarchy. The determination of Chirac and his principal supporters to conserve their right-wing constituency and appeal to FN supporters was made plain in the run-up to the second ballot of the presidential elections on 8 May 1988, when Charles Pasqua, the Interior Minister, affirmed that the FN and the RPR shared the same preoccupations and values, in a blatant attempt to persuade FN supporters to transfer their votes to Chirac in the second round. The failure of this policy was made manifest in the post-electoral analyses of why Chirac had failed to rally more than 46 per cent of the votes, and which suggested the possibility that 25 per cent of Le Pen's voters tranferred to Mitterrand in the second round and that 13 per cent of Barre's voters did likewise.

The high point for the 'rénovateurs' of the right was reached in the immediate aftermath of the municipal elections of March 1989, as a result of which Michel Noir and his supporters were swept to power in Lyon. The RPR hierarchy was now forced to contend with the member who had scored a notable victory by taking France's third most important town, but who it also regarded as 'incontrôlable'. [26] In the aftermath of the presidential elections, Charles Millon and Philippe de Villiers of the PR,

Dominique Baudis and Bernard Bosson of the CDS, and François Fillon and Alain Carignon of the RPR had made no secret of their meetings in the National Assembly to articulate their criticism of the 'partisan and sclerotic structures' which divided the Gaullists, the liberals and the Christian Democrats, keeping them in sterile opposition.[27] The same themes were to re-emerge more strongly after the municipal elections, and surfaced shortly afterwards at the RPR party sessions in Nice in April with calls for the renewal of party structures to facilitate the emancipation of the grassroots.

The calls of the 'rénovateurs' elicited a fierce reaction from the RPR old guard, led by Charles Pasqua and Bernard Pons, who unequivocally rejected any change which might, in their opinion, result in the absorption of the Gaullist right by the Giscardian centre. Though the 'rénovateurs' from the RPR were able to effect organizational changes in their party and force the acceptance of 'tendances' on the leadership, the frustration of 'rénovateur' ambition both in the RPR and UDF was in no small measure due to the lack of a coherent policy, organization, common strategy and a single leader to rally around. One may even suggest that the 'quadragénaires' were further undermined in their ambition by a crucial but unacknowledged consideration: their own long-term prospects as leaders of the right, and for a handful of the most prominent ones, their long-term prospects as 'présidentiables'.

The 'quadragénaires' advocating a move away from partisan politics and the more effective federation of opposition forces found their voices again over an issue which was to put partisan loyalties and party discipline under considerable strain. In the campaign preceding the French referendum on the ratification of the Maastricht Treaty on European union, a group of approximately 40 'quadragénaires' met three weeks before the referendum, under the leadership of Alain Juppé, general secretary of the RPR, and François Bayrou, general secretary of the UDF, and invited the press to witness their support for a 'yes' vote in the referendum and their commitment to greater unity among the parties of the mainstream right in France.[28]

Ironically, the European cause which the 'quadragénaires' had met to promote was also being vigorously contested by two of the most high profile figures originally identified with the group: Philippe Séguin of the RPR, and Philippe de Villiers, who departed the ranks of the UDF to launch his own, highly moralized movement to rescue the right, *Combat pour les valeurs*, at the head of the electors he described as 'la génération Soljenitsyne'.[28] As for the elders in the RPR and the UDF, the prelude to the referendum on Maastricht served to highlight the differences, in terms of policy and personality, which made the quest for enduring success in the co-ordination of the forces of the mainstream right, and the restoration of its ability to inspire the confidence of the electorate, such a difficult enterprise. The summer leading up to the referendum was punctuated by a series of warnings on the part of the pro-Maastricht UDF to the RPR and its leader regarding their equivocations on Maastricht, and on 4 July in Paris, in front of a gathering of party faithful largely hostile to the treaty, Chirac announced his decision to vote 'yes', but 'without enthusiasm'.[30]

Conclusion

The issue of Europe had exposed the difficulties encountered in attempting to coordinate the forces of the mainstream right in France, as the endeavours of the fortysomething 'rénovateurs' had revealed the structural and organizational factors which militated against its cohesion. A summary review of the succession of acronyms used by the opposition to christen their alliances after the triumph of the Socialists in 1981 provides succinct evidence of this: UNM (*l'Union pour la nouvelle majorité*), URC (*l'Union du rassemblement et du centre*), CCO (*Comité de coordination de l'opposition*), and into the 1990s with UPF (*l'Union pour la France*). Notwithstanding the landslide in the legislative elections of March 1993, tensions between the new government and the members of its parliamentary majority soon began to appear.

In the course of the summer following the installation of Edouard Balladur as the new Prime Minister from the RPR 'cohabiting' with a Socialist President, the dangers of controlling a large parliamentary majority containing powerful and potentially rival personalities became evident. On 16 June, after having been appointed President of the National Assembly, and during the course of a colloquium in Paris on new strategies for employment, Philippe Séguin denounced what he called a 'Munich social'; the capitulation by the Balladur government faced with the dictates of financial orthodoxy when what was needed was a fundamental revision of values and choices in favour of employment.[31]

The centrists were not slow in affirming their refusal to be taken for granted. Alarmed by the tough measures proposed by the Interior Minister, Charles Pasqua, aimed at ending clandestine immigration, and the even tougher amendment proposed by the RPR Deputy Alain Marsaud, the centrist Ministers Simone Veil (Social Affairs) and Pierre Méhaignerie (Justice) wrote to the Prime Minister expressing their concern in a letter which was subsequently leaked to the media.[32]

As for the eternal rivals Valéry Giscard d'Estaing and Jacques Chirac, they soon revived their inclination to be, or to allow others to perceive them, as alternative poles of attraction to Balladur. Giscard d'Estaing took his opportunity over the government's proposal to revise *La Loi Falloux*, passed in 1850 and aimed at securing the secular and republican nature of schooling in France by limiting the subsidy available to private (i.e. church) schools from public funds. When François Mitterrand refused to approve the parliamentary timetable allowing debate on government proposals for easing these restrictions, Giscard d'Estaing accused him of violating the constitution.[33] Implicit in the criticism, however, was doubt over Balladur's ability to manage the cohabitation with the President in a manner that was anything other than one of appeasement. The unease in the UDF was more than matched by the resentment among the traditionally Gaullist elements of the RPR over government policy on agriculture, Europe and the economy, leading to wistful reminders of the charismatic link characterizing Chirac's relationship with the RPR and which Balladur was incapable of fostering.[34]

In contrast to the 1980s, the tensions between the parties of the mainstream right in the 1990s stem from the realities of power, rather than the absence of it. However, as the final chapter of this study will show, the attempts of the established parties of left and right to restore their appeal vis-à-vis the electorate was also frustrated by profound shifts in France's underlying political culture; shifts which also help to explain the 'greening' of France.

Notes

1.   Giesbert, F.-O. (1990), *Le Président*, Points, Paris, p.454.

108

2.   Gaffney, J. (1990), 'Presidentialism and the Fifth Republic', in J. Gaffney (ed.), *The French Presidential Elections of 1988*, Dartmouth, Aldershot, pp. 10-11.

3.   Blondiaux, L. (1988), 'Une campagne insaisissable', *Le Monde, dossiers et documents: l'élection présidentielle*, May, p. 53.

4.   A. Laurens, 'De l'ouverture ratée à l'obligation d'ouverture, ibid., pp.42-3.

5.   Jaffré, J. (1988), 'France au centre, victoires socialistes', *Pouvoirs*, no. 47, pp. 158-81, p. 161.

6.   Findings summarized by Jaffré, ibid., pp. 172-3.

7.   Le Gall, G. (1989), "Novations et paradoxes des municipales 89', *Revue Politique et Parlementaire*, no. 940, pp. 8-13.

8.   Jaffré, J. (1990), 'Après les municipales et les européennes. Le nouveau décor électoral', *Pouvoirs*, no. 55, pp. 147-62, p. 152.

9.   Frappat, B., 'Désaveu et désarroi', *Le Monde*, 24 March 1992.

10. Dupin, E., 'Sanction pour le PS et stagnation pour l'UPF', *Libération*, 23 March 1992.

11. For an analysis of these figures see Le Gall, G. (1992), 'Elections: les handicaps du pouvoir face à 1993', *Revue Politique et Parlementaire*, no. 958, pp. 3-13.

12. Courtois, S. (1992), 'La marginalisation accrue du parti communiste français', *Revue Politique et Parlementaire*, no. 958, pp. 24-27.

13. It was a landslide which could be considered historic in terms of the size of the parliamentary majority it created and which was the sixth of its kind, following those of 1815, 1871, 1919, 1968 and arguably 1981. See J. Julliard, 'Le sixième raz de marée', *Le Nouvel Observateur*, 25 March 1993.

14. These findings are summarized by Bauby, P. (1993), in 'Les législatives en perspective', *Revue Politique et Parlementaire*, no. 964, pp. 59-63.

15. See Ponceyri, R. (1993), 'La victoire de la droite ou le triomphe par défaut', *Revue Politique et Parlementaire*, no. 964, pp. 20-33.

16. For a fuller discussion of the pressures for change within the PCF during the 1980s, see G. G. Raymond, 'The PCF: the Party of the Masses and its Marginalisation', in Cole, A. (ed.) (1991), *French Political Parties in Transition*, Dartmouth, Aldershot, pp. 42-60.

17. Juquin had criticized this aspect of the Communist mentality at length in (1985), *Autocritiques*, Grasset, Paris, Chapter 9.

18. For a fuller account of the campaigns led by the two Communist candidates in the presidential election of 1988, see G. G. Raymond, 'His Master's Voice? André Lajoinie', in Gaffney, J. (ed.) (1990), *The French Presidential Elections of 1988*, Aldershot, Dartmouth, pp. 158-86.

19. 'L'ancien ministre invite les communistes à un "énorme travail idéologique et politique" ', *Le Monde*, 15-16 October 1989.

20. Biffaud, O., 'La direction mobilise ses secrétaires fédéraux contre MM. Fiterman et Le Pors', *Le Monde*, 21 October 1989.

21. Courtois, 'La marginalisation accrue du parti communiste français', p.27.

22. See Courtois, S. (1993), 'Le succès en trompe-l'oeil du Parti communiste français', *Revue Politique et Parlementaire*, no. 964, pp. 49-53.

23. As Anne Stevens observes, it is in the nature of French politics that parties may arise principally out of a shared support for a particular leader rather than out of strongly held and coherently formulated beliefs, in which case the notion of intra as well as inter-party loyalty or discipline becomes less susceptible to a fixed and firm interpretation; in (1992), *The Government and Politics of France*, MacMillan, London, p.195.

24. As Catherine Nay describes in (1980), *La double méprise* (Grasset, Paris), Valéry Giscard d'Estaing appointed Jacques Chirac Prime Minister on 21 May 1974 for reasons which could not be reconciled with Chirac's own for accepting. Whereas Giscard d'Estaing had hoped that the appointment of Chirac would lead to a merging of the Gaullist movement with the presidential majority, Chirac had accepted the post in the hope of securing the survival of the Gaullist movement under his leadership. This was a key factor in explaining the degeneration of the relationship between these two figures into a bitter struggle for power. For a more detailed understanding of Chirac's motivation see F-O. Giesbert's biography of him (1987), *Jacques Chirac*, Seuil, Paris.

25. The current incarnation of the Gaullist movement is the result of a process of frequent mutation and occasional restructuring. Inspired by

De Gaulle in 1947 and designed to be a mass movement targeting the overthrow of the Fourth Republic, it began as the RPF (*Rassemblement du peuple français*), was reborn in the 1950s as the UNR (*Union pour la nouvelle République*), became briefly in the 1960s the UDVe (*Union des démocrates pour la Ve République*) before settling into its identity as the UDR (*Union des démocrates pour la République*), which was ultimately reborn as the RPR in 1976, opting for a style more reminiscent of its origins as the RPF. For its part, the UDF was born out of a confederation of non-Gaullist parties created in 1978 by Valéry Giscard D'Estaing to support his presidency, comprising principally the conservatively-inclined PR (*Parti républicain*), the Christian-Democratic CDS (*Centre des démocrates sociaux*), the *Parti radical* and other smaller formations.

26. Barjon, C., 'Le sacre de l'enfant terrible', *Le Nouvel Observateur*, 16 March 1989. However, in 1993 Michel Noir was to fall dramatically from grace as the leader of 'la génération morale' due to allegations of illegally profiting from his relationship with his son-in-law Pierre Botton, a financier who had become notorious for his dubious financial practices. See Sitbon, G., 'Lyon: le drame d'un homme pressé', *Le Nouvel Observateur*, 18 March 1993.

27. Algalarrondo, H. and Barjon, C.,'Les mutins de la droite', *Le Nouvel Observateur*, 16 April 1989.

28. Biffaud, O., 'Les "quadras" au château', *Le Monde*, 4 September 1992.

29. Carton, D., 'Le nouveau combat de M. de Villiers', *Le Monde*, 25 June 1992.

30. Biffaud, O., 'Le référendum sur la construction de l'Union européenne', *Le Monde*, 7 July 1992.

31. Biffaud, O., 'M. Séguin appelle à un "renversement" des choix du gouvernement', *Le Monde*, 18 June 1993.

32. D. Carton, 'M. Méhaignerie et Mme Veil veulent rappeler la vigilance du pôle centriste de la majorité', *Le Monde*, 22 June 1993.

33. Giscard d'Estaing, V., 'Un glissement constitutionnel', *Le Monde*, 8 July 1993.

34. Algalarrondo, H., 'Balladur-RPR: l'état de grogne', *Le Nouvel Observateur*, 17 June 1993.

Bibliography

Amouroux, H. (1988), *Monsieur Barre*, Hachette, Paris.

Algalarrondo, H. and Barjon, C., 'Les mutins de la droite', *Le Nouvel Observateur*, 16 April 1989.

Algalarrondo, H., 'Balladur-RPR: l'état de grogne', *Le Nouvel Observateur*, 17 June 1993.

Barjon, C., 'Le sacre de l'enfant terrible', *Le Nouvel Observateur*, 16 March 1989.

Bauby, P. (1993), 'Les législatives 1993 en perspective', *Revue Politique et Parlementaire*, no. 964.

Bell, D.S. (ed.) (1983), *Contemporary French Political Parties*, Croom Helm, London.

Biffaud, O., 'La direction mobilise ses secrétaires fédéraux contre MM. Fiterman et Le Pors', *Le Monde*, 21 October 1989.

Biffaud, O., 'Le référendum sur la construction de l'Union européenne', *Le Monde*, 7 July 1992.

Biffaud, O., 'Les "quadras" au château', *Le Monde*, 4 September 1992.

Biffaud, O., 'M. Séguin appelle à un "renversement" des choix du gouvernement', *Le Monde*, 18 June 1993.

Carton, D., 'Le nouveau combat de M. de Villiers', *Le Monde*, 25 June 1992.

Carton, D., 'M. Méhaignerie et Mme Veil veulent rappeler la vigilance du pôle centriste de la majorité', *Le Monde*, 22 June 1993.

Charlot, J. (1986), *Les partis politiques en France*, FNSP, Paris.

Cole, A. (ed.) (1990), *French Political Parties in Transition*, Dartmouth, Aldershot.

Courtois, S. (1992), 'La marginalisation accrue du parti communiste', *Revue Politique et Parlementaire*, no. 958.

Courtois, S. (1993), 'Le succès en trompe-l'oeil du Parti communiste français', *Revue Politique et Parlementaire*, no. 964.

Desjardins, T. (1986), *Les chiraquiens*, La Table Ronde, Paris.

Dupin, E., 'Sanction pour le PS et stagnation pour l'UPF', *Libération*, 23 March 1992.

Frappat, B., 'Désaveu et désarroi', *Le Monde*, 24 March 1992.

Gaffney, J. (ed.) (1990), *The French Presidential Elections of 1988*, Dartmouth, Aldershot.

Le Gall, G. (1989), 'Novations et paradoxes des municipales 89', *Revue Politique et Parlementaire*, no. 940.

Le Gall, G. (1992), 'Elections: les handicaps du pouvoir face à 1993', *Revue Politique et Parlementaire*, no. 958.

Giesbert, F.-O. (1987), *Jacques Chirac*, Seuil, Paris.

Giscard d'Estaing, V., 'Un glissement constitutionnel', *Le Monde*, 8 July 1993.

Jaffré, J. (1988), 'France au centre, victoires socialistes', *Pouvoirs*, no. 47.

Jaffré, J. (1990), 'Après les municipales et les européennes. Le nouveau décor électoral', *Pouvoirs*, no. 55.

Jouve, P. and Magoudi, A. (1987), *Chirac Portrait total*, Carrère, Paris.

Julliard, J., 'Le sixième raz de marée', *Le Nouvel Observateur*, 25 March 1993.

Juquin, P. (1985), *Autocritiques*, Grasset, Paris.

Juquin, P. (1987), *Fraternellement libre*, Grasset, Paris.

Lajoinie, A. with Passevent, R. (1987), *A coeur ouvert*, Messidor, Paris.

Le Monde, *Dossiers et documents: l'élection présidentielle*, May, 1988.

Le Monde, 'L'Ancien ministre invite les communistes à un "énorme travail idéologique et politique" ',15-16 October 1989.

Ponceyri, R. (1993), 'La victoire de la droite ou le triomphe par défaut', *Revue Politique et Parlementaire*, no. 964.

Remilleux, J.-L. (1987), *Les Barristes*, Albin Michel, Paris.

Stevens, A. (1992), *The Government and Politics of France*, MacMillan, London.

Szafran, M. (1986), *Chirac ou les passions du pouvoir*, Grasset, Paris.

Ysmal, C. (1989), *Les partis politiques sous la Vème République*, Montchrestien, Paris.

PART II
CULTURE

5 Cultural Policy and Democratization under Mitterrand

DAVID LOOSELEY

Introduction

The post-1981 period has been a fascinating one for French cultural policy. One of the more flaunted aspects of the Mitterrand years, it has also been one of the more controversial, despite the Socialists' success in creating a consensus about the political importance of culture today. Ever since the appearance of Patrice de Plunkett's acerbic book, *La Culture en veston rose*, in 1982, there has been a common view that the policy, in the image of the Minister who conducts it, is modish, media-conscious and electoralist. Alongside this has developed a further tendency, illustrated in Marc Fumaroli's *L'Etat culturel*, to censure the government for vulgarizing France's great cultural tradition.[1] The purpose of this chapter is not to controvert these public images, but rather to show that they are oversimplified.

To do so, it is important to look outside the Mitterrand years to the Ministry's beginnings. In 1989, its thirtieth anniversary provided a timely reminder that the De Gaulle era had also been an exceptional decade for cultural policy and that, despite appearances and the millenarian rhetoric of 1981, Mitterrand's 'cultural project' was not the result of an immaculate conception. A number of threads of continuity in fact weave through state

117

intervention across the decades, the most important of which, though one which assumes more than one form, is probably the preoccupation with the sociological and geographical democratization of culture. This provides a useful historical model with which to compare the main characteristics of policy in the eighties and nineties: the theories and practices which best illustrate its distinctiveness and the central debate to which it has given rise.[2]

Historical precedents

The tradition of state involvement in French culture goes back to the *ancien régime*. But Gaullist and Socialist cultural policies share a more recent parentage in the Popular Front government; the coalition of broad-left parties which briefly came to power in 1936. The Front was interventionist about culture. Within the frame of a broader concern to organize popular leisure, it believed in the need for access to the great works of art constituting France's national inheritance to be democratized and decentralized through state action. This contrasted sharply with the ambient liberalism of the Third Republic's *beaux-arts* policies, which were mainly limited to preserving the heritage and to unadventurous acquisitions and commissions.[3] Although the Front government had little time to enact its plans, some were taken up subsequently, firstly by Vichy and then by the left-oriented governments of 1944–47 which emerged from the Resistance. Between 1946 and 1952, the state official Jeanne Laurent was instrumental in setting up the first five regional theatre centres (*Centres dramatiques nationaux*, or CDNs) and appointed the champion of democratization Jean Vilar to head the restructured *Théâtre national populaire* (TNP). After that, she was nudged out of office and policy returned to its former liberalism.

Ironically, it was a Gaullist rather than left-leaning government which finally materialized the Front's democratizing ambitions. The first autonomous 'Ministry of Cultural Affairs' was set up under the novelist André Malraux by grouping together a number of government departments belonging to disparate ministries. Malraux embodied the ideological ambivalence of Gaullism. On the one hand, he had flirted in the thirties with revolutionary politics and had figured among the intellectuals close to the Popular Front and dedicated to bringing high culture closer to the people. On the other, his admiration for Gaullism had by 1959 led him to develop the Front's cultural humanism into a nationalist mystique in which democratization became a means of achieving national consensus.

Malraux's aims were reflected in the mission officially defined for the new Ministry: 'Rendre accessibles les oeuvres capitales de l'humanité, et d'abord de la France, au plus grand nombre possible de Français, assurer la plus vaste audience à notre patrimoine culturel, et favoriser la création des oeuvres de l'art et de l'esprit qui l'enrichissent'.[4] Three of the major directions for future state intervention are contained here: protecting the heritage; contributing to it by encouraging contemporary artistic and intellectual creation; and, dominating and embracing these first two, democratizing access to it. Behind this primacy of democratization lay Malraux's own conception of the metaphysical and civic purposes of art in the modern world. The highest forms of culture constitute 'un supplément d'âme', a spiritual rampart against both the absurdity of human destiny and the 'deluge of imbecility' issuing from the 'dream-factories' of mass culture, which cynically exploit the most primitive forces within human beings: 'sex, blood and death'. Cultural policy, therefore, must involve taking only the most spiritual forms of human achievement to the masses, in order to help them resist this deluge and find a form of transcendence in a godless universe. It was a cruel irony for Malraux that such a messianic vision was never deemed by the Finance ministry to merit even 0.5 per cent of state spending.[5]

Although he took up Laurent's initiative by considerably increasing the number of CDNs, the clearest expression of his philosophy was the setting up of a regional network of *Maisons de la culture*, cultural 'cathedrals' dedicated to decentralizing the arts. Soon condemned by some local authorities as hotbeds of left-wing sedition, the *Maisons* were also contested from within, along with Malraux's entire ideology, during the 'cultural revolution' of May 1968. May pointed up the failure of his democratization policies to attract working-class audiences to high-cultural events and the resulting need to define a new cultural democracy. Rather than prescribing a single, normative culture to an undifferentiated mass, the state should assist authentic popular creativity and recognize the plurality of cultural practices in different communities or groups. From the

119

late sixties to the late seventies, this polarity between 'democratization' and 'democracy' became a familiar theme of cultural policy debate.

After Malraux's departure in 1969, a succession of Ministers or Secretaries of State took up post at the rue de Valois. At first, Malraux's voluntarism prevailed, but the election of Giscard d'Estaing in 1974 marked a partial return to liberalism. The state budget for the arts remained low, diminishing as the years went by (0.47 per cent of state spending in 1981),[6] democratization was implicitly questioned when decentralisation was declared 'dépassée', and the cultural sector was generally required to be more responsive to market forces, a point clearly made in 1979 when the practice of fixing book prices (via the publisher's 'prix conseillé') was terminated, paving the way for a price war between small or specialist bookshops and *grandes surfaces* like FNAC which could afford to offer big discounts.

During this time, Mitterrand's rebuilt Socialist Party was evolving its own cultural doctrine. This came to combine the Popular Front and post-war preoccupation with democratization, constantly evoked by the Socialists in opposition, with a more recent commitment to popular and regional cultural practices learnt from May. Much of the experimentation on which this new policy drew took place after the municipal elections of 1977 in the Socialist-run municipalities, while cultural gatherings like Avignon and Jack Lang's Nancy Theatre Festival served as parallel centres of aesthetic and ideological exploration, generally conducted in a post-1968 spirit.[7] Culture was a key issue in the run-up to the 1981 presidentials and the whole Socialist programme for government was presented as a 'projet culturel', a grand design for a new civilization.

After 10 May, Jack Lang became the first minister since Malraux to come to the rue de Valois with a doctrine, albeit a somewhat imprecise one articulated like Malraux's with the due dose of *envolées lyriques*. Lang has not been allowed to forget the titters he caused on 17 November 1981 when he told the National Assembly that with Mitterrand's election France had crossed the frontier between darkness and light. Even so, the statement perfectly epitomized the Socialists' intention to make a dramatic break with the past. Where Lang particularly sought to do this was in the relationship between culture and its environment. The Malraux ministry was, as we have seen, concerned with a culture that was high in every sense, a 'culture cultivée' which hovered immaterially like a skylark above material, sociological and economic realities. Lang refused this view. His aim was to reconcile culture with its context, be it the state, society, or the economy and to emphasize the integral part it plays within everyday experience. All forms of national life, all political actions, all commercial goods and public services have a cultural dimension. Far from being an ornamental extra or Malraux's 'supplément d'âme', culture, he told the Assembly, was life itself and as such not the responsibility of one but of every government minister, all forty-four of whom were Ministers of Culture. More particularly, he was wont in the early days to present cultural activity as a lost key to the economic as well as spiritual regeneration of a France weakened by recession, inertia, and competition from US-dominated multinationals. The economic failure of the previous regime was itself 'cultural', the result of a subservience to market-oriented values and an indifference to 'la force de l'esprit'. Conversely, encouraging artistic creation and the presence of beauty in daily life will stimulate a surge of creative imagination in all fields which will in turn dynamize the economy.[8]

Clearly, the 'cultural' here is Lang's flexible friend, its meaning stretched far beyond the sense in which the Malraux ministry used it. Lang's usage, often woolly, is generally influenced by the much broader anthropological or ethnological meaning the term 'culture' has acquired in the social sciences, indicating the value systems, social rituals and general ways of life constructed by given communities. By extension, his ideas are also based on a rather dubious rapprochement of *création*, in the French sense of new creative work, with the much looser, '68-influenced *créativité*, which a deft pirouette has transformed into an entrepreneurial form of enthusiasm likely to reinvigorate commerce and industry. Indeed, by a kind of 'semantic boulimia', enthusiasm of every kind and ultimately life itself become the object of a ministerial remit.[9] The potentially Big Brother resonance of this outlook was to be incessantly seized upon by Lang's critics in the coming years.

From principle to policy

How, then, was the ambivalent doctrine outlined above translated into policy? Having begun by commissioning a number of reports that would serve as a basis for future initiatives (Bredin on cinema, Troche on the visual arts, Pingaud and Barreau on reading, etc.), Lang was anxious in the interim to symbolize the establishment of a truly Socialist alternative to Giscardian liberalism. His first gesture in this direction was to reverse the 1979 freeing of book prices by instituting 'le prix unique du livre'. Rushed through Parliament in July-August 1981, it aimed to protect the threatened smaller retail outlets by imposing a maximum discount of 5 per cent and is now well established.[10] In September of the same year, Lang signalled his intention similarly to protect French film production from US domination by controversially refusing to attend the American film festival in Deauville. His stand marked the beginning of a continuing crusade against what he described the following year, even more controversially, as 'cet impérialisme financier et intellectuel' and 'l'immense empire du profit', though this did not stop the American share of the French market rising to 57.4 per cent in 1990.[11]

But most importantly of all, Lang launched an ambitious programme of public spending by obtaining the doubling of his budget for 1982, which passed from some 3,000 to 6,000 MF to reach 0.76 per cent of overall spending. This was without doubt his most important achievement, and although as he implied in November 1981 it could not possibly be repeated, he was able in the following years, not without difficulty despite Presidential backing, to ensure that the government did not follow the example of other Western nations which sacrificed the arts whenever austerity measures were introduced. By the general election of March 1986, the budget had almost, though more slowly than originally envisaged, reached the legendary 1 per cent called for by the cultural left since 1968. After a cut imposed by the Chirac government on Lang's successor François Léotard (1986–88), the budget climbed steadily from 1988 to reach 0.95 per cent in 1991, with spending at some 13,000 MF.[12]

Amongst these first pointed gestures was a boldly stated fidelity to the left tradition of democratization, symbolized in the first visit of a President to the Avignon Festival in the summer of 1981, and reinforced by Lang's own background in regional theatre and his frequent references to Vilar and Laurent. Over time, however, their approach to that tradition began to appear more complex.

The Socialist Party had long voiced the need to 'décoloniser la province' and Lang soon claimed cultural decentralization as a major priority, though in the event it was not primarily pursued through Defferre's decentralization laws of 1982–83. These in fact had little impact in the cultural field, quite simply because the Culture Ministry, reflecting the reservations of many decentralized artists and professionals, refused to relinquish control over the central funds made over to the local authorities. Determined to approach decentralization on its own terms, it set up new regional acquisitions structures, the *FRACs* and the *FRAMs*,[13] improved the financial and human resources of its own regional services, and, most importantly of all, developed the 'conventions de développement culturel'. These extended a contractual policy launched under Giscard d'Estaing in which the state and a tier of local government undertook jointly to fund a programme of local cultural development over a fixed period of time. Throughout the 1980s, the contracts proved particularly successful in their aim of stimulating local cultural policies and increased spending, thereby enabling new cultural amenities to spring up throughout French territory, albeit unevenly spread. At the end of the decade the Ministry commissioned a report from René Rizzardo which recommended a further phase of cultural decentralization though still not full devolution.[14]

The contracts policy was conducted by a newly created ministerial department: the *Direction du développement culturel* (DDC), headed by a sixties student activist Dominique Wallon. The DDC was a complex unit which became the focus of a diversity of Socialist approaches to democratization. In charge of the *Maisons de la culture* and of the smaller provincial arts centres set up after Malraux (collectively known as *Etablissements d'action culturelle* or EACs), it reorganized them and doubled their budget.[15] But the DDC was responsible for democratizing sociologically as well as geographically. Thus, contracts were signed not only with local authorities but with other bodies, including various ministries and workers' organisations, with a view to bringing culture to new, diversified publics in their daily environment and more especially in those locations where cultural deprivation was acute: factories, prisons, hospitals, the army, youth organisations, suburban districts or rural areas. The DDC in fact became one of the Ministry's more dynamic departments and the most controversial politically. Unsurprisingly, it was effectively dismantled under Léotard and, significantly perhaps, was not restored when Lang returned.

123

One last area in which the democratization tradition can be traced are the *chantiers du Président* or *grands projets*. As Pascal Ory has pointed out, the gradual recognition that culture falls within the President's *domaine réservé* is a feature of the post-Gaullian era, beginning with Pompidou, extended under Giscard d'Estaing and taken to new heights by Mitterrand.[16] Much of the debate that has focussed on the *grands projets* has therefore concerned the quasi-monarchical personal power the President assumes in dreaming up and seeing through such massive and hugely expensive building projects. And even today with the *Bibliothèque de France*, this is still the hidden agenda beneath the current polemics regarding the suitability of Dominique Perrault's design, since its opponents' calls for a moratorium clash with the President's personal insistence that the project be completed before 1995. Such debates, and those concerning cost and architectural style, have tended to obscure the fact that, like the Pompidou Centre, some of the *grands projets* have aimed to widen access to the cultural heritage. The use of glass in the Louvre Pyramid and the towers of the *Bibliothèque de France*, for example, is designed to break with the imposing, aristocratic style of the traditional cultural institution and to enshrine a desire for openness and transparency.[17] In a different way, the Opéra-Bastille was intended as a 'popular', more approachable opera-house rivalling the ornate and hugely expensive Palais Garnier by offering lower seat-prices and an increased number of performances, but progress in this direction proved relatively limited.[18] Alongside these Parisian projects, a programme of decentralized *grands projets de province* was also launched to prompt local authorities to think in equally ambitious terms for their own localities. These included the comic-strip centre at Angoulême, the School of Photography at Arles, and a series of rock concert venues modelled on the Salle Zénith at La Villette.

Although in all these measures the democratizing tradition had been reaffirmed, it would nevertheless be misleading to suggest that it had been at the very heart of Socialist cultural policy, for in reality it had been overlaid with a number of more contemporary approaches. Much of the work of the multi-faceted DDC, for example, hinged on a notion of pluralism and cultural democracy closer to May than to Malraux, as it sought, not always successfully, to validate minority, regional and 'overseas' cultures within the general spirit of the Giordan report of 1982,

124

Démocratie culturelle et droit à la différence.[19] More importantly, as the *grands projets de province* listed above indicate, the notion of cultural democracy soon merged with more street-wise, more publicity-wise and more economy-wise preoccupations which better define the distinctiveness of the Socialist years and which, in the view of some disillusioned cultural militants, all but ousted the more classically socialist concerns they had hoped the new regime would demonstrate.

Lang's favourite term to describe his action was 'décloisonnement' or decompartmentalization. This of course does not preclude democratization but it also embraces another of the aims defined in the 1959 text, the encouragement of new work, or *création*. Lang aided *création* and artists in all disciplines and in a wide variety of ways. But *décloisonnement* particularly signifies a breaking down of barriers between elite art and mass culture, those industrially produced creative forms increasingly enjoyed by the majority but previously ignored by the Ministry as commercial activities undeserving of aid. Increasingly then, strip cartoons, fashion, pop music and pop videos, circus, even cooking were all legitimized as cultural forms alongside opera, literature and classical music by receiving ministerial support of various kinds.

Initially this pluralist position, referred to today in a pejorative short-hand as 'le tout culturel', had a certain theoretical, *soixante-huitard* ring, with its insistence on validating popular tastes rather than imposing an alien, 'bourgeois' culture from above. But this soon became indissociable from a concern with hard economic realities, as Lang's earlier reconciliation of the cultural and the economic underwent an ideological change of gear. In his November 1981 speech, he had already stressed that his ministry would make no hierarchical distinction between the traditional subsidised sector (EACs, CDNs, opera and so on) and the private cultural industries: publishing and bookshops, records, industrial design, etc., some of which, like French rock music threatened by US and UK competition, also needed protection from naked market forces. But between 1982–83, the government made its historic U-turn on economic policy. The resulting austerity measures, followed by the loss of a number of Socialist municipalities in the local elections of 1983, prompted the Ministry to pursue with renewed vigour a policy of openness to the rising cultural industries and the mass-cultural forms associated with them.

In the same spirit, it also encouraged private sponsorship and generally adopted a more *gestionnaire* approach to the subsidized sector, particularly the CDNs and EACs for which it drew up new agreements. Such establishments were encouraged to see themselves not simply as public services fulfilling a civic purpose *à la Malraux*, but as 'entreprises culturelles': run according to modern standards of managerial efficiency, required, in the case of the CDNs, to achieve a degree of economic independence by earning 20 per cent of their revenue, and financed on a selective rather than automatic basis according to a specifically agreed project of creative excellence. Some believed that these changes encouraged a trend towards ever more extravagant, star-studded and less challenging productions.[20] The high costs involved, together with a surplus of supply over demand, produced a serious financial crisis for the public theatre sector in the late 1980s which prompted the Ministry to take its reform further still by redefining the focus and managerial standards of all EACs (subsequently called *Scènes nationales*).

This new stress on industry and enterprise did not, however, put an end to protectionism. This was particularly evident in television, where the will to regulate remained strong, though to relatively little effect as rampant competition for advertising revenue steadily eroded standards after privatization. Having first failed to impose conditions favourable to the cinema industry concerning the time-lapse between a film's release and its showing on the new pay-channel Canal Plus (1984), Lang's disapproval of the even greater indifference to cultural criteria demonstrated in the setting up of two further private channels, la 5 and TV6, in 1986 brought him close to resignation and his Ministry continued to battle on this front after 1988. After France watered down its call for a mandatory quota system for the European directive 'Télévision sans frontières' in 1989, much to the fury of professionals and artists, Lang and Catherine Tasca (in charge of Communication at the Ministry until May 1991), did succeed in January 1990 in tightening France's own regulations in this regard. After 1987, all French channels had to include a fixed quota of European and French productions (60 per cent and 50 per cent respectively) in their schedules. But after 1992, Tasca's decrees required the majority of these productions to be shown between 6.00 p.m. and 11.00 p.m.[21]

Despite this objection to unbridled commercialism in television, the Ministry demonstrated more generally an awareness of the power of the media to give culture a higher public profile. Lang was an astute media manipulator following his early Nancy days and these skills, combined with those of his department directors, succeeded in transforming the Ministry's entire image. A turning point came in 1982 when several of his staff improvised the first *Fête de la musique*, during which France's five million amateur and professional musicians were encouraged to come out into the streets and do their thing. Despite Lang's own reservations, the event was a media success and continued to go from strength to strength,[22] spawning a number of similarly spectacular jamborees: *Fête du cinema*, *Journée portes ouvertes dans les monuments historiques*, *Fureur de lire* and *Photofolies*. After 1982, however, the meaning of such events subtly shifted. Once again, the first *Fête de la musique* looked back to 1968, a spontaneous street festival founded on authentically popular practice and self-expression. Afterwards, the obvious artificiality in the state-prompted 'spontaneity' of such occasions became more pronounced, as did their image-conscious quality, both characteristics reaching their apogee in the Jean-Paul Goude procession which ended the Bicentenary celebrations on 14th July 1989: 'un ballet gracieux et gratuit', said Le Monde, as stylized as a pop video, devised by a star of advertising and fashion, and apparently signifying only the desirability of 'le métissage culturel': 'the real revolution', Goude told Le Monde, is world music.[23]

In much the same vein, after appearing at Avignon in 1981 in the pink jacket that gave Plunkett's book its title, Lang seemed increasingly intent on turning himself into a kind of ministerial Gilbert and George, a walking cultural statement signifying in his clothes, his hairstyle, and his presence at key media or youth events the post-modern eclecticism of his policies.[24] This resolute appeal to the young in particular continued but by the end of the 1980s Lang seemed to have toned down much of his sartorial semiology. There was a sense too that the really ground-breaking days of his administration were also over and that, inevitably perhaps, it was largely fine-tuning its earlier achievements, while the real battle raged next door in Communication. Curiously however, it was during this post '88 lull that Socialist cultural policy found itself at the heart of a vigorous debate.

Criticism of the policy and its style grew as the 1986 elections approached, some of it ideologically inspired. Lang was accused of encouraging an official art, of seeking to control minds, of being, as one

127

observer put it, 'un pourrisseur inégalé de la culture qu'applaudissent les esthètes décadents et les jeunes gens inconscients'.[25] Since then, however, more measured assessments have been made and it is probably true that judgments of cultural policy today are less polarized than in the run-up to the legislative elections of 1986. Beyond perceived success or failure with particular disciplines, the general consensus is that the Socialists did well to increase public spending on culture and move it up the national and local agenda, but were guilty of neglecting the heritage by favouring a new academicism of the avant-garde, the fashionable and the spectacular,[26] and of failing to redress the balance of spending between Paris and the provinces because of the Parisian *grands projets*.

The meaning of 'culture'

But beyond pragmatic assessments of Socialist cultural policy, there is a recurrent and as yet unresolved theoretical debate. This centres on the belief that 'le tout culturel' has contributed to a confusion in France about cultural values, that cultural policy has given governmental approval to a trend, set in train by the social sciences, structuralism and more recently post-modernism, towards an aesthetic relativism in which, as Alain Finkielkraut put it some some years ago in *La Défaite de la pensée*, there is nothing to choose between Shakespeare and a pair of boots. Culture, Finkielkraut argues, in its highest sense has been confused with mass entertainment, democracy with Disneyland. This confusion is embodied, according to Marc Fumaroli in 1989, in the very conception of the proposed *Bibliothèque de France*. Here, Disneyland meets Alexandria, as France's great literary heritage is to be transferred from the *Bibliothèque Nationale* into what Fumaroli sees as a vast cultural supermarket, open to the general public and full of the latest technological gadgetry and other amusements.[27] Clearly in this perspective, the prospect of a Socialist regime with a supposedly anti-American Minister of Culture inaugurating the actual Eurodisneyland in 1992 was no longer incongruous but the natural culmination of the trend towards an undiscriminating consumer culture in which art becomes leisure.

Finkielkraut and Fumaroli rightly identify the dangers of this trend. From a ministerial point of view, however, they highlight only one half of a

128

complex equation. From the standpoint of the other half, Socialist policy can be better understood as a pragmatic assessment of the cultural realities of the 1980s and of the Ministry's own limitations. Central to this was, once again, democratization, the messianic crusade on which the Ministry was founded, and the god that transparently failed. This failure was already clear to the militants of May, echoing Bourdieu, and it was confirmed subsequently by surveys of cultural practice including the Ministry's own, published in 1990. Although cultural supply rocketed, demand for *la culture cultivée* from those not already 'customers' generally did not.[28] The Ministry has been able to do relatively little about this over the last thirty years, simply because by the very nature of its remit it can largely influence only the material obstacles to wider access, not those sociocultural forces which shape the individual's imaginative capacities: the family, the education system, the broadcasting media. Where the last two are concerned, Lang, like Malraux before him and despite his euphoric faith in the forty-four 'Ministers of Culture', was unable between 1981 and 1986 to persuade the Ministry of Education to undertake the costly reform required to introduce a full-blooded creative arts curriculum throughout the state system, today universally recognized as the only means of true democratization. Despite progress made after 1981, such as the introduction of music, cinema and theatre options (*baccalauréat* A3) in a number of *lycées* and of 2,200 art workshops in primary and secondary schools, a law on artistic education, introduced under Léotard in December 1987, years later was still felt to have made only a modest impact.[29]

But hard on the heels of this realization of ministerial limits comes another reality which puts a new complexion on the matter. Olivier Donnat, co-author of a Ministry survey of cultural practices, has identified a rationale for Socialist policy in the idea that it merely responded to a process of rapid technological, economic and sociological change since the sixties which has drained the Malraucian sense of the word culture and transformed the entire problematic. New technologies have altered the relationship between artistic production and the means by which it is disseminated, and have introduced commercial and industrial interests into the hermetic world of the artist, with the result that the distinction between 'work of art' and 'cultural product' has, in Donnat's view, become obsolete. Similarly, the walkman, for example, has arguably democratized music far more successfully than all the subsidized regional orchestras and opera houses together, by allowing direct, unmediated access to it whenever and wherever it is required. There was, then, a kind of absurdity in the Ministry's former insistence on propping up and promoting traditional art forms which all but a small percentage of the population refused to take any interest in, while at the same time ignoring those cultural practices and industries which were part of most people's everyday experience.[30]

From Donnat's vantage-point, Lang thus became the first Minister to take stock of this absurdity, to acknowledge the new complexity of the cultural, and to shape policy accordingly. Rather than perpetuate the cleavage between the mass-cultural industries and the more traditional subsidized sector, he tried to 'decompartmentalize' them. This certainly meant validating existing tastes and encouraging artists to learn from the brash entrepreneurialism of the 1980s, but it also meant attempting to prevent that entrepreneurialism from obliterating all aesthetic values and leading to standardization. In a sense then, the Socialist ambition, midway between Malraux's mysticism and Giscard d'Estaing's liberalism, was to bring two worlds together in order to save each from itself.

Conclusion

Of course, such a reading does not so much answer Finkielkraut and Fumaroli as rephrase the question; the fear remains that the new age of cultural democracy it postulates is merely another name for the consumer society.[31] But it does help confirm our initial premise that there is a somewhat greater consistency between Gaullist and Socialist policy than meets the eye. The Socialists did not so much abandon the Popular Front's or Malraux's concern with democratization as absorb it into a more pluralist definition of cultural action.[32] Rather than seeing the state's role as being simply to batter heroically at a closed door, Lang's décloisonnement tackled democratization by other routes, addressing the problem of elitism not only in terms of audiences but also of cultural forms and seeking to validate in a spirit of festivity and participation the diversity of practices people identify with and find meaningful. It remains to be seen to what extent the comparison with the right-wing administration elected to power in 1993 will serve as a retrospective validation of Socialist cultural policy, or cause it to be perceived as a misguided attempt at a kind of democratization which in the end merely aggravated the tendency to consider anything that is traditional or difficult as elitist or marginal.

Notes

1. De Plunkett, P. (1982), *La culture en veston rose*, La Table Ronde, Paris. Fumaroli, M. (1991), *L'Etat culturel: essai sur une religion moderne*, Fallois, Paris. Fumaroli's analysis in fact embraces the cultural policies conducted throughout the Fifth Republic.
2. Limited space precludes a more comprehensive assessment of individual policy areas; my aim here is rather to outline a possible reading of Socialist cultural policy as a whole, in relation to that of Malraux. This reading is currently being investigated more fully for a forthcoming book to be published by Berg. The research is funded by the Leverhulme Trust, whose assistance I would like to acknowledge in the writing of this chapter.
3. This liberalism is sharply criticised in Jeanne Laurent's (1955), *La République et les beaux-arts*, Julliard, Paris. One concern of Fumaroli's book (see Note 1) is to argue, not altogether convincingly, that Laurent's indictment is unjust and that Third Republic liberalism was considerably less dangerous than Fifth Republic voluntarism: see pp. 59-80.
4. Decree of 24 July 1959, quoted in Ritaine, E. (1983), *Les Stratèges de la culture*, Fondation Nationale des Sciences Politiques, Paris, p. 65. The term 'patrimoine', or 'heritage', as used by the Ministry embraces the great art of France's past as well as its historic monuments, districts, buildings, etc.
5. Malraux's ideas were articulated in a number of speeches but particularly clearly in that inaugurating the Maison de la culture of Amiens, 19 March 1966, reproduced in full in the Ministry of Culture dossier, 'Trentième Anniversaire du Ministère de la culture: journées d'étude sur la création du ministère de la Culture, 30 novembre-1 décembre 1989'. For details of the Ministry's budget during the sixties, see Wangermée, R. and Gournay, B. (1988), *Programme*

européen d'évaluation: la politique culturelle de la France, La Documentation Française, Paris, pp. 67-8.

6. Wangermée and Gournay, pp. 67-8. For a more detailed breakdown of the evolution of the Ministry's budget since 1971, see Ministère de la culture, 'La politique culturelle 1981-1991', April, 1991, booklet with same title, p. 5 and following page (unnumbered).

7. On the importance of Lang's work at Nancy, see Looseley, D.L. (1990), 'Jack Lang and the politics of festival', *French Cultural Studies*, vol.1, no.1, pp. 5-19.

8. The preceding analysis of Lang's ideas is based largely on the speech to the Assembly of November 1981 (unpublished Ministry typescript) and on another given in Mexico City, 27 July 1982, reproduced in *Après-demain*, no.250, 1983, pp. 4-7.

9. *Le Monde*, 19 November 1981. The phrase 'boulimie sémantique' is from Fumaroli's *L'Etat culturel*, p. 169.

10. Popular among many bookshops and publishers, the new law was not universally welcomed and was strongly opposed by FNAC. See Wachtel, D. (1987), *Cultural Policy and Socialist France*, Greenwood Press, New York, pp. 54-7. On the situation of books and publishing today, see 'La politique culturelle 1981-1991', booklet entitled 'Le livre et la lecture'; and 'Dix ans de prix unique', *Politis*, no.121, 1991, pp. 70-1.

11. Ministère de la culture, *Lettre d'Information*, no.294, 24 December 1990, p. 6. The quotations are from the Mexico City speech (see Note 8), in which the USA was never specifically named.

12. See *Lettre d'Information*, no.288, 1 October 1990, p. 6 for further details of 1991 budget.

13. FRAC: *Fonds régional d'art contemporain*. FRAM: *Fonds régional d'acquisition des musées*.

14. Rizzardo, R. (1991), *La Décentralisation culturelle: rapport au ministre de la Culture et de la Communication*, La Documentation Française, Paris. From 1984, contracts with the Regions (as opposed to Departments or communes) were made via 'volets culturels' included in the ninth Plan. For a fuller discussion of the government's cultural decentralization measures, see Looseley (1993), 'Paris versus the provinces', in M. Cook (ed.), *French Culture since 1945*, Longman, London.

15. The CDNs were not included in this network and were the responsibility of the Ministry's *Direction du théâtre et des spectacles*. Nevertheless, they were similarly reformed, received extra funds and were greatly increased in number. For details of the DDC's activities, see *Ministère de la culture*, 'Dossier d'information: la politique culturelle 1981-1985', booklet entitled 'La décentralisation et le développement culturel'. For a closer analysis of its complex role, see Saez, G. (1985), 'Politique culturelle: suivez le guide!', *Pour*, no.101, pp. 36-45.

16. Ory, P. (1989), *L'Aventure culturelle française 1945-1989*, Flammarion, Paris, pp. 60-1.

17. On glass and democratization in the Louvre Pyramid, see Riggins, S.H. and Pham, K. (1986), 'Democratizing the arts: France in an era of austerity', *Queen's Quarterly*, vol.93, no.1, pp. 150-3; and on the proposed library, see Perrault, D. (1990), 'La place et le cloître' (interview), *Le Débat*, no.62, p. 32 and p. 36. On this and other aspects of the library debate, see Looseley (1991), 'The Bibliothèque de France: last of the grands projets', *Modern and Contemporary France*, no.46, pp. 35-46.

18. A survey conducted at a decent interval after its opening showed that a respectable 30% of those without a season-ticket attending performances of Manon Lescaut had never been to an opera before. However, top category seat prices for the '91 season were as high (560 francs) as at the Palais Garnier according to *Le Monde*, 19 June 1991.

19. Giordan, H. (1982), *Démocratie culturelle et droit à la différence: rapport au ministre de la culture*, La Documentation Française, Paris. An example of this strategy was the 'Quartiers Lumières' project of summer 1991 which sponsored events encouraging youth cultures (rap, graffiti) in the 400 'quartiers défavorisés' identified in Michel Delebarre's 'politique de la Ville', *Lettre d'Information*, no.302, 22 April 1991, supplement.

20. See, for example, Colin, J.-P. (1990), 'La Culture et son administration', *Commentaire*, no.50, p. 345.

21. On the various TV battles, see Hunter, M. (1990), *Les Jours les plus Lang*, Odile Jacob, Paris, pp. 184-90 (Canal Plus), pp. 237-40 (la 5), and pp. 290-7 (European quotas). Hunter claims that Lang himself

lost interest in the whole quotas issue, p. 289. See also on quotas, *Politis*, no.121, pp. 7-8 & p. 13.

22. Hunter, pp. 143-51.

23. *Le Monde*, 16-17 July 1989.

24. These events were frequently concerts with a message, such as the *SOS-Racisme* gatherings, the open-air *Droits de l'homme* event under the Arche de la Défense in August 1989, or the Gipsy Kings' show at Wembley, a group Lang described as the symbol of French culture (*Le Monde*, 3-4 December 1989).

25. Jacques Baumel in *Le Figaro*, 2 March 1986.

26. After 1988, Lang attempted to rectify this imbalance by making 'le patrimoine' a government priority.

27. Finkielkraut, A. (1987), *La Défaite de la pensée*, Gallimard, Paris, p. 152. Fumaroli, M., 'Alexandrie ou Disneyland', Le Figaro, 21 July 1989. For a fuller account by Fumaroli's of his views see (1990), 'La Culture et les loisirs: une nouvelle religion d'Etat', *Commentaire*, no.51, pp. 425-35, an essay which summarizes the main argument of his book (see Note 1). Fumaroli's view of the new library dates from a period when the plans for the public facilities which are to adjoin the former Bibliothèque Nationale's collections were considerably more ambitious than they are today: see Looseley, 'La Bibliothèque de France', pp. 41-3.

28. The Wangermée and Gournay report of 1987 (see Note 5) found some signs of progress in museums and music (see Gournay's digest of the report in *Commentaire*, no.48, 1989-90, p. 705). However, a Ministry survey shows only a 3 per cent increase from 1973 to 1988 in the numbers visiting a museum once in the previous year (a 4 per cent drop for historical monuments). And though it does speak generally of a 'boom musical' during the same period and demonstrates that the audience for classical music is up 7 per cent, the social composition of this audience has changed little in fifteen years: Donnat, O. and Cogneau, D. (1990), *Les Pratiques culturelles des Français 1973-1989*, La Découverte/La Documentation Française, Paris, p. 103 (museums) and p. 67 (music).

29. See *Ministère de la culture*, collection of booklets called 'La politique culturelle 1981-1991', booklet entitled 'Développement et formations', pp. 19-22. On 2 October 1991, Lang and the Education

Minister L. Jospin presented a package of further measures to the Conseil des ministres: see *Lettre d'Information*, no.314, 25 November 1991, supplement, which also reviews progress since 1981.

30. Donnat, O. (1988), 'Politique culturelle et débat sur la culture', *Esprit*, November, pp. 90-101, to which I am particularly indebted for this analysis.

31. See Finkielkraut, pp. 166-8 and Fumaroli, *Commentaire*, p. 433-4. It should be stressed that Donnat too, who writes not as a Ministry mouthpiece but in his own name, is fully aware of this ambivalence, as is clear from his more recent analysis of the question of democratization (1991), 'Démocratisation culturelle: la fin d'un mythe', *Esprit*, March-April, pp. 65-79.

32. This need to include traditional democratization in a wider definition is clearly articulated in a report produced in the context of the ninth Plan : Commissariat Général du Plan (1983), *L'Impératif culturel: rapport du groupe Long Terme Culture*, La Documentation Française, Paris, pp. 80-1.

Bibliography

Baumel, J., ' "Supprimons le monopole du ministère et décentralisons" ' (interview), *Le Figaro*, 2 March 1986.

Commentaire, no. 48 (winter 1989), no. 49 (spring 1990), no. 50 (summer 1990).

Commissariat Général du Plan (1983), *L'Impératif culturel: rapport du groupe Long Terme Culture*, Paris: La Documentation Française.

Donnat, O. (1988), 'Politique culturelle et débat sur la culture', *Esprit*, November.

Donnat, O. (1991), 'Démocratisation culturelle: la fin d'un mythe', *Esprit*, March-April.

Donnat, O. and Cogneau, D. (1990), Les pratiques culturelles des Français 1973-1989, La Découverte/La Documentation Française, Paris.

Finkielkraut, A. (1987), *La défaite de la pensée*, Gallimard, Folio/Essais, Paris.

Fumaroli, M., 'Alexandrie ou Disneyland', *Le Figaro*, 21 July 1989.

Fumaroli, M. (1990), 'La culture et les loisirs: une nouvelle religion d'Etat', *Commentaire*, no. 51.

Fumaroli, M. (1991), *L'Etat culturel: essai sur une religion moderne*, Fallois, Paris.

Giordan, H. (1982), *Démocratie culturelle et droit à la différence: rapport au ministre de la culture*, Collection des rapports officiels, La Documentation Française, Paris.

Hunter, M. (1990), *Les jours les plus Lang*, Odile Jacob, Paris.

Lang, J., Speech to National Assembly, 17 November 1981 (unpublished Ministry typescript).

Lang, J., speech in Mexico City, 27 July 1982, reproduced in (1983), *Après-demain*, no. 250, January.

Laurent, J. (1955), *La République et les beaux-arts*, Julliard, Paris.

Looseley, D.L. (1990), 'Jack Lang and the politics of festival', *French Cultural Studies*, vol. 1, no. 1, February.

Looseley, D.L. (1991), 'The Bibliothèque de France: last of the *grands projets*', *Modern and Contemporary France*, no. 46, July.

Looseley, D.L. (1993), 'Paris versus the provinces', in Cook, M. (ed.), *French Culture since 1945*, Longman, London.

Ministère de la culture, *Lettre d'Information*, no. 288, 1 October 1990; no. 294, 24 December 1990; no. 302, 22 April 1991, supplement; no. 314, 25 November 1991, supplement.

Ministère de la culture, 'Trentième anniversaire du Ministère de la culture: journées d'étude sur la création du Ministère de la culture, 30 novembre-1 décembre 1989' (dossier).

Ministère de la culture, 'Dossier d'information: la politique culturelle 1981-1985' (collection of booklets).

Ministère de la culture, 'La politique culturelle 1981-1991', April 1991 (collection of booklets).

Le Monde, 19 November 1981; 16-17 July 1989; 19 June 1991; 31 October 1991; 15 November 1991.

Ory, P. (1989), *L'Aventure culturelle française 1945-1989*, Flammarion, Paris.

Perrault, D. (1990), 'La place et le cloître' (interview), *Le Débat*, no. 62, November-December.

De Plunkett, P. (1982), *La culture en veston rose*, Collection Place Publique, La Table Ronde, Paris.

Politis, no. 121 (special issue), 3-10 January 1991.

Riggins, S.H., and Pham, K. (1986), 'Democratizing the arts: France in an era of austerity', *Queen's Quarterly*, vol. 93, no. 1, spring.

Rioux, J.-P. (1991), 'L'Impératif culturel', *L'Histoire*, no. 143, April.

Ritaine, E. (1983), *Les stratèges de la culture*, Fondation Nationale des Sciences Politiques, Paris.

Rizzardo, R. (1991), *La décentralisation culturelle: rapport au ministre de la culture et de la communication*, Paris: La Documentation Française.

Saez, G. (1985), 'Politique culturelle: suivez le guide!', *Pour*, no. 101, May-June.

Saez, G., 'La politique de développement culturel de 1981 à 1986', paper read to the *Séminaire du Centre des Recherches Administratives, Fondation Nationale des Sciences Politiques*, 31 January 1987, typescript, 15pp.

Télérama, 9 January 1991.

Wachtel, D. (1987), *Cultural Policy and Socialist France*, Contributions in Political Science, no. 177, Greenwood Press, New York.

Wangermée, R. and Gournay, B. (1988), *Programme européen d'évaluation: la politique culturelle de la France*, La Documentation Française, Paris.

6　The Return of the Clerics?

JOHN FLOWER

> Intellectuel, nom masculin, catégorie sociale et culturelle, née
> à Paris au moment de l'affaire Dreyfus, morte à Paris à la fin
> du XXe siècle; n'a apparamment pas survécu au déclin de
> l'Universel.[1]

Thus wrote Bernard-Henri Lévy in 1987 in his controversial essay *Eloge
des intellectuels*. Taken together, this quotation and title of the book might
well suggest not so much despair as nostalgia, the regret of the passing of
an age when values of an absolute nature had been held to exist and had as
well been recognized as providing the norms against which all actions
could be measured. Lévy's position is shared by a number of his
contemporaries who are often (though not always usefully) grouped
together and referred to as *les nouveaux philosophes*. But any discussion of
the reasons for their attitudes and consequently of the changing nature, role
and influence of the intellectual during the last quarter of the twentieth
century, is not quite as final and as straightforward as Lévy's words might
at first have us believe. Where precisely the fundamental causes for the
intellectual's changing role during this period are to be found is not
something upon which there is unanimity. For some, for example, they lie
in the aftermath of the 'failed revolution' of May 1968, for others they are
attributable quite precisely to the long-standing debate between Sartre and
Raymond Aron, for others again and more broadly they have something to
do with the gradual discrediting of communism; not, of course, that these

three factors are without connection. Nor should it be forgotten that the circumstances and conditions in which the intellectual now has to function have changed significantly. Technological advances, creating what Régis Debray in his study of the French intelligentsia has called the 'cycle média',[2] have not only provided new means of communication for him to exploit but have altered the perception and expectation of those to whom he addresses himself.

What I hope to do in this brief survey is to examine some of the attitudes expressed about intellectuals after the return to government of the Socialists in 1981 and offer a few tentative comments about their evolution and possible role in the future.

The subject of 'the intellectual' in France has since 1981 received a good deal of critical attention.[3] There is neither the space nor indeed the need here to rehearse this in any detail, though a few principal points might usefully be recalled. As a noun the word 'intellectuel' first appeared in the French language towards the end of the nineteenth century. For long it was thought to have been used by nationalists as a term of abuse to describe those who took the side of Dreyfus and propounded the rights of Man. Recent research, however, has shown that in fact the word was used across the complete spectrum of political discourse. In broad terms, whether to the left or to the right, the 'intellectuel' was one who defended a position or an issue with reference to a set of general principles, a belief or an ideology. Emile Zola and Anatole France were essentially no more or less 'intellectuals' for their belief in the primacy of the freedom and dignity of the individual than were Brunetière or Maurice Barrès for theirs in national traditions and in those institutions in and by which they considered such traditions to be enshrined and best protected. The essential difference between the two sides was one of degree. While the latter in their support for the Church or the Army were specific, the former remained vague, maintaining a belief in principles whose origins lay, of course, in the values underpinning the Revolution of 1789. These would and indeed should if necessary, they argued, transcend matters of local and national self-interest. Such a position was effectively destroyed, however, by the immense, unprecedented upheavals caused by the First World War and by the hardening of ideological allegiances which followed. The norm rapidly became one of extreme partisanship. Intellectuals were allowed to exist and indeed to be the depository of Truth, but only within a particular political

139

perspective. Thus from the extreme left we find Henri Barbusse in 1921 claiming that:

> ....leur métier éternel est de fixer et de mettre en ordre la vérité innombrable, par des formules, des lois et des oeuvres [...] Pour eux, la vérité s'avoue, s'ordonne et s'augmente, et la pensée organisée sort d'eux pour rectifier et diriger les croyances et les faits.[4]

From the opposite end of the political spectrum and with no less conviction, Drieu la Rochelle considered that intellectuals had 'des devoirs et des droits supérieurs aux autres'.[5] Within this climate in which ideological criteria and their translation into practice assumed ever-increasing importance, one voice in particular stood out in resistance, that of Julien Benda whose essay *La Trahison des clercs*[6] is significantly a point of reference for several of the *nouveaux philosophes* of recent years. For Benda, the cleric or intellectual, a mixture of scribe, man of learning and priest, had a duty, precisely at a time when partisanship was increasingly the norm, to sustain an awareness in others of the absolute values of Truth and Justice. He did acknowledge, however, that because of the pressures that developed after the war and of the willingness of intellectuals to succumb to them and to participate unequivocally in the arena of political debate, such an ideal, platonic position was no longer tenable. What effectively happened, of course, was that it was those on the left, who, looking to the principles of the Revolution for inspiration assumed the mantle of this particular responsibility. Whatever the degree of their allegiance to socialist views, they considered their task to be to instruct through actions and words, and it is here that the origins of the engaged or committed intellectual are to be found.

By the 1950s and 1960s this notion of commitment had become the order of the day, distinctly left-wing and oppositional. The degree of opposition varied considerably, from the extreme and revolutionary to the more traditional. The former found expression especially in the statements by the Communist Party's spokesmen on cultural and intellectual matters: Kanapa, Casanova and, of course, Aragon. The latter is best described, to quote a more recent phrase from 1988 by René Rémond, as a position of 'contre-pouvoir'.[7] In the same year Michel Foucault referred to the intellectual's essential 'fonction critique'[8] and more recently still, one of Foucault's close friends and admirers Claude Mauriac, saw the intellectual's duty to be to 'mettre en cause'.[9]

The best discussion and definition of this position at the time came from Sartre whose book *Plaidoyer pour les intellectuels* published in 1973 reproduced the celebrated lectures he had given in Japan seven years before. While he was not a member of the Communist Party, Sartre's sympathies for many of their policies was considerable. In these lectures, however, he is more concerned with the theoretical role of the intellectual. He argues that the true intellectual is someone who has become aware of the conflict between the loyalty he has to his cause or belief and the way that he and it are manipulated by society so that it can perpetuate its own system of values. The tension and contradiction which result from this conflict are made public by the intellectual who in so doing is potentially subversive and therefore dangerous. The intellectual who claims, no matter how much he tries to oppose certain political or social developments, that they remain too powerful, is false, guilty of bad faith. The intellectual's duty is to remain in permanent, radical opposition and to facilitate this should identify himself with the least privileged members of society since all they can do is revolt against whatever oppresses them. Yet even if he manages to arrive in this way at what he calls a 'dialectical agreement' with society, the intellectual remains a lone figure and is fully aware of this. Two years before the publication of these lectures in an interview which he gave to Hallier's *L'Idiot international* Sartre had fine-tuned this position into a definition which risked being circular if not self-destructive:

> L'intellectuel [...] dans notre société ne peut avoir de sens qu'en étant en contradiction perpétuelle, en faisant le contraire de ce qu'il veut, qu'il se supprime en tant qu'intellectuel.[10]

In addition to the debate at the time schools or movements developed headed by individuals who enjoyed fierce allegiance from disciples whose activities took them beyond the field of the narrowly political. This was in broad, simple terms the kind of intellectual climate which prevailed through the 1970s and the beginning of the 1980s. But a vital new factor was introduced with the Socialist victory at the ballot box in May 1981. With the election to power of the erstwhile opposition party which had enjoyed the sympathy of left-wing intellectuals, some of them felt either that they were redundant or that close association with the government would be counter-productive. The situation quickly provoked comment and debate: for a variety of reasons the intellectual was suddenly a matter of renewed interest.

In the early 1980s three surveys in particular about the current status and role of the intellectual were published by the quality press. The first appeared at the end of July 1983 as *Le Monde* attempted for that year to retain the interests of its regular readers (not to mention their custom) during that sybaritic period known as the *grandes vacances*. As some readers were to observe mid-way through August, such a topic made for less than riveting holiday reading and its success in guaranteeing that people would not be weaned away, if only temporarily, by the multi-coloured delights of *Le Provençal* or *Sud-Ouest* for example must have been limited. Even so the debate, taking place two years after the Socialists' arrival in power, was important.

Organized by Philippe Boggio, it was launched in a somewhat blunt if reasonably accurate way on 26 July 1983:

> Les grandes figures de la vie intellectuelle, que l'on avait coutume de voir en premier rang des combats de la gauche, se sont tues, semble-t-il, depuis que celle-ci a accédé au pouvoir.

The task of responding initially to this assessment fell to Max Gallo, at the time the government's spokesman on cultural and intellectual matters. Gallo began by bemoaning the fact that intellectuals who had once traditionally considered it their duty to voice matters of general concern, were no longer in evidence. 'Où sont les Gide, les Malraux, les Alain, les Langevin d'aujourd'hui ?' he asked rhetorically. His answer was not in fact particularly enlightening. Since the 1960s, the end of the Algerian War, the events of May 1968 and in particular with the decline of marxism on a large scale and of the French Communist Party nationally, intellectuals he said had become disillusioned. More recently, they had not been called upon to play a significant role in the election of the Socialists to government in 1981 and were left with a sense of having been misunderstood or, even worse, forgotten. And yet at a time of social and economic conservatism, Gallo suggested, they were needed perhaps more than ever. The problem for the left, which intellectuals could help solve, was one of vision: 'Moderniser, adapter, sans saccager le passé, créer une société ouverte, dynamique et vivante.' But faced with this invitation to join ranks even if only in a semi-official way, was not, as I have already hinted, everyone's idea of how best to proceed. Emmanuel Le Roy Ladurie expressed his own *méfiance* in the paper on 27 July:

> Il est difficile pour nous de devenir des intellectuels organiques d'Etat, d'avoir, même avec des gens qui nous sont proches, un rapport administratif. Il faut maintenir la frontière entre ce qu'on appelait en Inde, le Dharma, l'ordre sacré, et l'Artha, l'ordre guerrier.

In the event his personal response, he said, was to have opted for 'une cure de silence'. In the same issue Régis Debray's perception, if substantially the same, at least had a touch of healthy cynicism about it:

> Il est évidemment un peu moins chic qu'avant d'être à gauche. Qu'avaient-ils à gagner à travailler pour l'effort national en cours ?

As the summer drew on the debate developed and other factors were introduced, notably society's preoccupation with a new materialism and the role played in the diffusion of ideas by the media. Alfred Grosser (5 August) was one who claimed that: 'Le goût du gadget, du coup d'éclat, règne plus que jamais'. The day before, with an allusion to French television's popular test of mental agility Jacques Cellard had quipped that 'les chiffres font taire les lettres'. Rather more seriously he had also observed that whereas during the Enlightenment, the Dreyfus Affair or the rise of Nazism, intellectuals were confronted by 'un ennemi à leur mesure' all that appeared to matter now were 'le cours du dollar ou la semaine de trente heures'. A fortnight later (29 August) echoing Marc Riglet who had already accused intellectuals of commercializing culture, Thomas Ferenczi argued that such was their concern for instant communication that ideas of real worth were in danger of becoming distorted and trivialized. While there was undoubtedly need for this new style intellectual (whom he interestingly defines as *le clerc*), the old style one or *le moine*, whose task is to reaffirm 'les droits d'une pensée libre et exigeante', should not be forgotten or allowed to disappear.

By the beginning of September discussion had become largely repetitive if not sterile. Even calls for a vigorous, even revolutionary, response to the present state of affairs by the late Henri Lefèbvre or by that *enfant terrible* Jean-Edern Hallier early in August provoked little reaction. Two months later in a long article in *Le Débat*, the editor in chief of *Le Nouvel Observateur*, Jean Daniel, attempted to situate the issue more firmly in a political context. Within two years of Mitterrand's coming to power his policies had shifted and, Daniel argued, the revolutionary tradition to the left had been diluted if not lost and intellectuals found themselves in a kind of vaccum. While echoing Boggio's opening remark in *Le Monde* this hardly advanced the debate much further than Gallo's article had done:

> Délivrée de ses mythes, cette gauche est nue. C'est l'heure de l'imagination idéologique, c'est-à-dire, peut-être et encore, celle des intellectuels.[11]

While in the same article Daniel dismissed the kind of survey conducted by *Le Monde* as a 'summer frivolity', his own weekly magazine gave the debate further impetus with the publication in June 1986 of the second of the contributions to which I referred earlier entitled 'Idées, universités, culture: la grande lessive'. Here, as the title suggests, the context was significantly broadened. Moving beyond the immediately political Jacques Julliard in an introductory article linked the demise of the intellectual with that of society's rejection of all forms of systematization (linguistic, anthropological, economic, psychoanalytic and so on) which, during the 1960s especially he argued, had been seen to offer global explanations (*explications* would be a better word) for individual behaviour. Marxism and structuralism in particular are singled out though, as Gérard Genette remarks in another contribution, the former in particular has had such an impact on modern thinking that to see the eclipse of its most immediate, superficial manisfestations in the form of political systems as an indication of its disappearance altogether would be misguided. None the less the general thrust of a large number of opinions expressed in the *dossier* was, in François Furet's words, the re-emergence of a 'discours anti-totalitaire, au nom des droits de l'homme'. In view of the assumption by the left of responsibility for this very concern around the beginning of the century an important shift of emphasis had clearly taken place. What was also being witnessed, several contributors argued, was a new fragmentation, an unwillingness on the part of intellectuals to participate in and still less to claim authority for any single system. A year before Pierre Nora, editor of *Le Débat* had made the same point quite succinctly:

> Chaque intellectuel tend à être à soi seul son début et sa fin. Il y avait autrefois des lieux de culte, une langue et des services du culte. Aucune université, aucune chapelle, aucune académie n'oserait aujourd'hui prétendre à ce rôle.[12]

In December 1987 the monthly *Magazine Littéraire* picked up the debate and took it a stage further with an *enquête* based on five questions:

> 1.L'intellectuel doit-il s'engager ? Au risque de se tromper ? Au risque qu'on lui reproche cette erreur, des années plus tard, quand les circonstances ont changé ?

> 2.L'Opposition droite-gauche a-t-elle aujourd'hui, aura-t-elle demain encore, un sens, du point de vue de la conduite des intellectuels ?

> 3.Le rôle de l'intellectuel doit-il se limiter à dénoncer les injustices, les atteintes aux droits de l'homme ? Ou doit-il aussi dire le vrai, le bien, le beau ?

> 4.Où se trouve, aujourd'hui, le courage pour un intellectuel ?

> 5.N'y a-t-il pas dans la nostalgie et l'affirmation des 'vraies valeurs' une tentation passéiste, voire réactionnaire ?

From the responses of a group of modern-day intellectuals of all disciplines and political persuasions two themes in particular become evident. The first picks up the debate about the status of the intellectual. Some, like André Glucksmann and the economist Alain Minc, echo the view that as one who speaks on behalf of 'la Beauté', 'la Vérité and 'le Bien' the intellectual may well believe in himself but is in fact talking nonsense in a modern society for which such absolute, eternal concepts (Minc refers to such people in a platonic allusion as 'gardiens du temple') have not so much no value as no relevance. In contrast, Lévy, making use of the same classical reference claims the opposite: only by promoting a return to such values does the intellectual have a chance of survival himself, and moreover, of being of positive benefit in a society which has for too long suffered from the abuse of enforced systematization. The second, though not unconnected point, already touched on by some of the contributors to *Le Monde*, concerns culture or rather cultural levelling (what is commonly referred to as 'le tout culturel') and the need which the public increasingly seems to feel and to express for material which lends itself to instant consumption. This problem is essentially the result, it is suggested by several, of social democratization and of the unprecedented developments in the exploitation of modern technology.[13] It should be the intellectual's task in this context at least, to fight for the preservation of values whose roots lie in the distant traditions of art and philosophy: basically, to preserve high culture rather than low, Racine rather than Astérix, Mozart rather than Wolfie. Such a task is not, as I hope to suggest, without a certain paradoxical element, but before looking more closely at this new *fin de siècle* figure I should like to return to the problem of the growing silence of the intellectuals under the Socialists.

The kinds of reasons offered and to which I have already referred clearly are significant: the absence of issues which have galvanized national consciousness and conscience, the paradox of finding the party with which one sympathizes in opposition now itself in power and required, or worse, prepared to compromise its own values, even the disappearance of a generation of figures (Aragon, Sartre, Aron, Barthes, Althusser, Foucault for example) who created around them the kinds of sects and power groups to which Pierre Nora refers. Linking these but much more fundamental than any is the growing awareness on the part of left-wing intellectuals not of the inadequacies of marxism itself as a philosophical discourse in modern western society but of the way in which it has been betrayed and compromised. This has been referred to by a number of commentators as the *goulag* factor. Purges, persecutions, labour camps, psychiatric hospitals, arranged trials, privilege and corruption in the Soviet Union had, over the years, been overlooked or forgotten. Even the Kruschev report in 1956 with its account of Stalinist atrocities tended for many French intellectuals to slip from view or had been denounced as fabrication; Kostler's *Darkness at Noon* which had been translated into French in 1946 was dismissed by many as blinkered and reactionary. This kind of oppressive regime was moreover not relevant in the political history of France with its roots in a democratic, liberal tradition which had evolved over more than a century and in the not too distant past had had the likes of Jean Jaurès and Léon Blum amongst its proponents. And in fact even to attempt to suggest that it was relevant was argued to be a move by those on the right to split their opponents' camp.

Yet through the late 1960s and early 1970s the *goulag* factor became increasingly significant. At a time when the intellectual influence on the French Communist Party was already waning at some speed, the appearance in the bookshops in 1974 of the translation of Solzhenitsyn's *Goulag Archipelago* was significant. Essentially it reaffirmed what many had known for a long time to be the truth about the Soviet Union; but what was now much more disturbing was the way in which those principles of 1789 were then discredited or at best seen to be little more than empty slogans.[14]

More recently in *Le Monde* (18 September 1991), Bertrand Poirot-Delpech recalled this climate when he suggested that anyone who has shown sympathy for communism is now, in the wake of the disintegration and discrediting of communist régimes, in danger of being automatically the victim of a witchhunt, of a new *épuration* or of 'un maccarthysme à retardement et à la française'. Although he does not mention any names Poirot-Delpech's target is clearly the new right wing as it has developed especially since the mid-1970s and in which people like Jean d'Ormesson, Alain de Benoist or Marc Fumarolli, often under an appeal for intellectual independence or disinterestedness, in fact advocate a return to tradition and conservatism. Their ideas are disseminated through books (Fumarolli's *L'Etat culturel* is an example),[15] reviews such as *La Nouvelle Ecole*, *Eléments*, and even the *Figaro-Magazine* or groups such as the 'Club de l'Horloge' or GRECE *(Groupement des recherches et études pour la civilisation européenne)*.

It is within this context that the label of *nouveaux philosophes* has emerged, being attributed to a number of young thinkers amongst whom pride of place has generally been awarded to Bernard-Henri Lévy.[16] While he himself (though not perhaps without a degree of assumed innocence) has

147

observed 'je n'ai toujours pas bien compris moi-même ce qu'on entend par nouveaux philosophes, ou nouveaux gourous ou nouveaux oracles',[17] he has expressed views which have led some to suggest that his natural political home was to the right of centre. In May 1990 a review entitled *La Règle du jeu* appeared, its preoccupations very much to do with a world in which communism was in the process of decay. Lévy is the founding editor of this review and while its first editorial is anonymous, its inspiration is clearly his. In it 'le modèle *engagé* de l'intellectuel sartrien' is considered at best moribund or sick, not likely to outlive the demise of communism. This, of course, is the kind of intellectual to whom he refers in *Eloge des Intellectuels* and with which I began. The unattached or uncommitted intellectual, however, the 'intellectuel dégagé' who deals in pure ideas and knowledge for its own sake will remain: 'Ce modèle-ci n'est pas mort. Il ne le sera peut-être jamais.'[18]

To assimilate Lévy too readily with the political right wing is premature. In his first major contribution to the intellectual climate of the late twentieth century, *La Barbarie à visage humain* (1977), he did attempt to target *all* forms of totalitarian oppression to which the intellectual has fallen prey. Four years later his *Eloge des Intellectuels* (a title which at once echoes and challenges that of Sartre's essay from the early 1970s) rehearses the same basic argument. Willingness to become engaged with any system necessarily results in a loss of individual freedom. Only in isolation, by maintaining his independence can the intellectual remain true to himself and to his vocation:

> L'intellectuel, enfin, est un homme seul. Un homme qui parle, pense, opine seul [...] L'intellectuel (est) contre la dictature de l'opinion [...] contre la religion des majorités.[19]

Only from such a position is he able to have the courage to speak and act on behalf of the cause which he alone has chosen. More recently, in 1991, in *Les Aventures de la Liberté* the same thesis is rehearsed again through a series of short reflections and interviews (both real and imagined) relating not only to communism and fascism, but to movements such as surrealism ('cette police de la pensée') for example or structuralism 'qui aurait en effet fini par empêcher de penser'.[20]

In the same year as Lévy's *Eloges des Intellectuels*, Alain Finkielkraut's *Défaite de la pensée* was published. A rather more substantial work than Lévy's, this argues in the early sections that the individual is inevitably absorbed into the collectivity of his nation to the point where he loses all sense of intellectual independence and critical resistance. Under the influence of Marxist sociologists and structural anthropologists, Finkielkraut argues, this process has developed on a larger scale to the point where all nations and cultures are held to be potentially equal and valid, and has resulted in growing banality and in the erosion of critical faculties. Fundamental to both books and especially to *Défaite de la pensée* is a nostalgia for a golden age when values (whether political or cultural) were somehow absolute, self-defining, self-evident, resistant and incorruptible. Are Lévy and Finkielkraut then the Bendas of the late 20th century? In terms of allegiance Lévy in particular certainly makes no effort to hide his allusions to the author of *La Trahison des clercs* and to the explicit platonism of that essay. But there is another element to consider which, as we have already seen, was a matter of concern for several of the contributors to the debate which was carried on in the columns of *Le Monde*, namely that of modern technology. Finkielkraut is adamant in deploring its effort on culture:

> Quand ce n'est pas l'identité culturelle qui enferme l'individu dans son appartenance et qui, sous peine de haute trahison, lui refuse l'accès au doute, à l'ironie, à la raison - à tout ce qui pourrait le détacher de la matrice collective, c'est l'industrie du loisir, cette création de l'âge technique qui réduit les oeuvres de l'esprit à l'état de pacotille (ou, comme on dit en Amérique, *d'entertainment*).[21]

Moreover, shallowness of ideas is paralleled by an inability on the part of the consumer to maintain concentration for long: the *télécommande*, the zapper rules supreme, giving rise to what has become known in the Anglo-Saxon world as the three minute culture. While Finkielkraut himself resorts to radio, television and the superficial interview only sparingly, Lévy shows himself willing to exploit such channels of communication with unabashed zeal. His works are accompanied by much hype, and it is also noticeable in *Les Aventures de la liberté*, a text of 431 pages, that the 69 entries (some of them subdivided) produce an average length of just over six generously printed pages each. Where Finkielkraut appears cautious and considered Lévy is busy, direct and not infrequently superficial and inaccurate.[22] But in a strange, almost paradoxical way does it really matter? Many years before the noun *intellectuel* appeared in the French language Victor Hugo wrote in *Les Contemplations*, 'le mot, qu'on le sache, est un être vivant'.[23] At a time when there were no extensive means of achieving rapid and instant large scale communication of an audio or visual kind the printed word was paramount. This was a situation which in essence hardly changed for almost a century. For Benda as for Gide or Barbusse or Nizan and for countless others the essay, the pamphlet and the periodical were the principal ways of broadcasting ideas; as Barthes once remarked with a slightly narrower frame of reference: 'l'oeuvre écrite est un acte'.[24] With the technological explosion of the late twentieth century there has clearly been a change, but whether we should go quite as far as some commentators have done and argue that quality has, as a result, given way to notoriety[25] may, I think, be too hasty a judgment or at least be to base it on criteria which are no longer applicable or are less easily tenable. As long ago as 1968 Edgar Morin suggested that what was already being witnessed was a new phase or shift in intellectual history.[26] We are free to deplore such a shift but it may be that the Socialist years in France were concomitant with the effective end of the old-style 'intellectuel engagé' and witnessed the re-emergence of the cleric with his faith in absolute values, identifiable not so much by his habit and quill as by his open-necked shirt and word-processor, having returned to form what Serge Daney in *Libération* defined as the 'intellectuel(s) du troisième type' or, perhaps more aptly, the 'télé-clergé'.[27]

Notes

1.   Lévy, B-H. (1987), *Eloge des intellectuels*, Grasset, Paris, p. 48.
2.   Debray, R. (1979), *Le Pouvoir intellectuel en France*, Ramsay, Paris.
3.   See in particular: Bourdieu, P. (1984), *Homo academicus*, Editions de Minuit, Paris; Ory, P. and Sirinelli, J.-F. (1986), *Les Intellectuels en France de l'Affaire Dreyfus à nos jours*, Colin, Paris; Ory, P. (1989), *L'Aventure culturelle française*, Flammarion, Paris; Sirinelli, J.-F. (1990), *Intellectuels et passions françaises*, Fayard, Paris; Charle, C.

(1990), *Naissance des Intellectuels*, Editions de Minuit, Paris. Nor should we forget: Bodin, L. (1962), *Les Intellectuels*, P.U.F., Paris; Johnston, W. (1974), 'The Origin of the term "intellectuals" in French Novels and Essays of the 1880s', *Journal of European Studies* IV, No 1, March, pp. 43-56.

4. Barbusse, H. (1921), *Le Couteau entre les dents*, éditions Clarté, Paris, pp. 5-6.

5. Drieu la Rochelle, P. (1961), *Récit secret*, Gallimard, Paris, pp. 67-8.

6. Benda, J. (1927), *La trahison des clercs*, Gallimard, Paris.

7. *Le Figaro*, 9-10 January 1988.

8. *L'Express*, 27 May 1988.

9. Mauriac, C. (1991), *Le Temps accompli*, Grasset, Paris, p.324.

10. Quoted in Ory and Sirinelli, *Les intellectuels en France*, p. 217.

11. *Le Débat*, November 1983.

12. Ibid., May 1985.

13. In a more limited survey carried out by *L'Express* (27 May 1988), 'Ne tirez pas sur les intellectuels', Lévi-Strauss defended the intellectual against charges that he should have opinions on all issues on the ground that the world had become too complex and fragmented.

14. For an interesting analysis of this climate see Diana Pinto (1982), 'Le socialisme et les intellectuels: le conflit caché', *Le Débat*, January.

15. Fumaroli, M. (1991), *L'Etat culturel*, De Fallois, Paris.

16. In addition to his own essays Lévy is the general editor of the *Collection "Figures"* published by Grasset. Many of the volumes are by writers who have become grouped under the label of *nouveaux philosophes*. Since the 1970s Lévy has carefully cultivated an image of himself in a series of interview articles. See, for example: *Le Point*, 4 July 1977; *Paris-Match*, 28 October 1977; *Le Monde*, 21 January 1980; *Le Quotidien de Paris*, 18 June 1984; *Globe*, March 1991. See too: *The Independent*, 1 February 1991.

17. In Paugam, Jacques (1977), *Génération perdue*, Laffont, Paris, p. 173.

18. Lévy, B-H., *Eloge des intellectuels*, pp. 6-7.

19. Ibid., pp. 99-100.

20. Lévy, B-H. (1991), *Les aventures de la liberté*, Grasset, Paris, pp. 84 and 346.

21. Finkielkraut, A. (1987), *Défaite de la pensée*, Gallimard, Paris, p. 165.
22. Quoted in Cocula, Bernard (1990), 'L'intellectuel bouge encore. Réflexions sur la naissance, l'essence et l'existence du substantif *intellectuel*', in *Mélanges de littérature comparée et de littérature française offerts à Simon Jeune*, Société des Bibliophiles de Guyenne, Bordeaux, p. 459.
23. See, for example: Quadruppani, Serge (1983), *Catalogue du prêt-à-penser français depuis 1968*, Balland, Paris, pp. 120-40; Aron, Raymond, in *L'Express*, 7-13 February 1981.
24. Barthes, R. (1953), *Degré zéro de l'écriture*, Editions du Seuil, Paris, p. 23.
25. Julliard, Jacques, in Furet, F., Julliard, J., and Rosanvallon, P. (1988), *La République du centre*, Calmann-Lévy, Paris, p. 116.
26. Morin, E. (1986), 'Ce qui a changé dans la vie intellectuelle française', *Le Débat*, September.
27. Daney, S., *Libération*, 25-26 April 1987.

Bibliography

Barbusse, H. (1921), *Le couteau entre les dents*, Clarté, Paris.

Barthes, R. (1953), *Degré zéro de l'écriture*, Seuil, Paris.

Benda, J. (1927), *La trahison des clercs*, Gallimard, Paris.

Bodin, L. (1962), *Les intellectuels*, P.U.F., Paris.

Bourdieu, P. (1984), *Homo Academicus*, Minuit, Paris.

Charle, C. (1990), *Naissance des intellectuels*, Minuit, Paris.

Cocula, B. (1990), 'L'intellectuel bouge encore. Réflexions sur la naissance, l'essence et l'existence du substantif *intellectuel*', in *Mélanges de littérature comparée et de la littérature française offerts à Simon Jeune*, Société des Bibliophiles de Guyenne, Bordeaux.

Le Débat, November 1983; January 1982; September 1986.

Debray, R. (1979), *Le pouvoir intellectuel en France*, Ramsay, Paris.

Drieu la Rochelle, P. (1961), *Récit secret*, Gallimard, Paris.

L'Express, 27 May 1988; 7 February 1981.

Le Figaro, 9-10 January 1988.

Finkielkraut, A. (1987), *La défaite de la pensée*, Gallimard, Paris.

Fumaroli, M. (1991), *L'Etat culturel*, De Fallois, Paris.

Globe, March 1991.

The Independent, 1 February 1991.

Johnston, W. (1974), 'The origin of the term *intellectual* in French novels and essays of the 1880s', *Journal of European Studies*, vol. IV, no. 1.

Juillard, J., Furet, F. and Rosanvallon, P. (1988), *La République du centre*, Calmann-Lévy, Paris.

Lévy, B.-H. (1987), *Eloge des intellectuels*, Grasset, Paris.

Lévy, B.-H. (1991), *Les aventures de la liberté*, Grasset, Paris.

Libération, 25 April 1987.

Mauriac, C. (1991), *Le temps accompli*, Grasset, Paris.

Le Monde, 21 January 1980.

Ory, P. and Sirinelli, J.-F. (1986), *Les intellectuels en France de l'Affaire Dreyfus à nos jours*, Colin, Paris.

Ory, P. (1989), *L'Aventure culturelle française*, Flammarion, Paris.

Paris-Match, 28 October 1977.

Paugam, J. (1977), *Génération perdue*, Laffont, Paris.

Le Point, 4 July 1977.

Quadruppani, S. (1983), *Catalogue du prêt-à-porter français depuis 1968*, Balland, Paris.

Le Quotidien de Paris, 18 June 1984.

Sirinelli, J.-F. (1990), *Intellectuels et passions françaises*, Fayard, Paris.

7 Freedom of Expression: the Case of Blasphemy

NICHOLAS HARRISON

Introduction

It may appear incongruous to use the term blasphemy in a discussion of modern, secular France, and perhaps especially in a discussion of France under socialist government. Nevertheless, blasphemy is a notion which has re-emerged within political discourse in recent years, most notably in connection with the debates around Godard's *Je vous salue, Marie* and Scorsese's *The Last Temptation of Christ*, and in the related case of Rushdie's *The Satanic Verses*. It is these three debates I will be discussing here. All three were international to a greater or lesser degree, of course, but were given a distinctive twist in France by various features of the political landscape.

Foremost amongst these, perhaps, was the political space occupied by the extreme right, who sought actively to manipulate the debates to their own ends. Their growing influence has gone a long way towards normalizing racism in contemporary France, a process articulated above all around the issue of immigration, and in the debates under discussion here this background meant that political rhetoric veered all the more readily into a vision of irreconcilable conflict between traditional French values and those of other social and religious groups, epitomized for many by North African Muslims.

A second salient feature was the idea of *laicité*, one which retains a certain force as a rallying cry despite suffering various shocks after the Socialists came to power in 1981. The most important of these came in 1984 with the Socialists' failure to mobilize the French people behind their slogan calling for an integrated, national and secular education system ('un grand service public, unifié et laïc de l'éducation nationale'), a failure which could be put down in part to the underestimated dynamism of the Catholic right and to a general tension between religion and state, but which, as Antoine Prost has argued[1] also indicated a fairly broad based opposition to centralized bureaucracy, boosted by a wave of anti-state liberalism and a fashionable faith in the private sector. A further shock came in 1989 with the affair of the islamic headscarves, which complicated the issue by cutting across divisions between the left and the right and by introducing the question of sexual politics into that of race relations. Although superficially it may seem that secularism and (perhaps) feminism finally gained the upper hand in this instance, the fact that the girls stopped wearing their scarves at the behest of the king of Morocco, and the way in which the whole incident was followed by an upswing in support for the *Front National*,[2] must suggest that this outcome was, at best, ambiguous, and points to a whole nexus of problems concerning the relationships between religion, the state and the individual, and more specifically any individual who is the object of prejudice or discrimination.

The final, specifically French feature of these debates lay in a particular interpretation of the idea of freedom of expression and the place of artistic expression within it, and it is on this feature that I will be concentrating here. The Socialists, distancing themselves from the Catholic right and with a historical penchant for a robust or even crusading version of secularism, tended towards positions of unequivocal support for both films and for Rushdie's book, and almost invariably sought to justify their stance in terms of the freedom of expression. My intention is to suggest that the questions the debates raised were more complex than was generally allowed by this stock response, however, and that a more nuanced, historically based understanding of the freedom of expression would permit greater perspicacity and sensitivity concerning the various obstacles to that freedom which exist in contemporary France.

The reception in France of *Je vous salue, Marie* and *The Last Temptation of Christ*

Je vous salue, Marie was banned within the municipality of Versailles by the mayor's office in January 1985. This decision was justified by the mayor's spokesperson in terms of the 'troubles sérieux de l'ordre public' likely to arise in response to a film which threatened to 'heurter les convictions d'une partie de la population versaillaise'.[3] At the same time, a national ban was called for by the *Confédération des associations familiales catholiques* and by the *Alliance générale contre le racisme et pour le respect de l'identité française et chrétienne*, an organization headed by Romain Marie, a prominent member of the FN. Both the Versailles decision and the aims of the pressure groups were immediately rebuffed by the Government, Jack Lang, the Minister for Culture, stating that only scenes depicting violence could justify censorship, and that it was unacceptable for any local or national authority to attempt to substitute itself for individual conscience. Just four days later the local ban was overturned in court. Demonstrations against the film continued, however, and occasionally became violent. Early in February, for example, a group of about two hundred and fifty protestors praying outside a cinema in Nantes came to blows with a group of about one thousand counter-demonstrators who objected to the incursion of so-called Catholic fundamentalism into the public space. Later that month a cinema in Tours where the film was showing was burnt down.

Even before its French release some three and a half years later in September 1988, *The Last Temptation of Christ* was causing still fiercer controversy, partly because the book on which it was based had been put on the papal index upon its publication in 1954. In France, opposition to the film became especially vehement after Jack Lang offered Scorsese some financial backing for the project; an offer he was forced to withdraw. When the film was finally released there were again widespread demonstrations, marked more widely than before by violent tactics including the use of tear gas, stink bombs and fire bombs. These led to numerous casualties, to the three-year closure of a Paris cinema which was gutted by fire, and to the arrest of a number of right-wing and predominantly FN activists, including Romain Marie.

Unacceptable as the far right's tactics were, however, it must be said that their opponents on the left did little to raise the tone of either debate, tending to obliterate any distinction between those who expressed themselves through violence, those who called for censorship, and those who merely voiced their disapproval of the films and of the offence they caused. Little attention was paid to the fact that some of the most favourable reactions to the films came from Catholic papers such as *La Croix* and *Témoignage Chrétien*, or that they had been passed for general release by a commission which included representatives of Catholic family associations. In *Libération*, for example, the Catholic right's anger was greeted with a rather puerile sense of glee, typical of which was the pun used for its headline for the Tours incident, 'La Marie de Godard a eu chaud aux fesses'.[4]

Comments such as this were doubtless all certain opponents of the film needed to feel they were the victims of a conspiracy, a feeling which was, unsurprisingly, intimately bound up with racial prejudice. In the case of *The Last Temptation* this led to overt anti-semitism; a development far less marked in France than in the United States and elsewhere in Europe. Franco Zeffirelli, for example, was quoted in *Le Monde* describing the film as the product of '[cette] chienlit culturelle juive de Los Angeles qui guette la moindre occasion de s'attaquer au monde chrétien'.[5] In France, on the other hand, the extreme right made a concerted attempt to appropriate the idea of racism for their own purposes, a tactic seen in the very name of the *Alliance générale contre le racisme et pour le respect de l'identité française et chrétienne*. Their aim in this was clearly to reveal and to undermine the perceived alliance between the left and those people (mainly non-white, non-christian immigrants) considered a threat to indigenous French and Catholic values. Typical of all this was an article published in *Le Figaro* in January 1985, whose author stated the following:

> ....les chrétiens, plus que les islamiques ou les juifs, doivent se montrer vigilants: dans le dessein de déstabiliser notre société, on multiplie contre eux les attaques.

> Jack Lang, à propos de Godard, plaidait pour une large liberté d'expression. Mais on comprend dans quel sens il va, si l'on sait que notre ministre de la Culture s'apprête à subventionner La Dernière

Tentation de Christ. [...] Après une Marie démythifiée on nous montrera un Christ homosexuel [sic], cédant à toutes les tentations de la chair. Le but suprême est toujours le même: remplacer le Credo par l'Internationale.[6]

Despite the crassness of such comments, however, and despite the acts of violence initiated by the FN, it would be a mistake to dismiss the campaigns against the films as nothing more than the paranoid rantings of the Catholic far right. Objections to both films were voiced not only by many Catholics other than those associated with the FN, but also by Muslims, and there was clearly a fairly widespread sympathy for the idea that if the sort of anti-discrimination law which could be used against so-called revisionist historians was truly just and impartial, then it might equally well be applied in some way to those who showed disrespect for Catholic doctrine. Indeed, the lawyer representing the three Catholic organizations who attempted to have *The Last Temptation* banned, invoked both the anti-racism law of 1 July 1972, and the precedent set by the prosecution of Le Pen for his dismissal of gas chambers as a mere detail of the history of the Second World War.

The parallel between Scorsese's film and Le Pen's political rhetoric was of course a flimsy one and was rejected in court, but it represented the culmination of this particular line of argument concerning the left's inconsistencies and hypocrisies, one which the left itself was perhaps too ready to ignore. A badge worn by protestors against Godard's film bore the words 'Touche pas à mon Christ', ironically appropriating the famous slogan coined by *S.O.S. Racisme*[7] and thereby attempting (quite successfully, it seems to me) to pose the question of why the respect the left generally seeks to accord to ethnic and religious minorities should not be extended to traditionalist Catholics, themselves certainly a minority since practising Catholics of every ilk form only about 7 per cent of the French populace.

Taking this question more seriously than did the French Socialists, then, I nevertheless wish to argue in the rest of this chapter that there is some justification for being less wary of causing offence to Catholics than to members of other religions in contemporary France. At the same time, I want to suggest that even if one follows the Socialists in approaching these issues in terms of the freedom of expression, a more sophisticated version than that which is normally invoked may lead to the conclusion that the responsible use of the freedom is at times more limited, at least with regard to religious sensibilities, than is allowed by the legal baselines and legalistic thinking which tend to dominate debates on the subject.

Liberté d'expression: some historical background

The framework within which debates over freedom of expression take place in modern France was given its basic shape by the *Déclaration des droits de l'homme et du citoyen of 1789* and the subsequent constitution of 1791, whose article XI stated that: 'La libre communication des pensées et des opinions est un des droits les plus précieux de l'homme, tout citoyen peut donc parler, écrire et imprimer librement, sauf à répondre de l'abus de cette liberté dans les cas déterminés par la loi.' If the basic formulae of today's constitution on this issue are close to those just quoted, however, this should not disguise the fact that the underlying notions concerning the nature of the citizen's participation in and accountability to her or his society, the criteria by which certain uses of the right are deemed abuses (and as such, actionable), and the nature of the authority possessed by those placed to make such judgments, are far from being constant. Indeed, the very fact that the right is now generally referred to and conceived of as the freedom of expression marks an exemplary and fundamental shift in its application, moving the emphasis away from the freedom to participate intellectually and politically in society's affairs, and towards a greater accent on autonomy. The latter version makes the right a broader one, but often obscures the reasons why freedom of expression should be considered important in the first place.

The Third Estate's appreciation of the importance of what it termed the right to the free communication of thoughts and ideas was born of its own oppression at the hands of the monarchy and the Church, and its confidence that rationality, diffused via the printed word, was on its side and had helped to make it a triumphant force of opposition. This confidence undoubtedly set the tone of the *Déclaration*, whose rhetoric betrayed an inordinate faith in the performative power of its own formulations to deliver the freedoms it described. It presented itself as revealing, 'en présence et sous les auspices de l'être Suprême', rights which were deemed 'naturels, inaliénables et sacrés', and its quasi-visionary quality was underlined by the fact it was published at first in the format of a breviary, and prompted various commentaries which treated it as a catechism, including Mirabeau's *Catéchisme de la Constitution*. The religious vocabulary was chosen no doubt partly to appease the clergy, and partly to help win over a largely Catholic populace: but also, no doubt, partly because it seemed appropriately transcendent and because a particular Christian framework of thought (summarized by Michel de Certeau as 'messianisme, évangélisme, croisade')[8] had been unconsciously inherited. Nevertheless, opponents of the *Déclaration* considered it, unsurprisingly, too radical a break with the past, and expressed justifiable fears that the rights it affirmed in the abstract were not sufficiently securely anchored in actual social structures.

It was perhaps unsurprising, consequently, that having remained almost absolute for the first three years after the Revolution, the right soon proved far from secure. Nevertheless, the Revolution had succeeded in redefining the discourse of government on this issue to such an extent that post-revolutionary censorship generally attempted to cover its tracks, in contrast both to that of late medieval or early modern France, where the authority of the censors was metaphysically guaranteed, and to that of the latter-day *ancien régime*, under which it was excessive permissiveness which the authorities sought to conceal.

Through the nineteenth century the right continued to evolve and was fiercely debated in Parliament, where there was extensive agreement that free speech should be considered an exercise of power. Disagreements arose over differing versions of the division of the public from the private, which proponents of censorship understood to circumscribe the appropriate field of action of the individual, while its opponents emphasized instead the acceptable limits of state power. This interpretation no doubt contained the seeds of the freedom's contemporary emphasis on individualism and autonomy, but its champions also stressed the fact that the shared context of discussion which free interlocutors are obliged to negotiate, is one of the freedom's great benefits. This point is often missed by fans of unbounded self-expression, who tend nonetheless to object to the type of self-expression offered by burning books.

Another medium of expression which was particularly closely monitored in the nineteenth century was the theatre, largely because of the perceived strength of its influence on an often illiterate public, gathered together in an unruly mass for an occasion of dubious cultural worth. If theatre censorship disappeared only in 1906, this was partly because of the strength of the consensus supporting it, even the left welcoming the actions of the *Bureau des Théâtres* when faced with the type of jingoistic and anti-semitic plays which became common around the time of the Dreyfus affair. The vast majority of spectacles aimed only to entertain and to make money, anyway, which was why many theatre directors welcomed the relative financial security offered by pre-censorship, and why, even when they did express dissatisfaction with the system, their rallying cry tended to be 'la liberté industrielle' or 'la liberté d'entreprise', values clearly dearer to them than the freedom of expression.

After theatre censorship was abolished, the kind of fears which had fuelled it soon found an alternative object of attention, and a perennial one, in the cinema. In 1909 the Minister of the Interior banned a newsreel which showed four men who had been sentenced to death being killed, and granted mayors a power of censorship. As this system proved too lax by the standards of the government, it passed a decree in 1919 instituting a regulatory commission, whose existence did not, however, annul the right of mayors to censor locally. This they may technically still do either on the grounds that the projection of a film threatens to engender 'troubles sérieux' in the form of reactions hostile enough to lead to violence from a particular group of local people, or if it can be shown that the film will be 'préjudiciable à l'ordre public',[9] the latter a notion which has gradually come to refer only to quantifiable physical and economic categories. In the light of this, the residual right of mayors to act as film censors is, in effect, an empty one. In the case of *Je vous salue, Marie*, for instance, Jack Lang asserted quite specifically that: 'Le maire est responsable de l'ordre public matériel, non de l'ordre public moral',[10] and legal opinion now concurs that 'la seule atteinte à la moralité publique', equated with the reduced idea of 'le trouble dans les consciences',[11] is no reason for a ban. An exception to this can be made only if it can be proved that there are special local circumstances, but when dealing with ideas such as morality and *ordre public*, which strain towards the universal, such proof is hard to establish. A ban placed by the mayor of Nice on various films was annulled, for example, after the only local circumstance he could invoke in justification of his decision was 'la vague d'immoralité qui a déferlé sur la ville de Nice au début de l'année 1954'.[12]

Freedom of expression in context

The fact that the idea of a 'wave of immorality' could be invoked in this way less than forty years ago, and now sounds almost quaint, is an indication of how much broader the liberal consensus on this issue has become since that time. Nevertheless, there is yet to be a constitutional affirmation of freedom of cinematographic expression, and phenomena such as the visa system (first introduced in 1941) which differentiates cinema-goers by age, or the specially stringent fiscal régime to which pornographic cinema has been subject since 1975, suggest that the freedom is not absolute, and that a certain degree of governmental intervention in this area is widely accepted. The liberal consensus on freedom of expression is, then, more complex than it may at first appear.

As the example of the specially high levels of tax demanded of pornographic cinemas suggests, the notional gap left by the collapse of absolute moral authority and confidence has frequently been bridged by the market in its role as a moral mediator; one it has been perceived and manipulated to fulfil at least since the nineteenth century. The obverse of this role can be seen in an initiative which helped form one of the Socialists' flagship policies when they came to power, namely their massive increase in governmental support for the cinema, along with other arts. By the end of the 1980s their aims and rhetoric were a little less expansive and certain schemes were dropped, but the basic intentions (promoting pluralism, competition and creativity, and making French cinema and cinemas materially more accessible) remained the same.

What is notable about this policy in the present context is that it departs from the most widespread contemporary interpretation of the freedom of expression, which sees in that right a means of protecting the individual from the state, and so implies a recognition that the abstract right, coupled with a liberal market, does not necessarily entail meaningful freedom of expression for all members of a society. The perception of a need for action in favour of pluralism hinges on the insight that if the 'free market of ideas' is left unchecked, when it is indeed a market, then it will be

162

predominantly the ideas of the dominant socio-economic group which will find expression, and they will do so only insofar as they are suitable for consumption as a commodity that may be privately appropriated.

In the light of this tension between markets and pluralism, the supposed autonomy of all individuals protected by the freedom of expression is also revealed to be a misleading concept, in that the ideas and opinions particular individuals might wish or be able to express are determined, partially but fundamentally, by the society in which they live, at an individual level and also at the level of their insertion into socially defined collectivities. Individuals may not be free to act as such if they are prejudged as members of a group which is constructed as a group, and as inferior, within a certain hegemonic formation to which they are marginal. The fact that such determinations are frequently overlooked can again be linked back to the Déclaration's failure to think through the essential mediation between abstract law and an actual society, and in this instance more specifically the failure to recognize that the subject of that law was modelled on a particular version of the sovereign individual, primarily (and in some instances, legally) male, upper or middle class, white, Christian and adult.

Making allowances for social groups whose members do not fit this description is nowadays a fairly widespread practice amongst the left, of course, and one Mitterand endorsed tentatively in a speech made in April 1991, when he talked of the possibility of legislating for 'un statut des minorités en Europe'.[13] The justifications for such allowances, however, are often poorly thought out. The usual assumption is that most political decisions in a modern liberal democracy are underpinned by a kind of neutral utilitarianism, and that certain social groups need help in the form of positive discrimination because of the small number of their representatives within the utilitarian calculus. The fact that this assumption frequently leads to women being referred to as a minority reveals, however, that it is an oversimplification. Confusion arises from the failure to acknowledge this background utilitarianism as an egalitarian political ideology in its own right, rather than as a mere precondition for a set of political values which are those of the majority. The latter version provides no grounds for discounting those political preferences of Nazis which require the preferences of Jews, gays etc. to be ignored, for example, whereas the stronger version does not rely solely on headcounting and must equip itself to discriminate between the contents of different preferences on the basis of its own values – most fundamentally, that of equality. This approach also has the merit of discouraging proponents of positive discrimination from treating 'minority' cultures as absolutely and homogeneously other and so offering them a blanket acceptance which, when rendered problematic by something such as the Satanic Verses affair, flips over all too easily into blanket rejection.

In terms of the freedom of expression, this means that a pluralist approach should be adopted which safeguards diversity while aiming to promote the norms of public discourse to which different groups must submit. Generally, however, the freedom is understood as an individualist one, and consequently, as Robert C. Post has argued, can 'redress audience outrage only when that outrage stems from characteristics potentially shared by all individuals, rather than from characteristics that are constitutive of particular social or religious groups'.[14] In other words, this individualist approach recognizes no dissymmetry between Catholics and Muslims or members of any other religion, though in reality the very different socio-historical status of Islam and Catholicism means there are sound reasons for treating Islam with more caution than Catholicism in modern France.

Amongst these reasons it should be recognized, firstly, that the contemporary context within which criticism of any religion can take place is one which the Catholic church itself has had an important role in shaping, both through its influence on such mainstays of secularism as the *Déclaration*, and through the internal evolution of its attitude to self-expression, since the Reformation. Islam, on the other hand, had no place in French society when the present 'secular contract' (to borrow a phrase from Jean Baubérot) was beaten out, and, as Richard Webster has argued, has passed through no equivalent 'conscience-centred revolution'.[15] Consequently the phrase a 'God-shaped hole' which Rushdie once used to explain the sacred space filled for him by literature,[16] has little resonance for Muslims unfamiliar with a particular Christian tradition. Secondly, to insult others' religious faith is, according to Webster, to perpetuate one of the distinctive and worst characteristics of the Judeo-Christian tradition, within which such a contemptuous attitude to other religions is an ancient custom. Thirdly, it should be noted that the idea of 'blasphemy' is itself culturally specific and has no exact equivalent in Islam, and that the hierarchy of linguistic practices found in 'western' cultures, in which people feel free to write things they would not dare to say, is, according to Simon Lee, the inverse of that which generally holds in Islamic countries. As a result, the very idea of fictionalizing the life of Mohammed is offensive to many Muslims. Having said all this, it is also true that to reveal the connections between contemporary consensus on freedom of expression and a specifically Catholic tradition does not automatically invalidate that consensus, and that the inherent difficulty for Islam in finding a place within it can easily be overestimated. What is called for, above all, is a greater sensitivity to these issues than that shown by Pierre Joxe, for instance, who, when he was Minister of the Interior and the Minister in charge of religious affairs, remarked that, 'Ceux dont la foi religieuse est sincère, et fondée sur des convictions personnelles, ne peuvent sentir leur foi, selon moi, atteinte par une oeuvre d'art'.[17]

If Joxe's remark would fail to jar in most French ears, however, this is as much because of a specific artistic tradition as because of a particular religious one, since it draws on the widespread perception of art as ultimately inconsequential . Rushdie himself played on this when, a week before *The Satanic Verses* was first published, he remarked in an interview that, 'it would be absurd to think that a book can cause riots'.[18] Again the expression/action dualism comes into play here, but what is more specifically at stake is the protection of a sacred artistic space in which the artist's primary aim and responsibility is unfettered self-expression. This use of the term 'sacred' is not gratuitous, since artistic vision is often conceived of in terms reminiscent of those of the religious visionary. Godard, for example, in discussing *Je vous salue, Marie*, commented that, 'Je ne crois pas en Dieu. Je ne crois qu'en moi et au cinéma. Cela dit, à force de fabriquer des images, je me suis demandé cette fois-ci d'où elles viennent'.[19] Indeed, *Je vous salue, Marie* seems to invite interpretation as a reflection on mysteries of creation, playing on analogies between procreation and artistic creation and on the idea of cinema as soul made flesh, in this case via Godard who imagined his role on one hand as that of the doctor, the mother or the vagina, and on the other hand as that of the angel of annunciation, as the film's title suggests. This particular interpretation should not necessarily be taken as the trace of any coherent intention on Godard's part, of course; in interview he suggested that the film's subject had chosen him, rather than vice versa, and explained: 'Je ne sais pas ce que je veux, je fais ce que je peux.'[20]

Given the relation of the artist's space to a conscience-centred Christian tradition, then, and given the currency of this sort of disregard for any question of communication (a disregard made quite explicit in Godard's case by his comment: 'Il faudrait pouvoir dissocier le film [in general] du public. Si le public vient, tant mieux, mais ce n'est pas si important que ça'),[21] it is unsurprising that that space is often conceived of, paradoxically, as a private one, and that the question of whether a particular act of expression is moral, or responsible, or worthwhile, is a difficult one to pose. Those who objected to Godard's film or the other works in question consequently found it hard to criticize them on the basis that they flouted the necessary norms of public discourse, and were told by Jack Lang, amongst others, that they should simply avoid personal contact with them. A blasphemous publicity poster for the film *Ave Maria*, on the other hand, was banned in 1984, because unlike a film it imposed itself on its audience and did not enjoy the special privileges extended to art.

The distinctions drawn between these two cases are of course reasonable ones, constructed on a particular version of such binary oppositions as action/expression, public/private and art/reality. These help define the conventions of public discourse that make cultural heterogeneity possible in a modern democracy, by allowing the co-existence of doctrines such as Christianity and Islam which are, one one level of ideology, incompatible. All the same, these conventions and the oppositions which underpin them are not necessarily valid outside a particular socio-cultural context, something Rushdie wilfully ignored in his sweeping remark about the inability of books to provoke riots.

Despite this, Rushdie's remark may nonetheless have been right to the extent that those who riot in response to a book are almost invariably responding simultaneously to other frustrations and provocations too. If people fail to respect the so-called decencies of controversy, this may be because they were not invited to take part in the controversy in the first place, and see no benefit in respecting its conventions. Perhaps out of sensitivity to this, French jurisprudence on the issue of *ordre public* seemingly recognizes the importance of allowing people their say, since the police's responsibility, when faced with violent reactions to a particular act of expression, is simply to prevent the violence. This makes it all the more notable that a demonstration in Marseille against the publication of *The Satanic Verses*, which was planned by five İslamic organizations in March 1989, was banned, presumably because of fears concerning the disruption it might cause.

It is difficult not to conclude that this is one instance of the marginalization which Muslims and Arabs in France suffer because of the widespread prejudice against them, the extent of which was revealed by the reports and comments on the *Satanic Verses* affair in a liberal paper such as *Le Monde*. These included an article asking if Islam was ultimately incapable of being incorporated into French secular democracy, numerous references to Islam's archaism (frequently backed by facile parallels between the Christian middle ages and the current fifteenth century of the Islamic calendar), attempts to explain away demonstrations as being manipulated by fanatical Muslim leaders, and an open letter addressed to 'les musulmans de France' from the head of the *Grand Orient* notifying them glibly that 'la liberté d'expression est inconditionnelle ou elle n'existe pas'.[22] Nearly all such articles, even if describing Parisian demonstrations, elucidating French laws or providing statistics on Muslims in France, were lumped together in the section of the paper headed *Etranger*.

It is impossible, then, to understand the *Satanic Verses* affair as it unfolded in France without reference to the marginal status of Muslims in French society. Substantively, their freedom is undercut more significantly by the prejudice which marginalizes them than by anything else, and it is not helped by a version of freedom of expression which sees nothing wrong, and much to be admired, in the publication of such a book. This holds true, it seems to me, even if freedom is conceived of within a secular framework which sees religion as inherently antinomic to it.[23] The situation of Catholics, on the other hand, is clearly very different. Having said this, it may be that the iconoclastic appeal which *Je vous salue, Marie* and *The Last Temptation* hold for many liberals is itself something of an anachronism in contemporary France, and smacks of nostalgia for an era (still recent, admittedly) when those militating for freedom of expression had an easily recognizable and confrontable enemy in the shape of the French Catholic Church. Similarly, the fact that the government is not always a reactionary force can be disorienting for some. A typical complaint is that of Serge Toubiana who, in commenting on the notion of *liberté d'expression* with regard to the Rushdie affair, wrote that:

'aujourd'hui, c'est le monde à l'envers: c'est l'Etat qui se trouve du côté de la liberté artistique, face à une partie de l'opinion ou de la société civile qui s'accroche à des valeurs archaïques et puritaines.'[24]

Conclusion

Comfortable antagonisms of the type which Toubiana seems to miss are justifiably revitalized by such occasional alliances as emerge between the Catholic church and the far right, of course, but the enthusiasm with which the flames of controversy in such instances are fanned by many on the left belies their failure to come to terms with the numerous other forms which threats to freedom of expression can take. In some cases these are part of broader social structures and developments, such as the concentration of media ownership, an issue which the Socialists in government recognized as problematic but which they failed to confront effectually. In other cases, however, the problem still stems directly from the government, whether left or right, which too frequently practises its administration as an exercise in public relations carried out via resolutely non-transparent bodies, and which has shown itself all too ready to disregard the freedom of expression when it risks interfering with the smooth running of certain affairs of state. As was the case during the years of Socialist government with the Rainbow Warrior affair, the persistent banning of foreign publications based in France which threatened diplomatic links, or the Gulf War, during which Mitterrand stated categorically that press freedom was far from being a priority.

In many respects, then, the record of the Socialists in this area during their years of government is unimpressive, and is a sign that their occasional invocation of the freedom of expression should be treated with suspicion, even in the case of an issue such as blasphemy where the enemies of that freedom seem easy to identify. As I have tried to suggest, many of the forces which today form an obstacle to a genuinely pluralistic freedom of expression are more diffuse and make a less easy target than do certain rigid versions of Catholicism or Islam, and can be understood only in terms of deep-rooted social, political and economic inequalities. What was not clearly appreciated by the left, and more generally, in France during the Socialist years was that if the power of the idea of freedom of expression is to be harnessed in order to help dismantle such inequalities, then the individualistic assumptions on which that freedom is generally constructed must be substantially rethought.

Notes

1.   Prost, A. (1987), 'The Educational Maelstrom', in Ross, G., Hoffmann, S. and Malzacher, S. (eds), *The Mitterrand Experiment*, Polity Press, Cambridge, pp. 229-36.
2.   Hereafter referred to as the FN.
3.   *Le Monde*, 25 January 1985.
4.   *Libération*, 28 February 1985.
5.   *Le Monde*, 13 August 1988.
6.   *Le Figaro*, 26 January 1985.
7.   *S.O.S. Racisme* is an anti-racism movement which was founded in 1984. Part of its highly successful first campaign was inspired by the impact of the *Solidarnosc* logo during its period of fashionable ubiquity, and entailed getting as many people as possible to wear its own logo, a hand-shaped badge (reminiscent of the traditional islamic 'hand of Fatima' design) bearing the slogan 'Touche pas à mon pote'.
8.   De Certeau, M. (1975), *L'Ecriture de l'histoire*, Gallimard, Paris, p. 195.
9.   Long, M., Weil, P. and Braibant, G. (1984), *Les Grands Arrêts de la jurisprudence administrative*, eighth edition, Sirey, Paris, p. 485.
10.   *Quotidien de Paris*, 25 January 1985.
11.   Long, Weil and Braibant, *Grands Arrêts*, p.484.
12.   Ibid, p. 486.
13.   *Nouvel Observateur*, 2 May 1991.
14.   Post, R.C. (1988), 'Cultural Heterogeneity and Law: Pornography, Blasphemy and the First Amendment', *California Law Review*, vol. 76:297, pp. 297-335. The different versions of utilitarianism discussed above are sketched out by Ronald Dworkin in his essay 'Do We Have a Right to Pornography'in (1985), *A Matter of Principle*, Harvard University Press, Cambridge, Mass. The issue of pornography is another which, in France and elsewhere, has raised questions concerning the definition of norms of public discourse and

concerning the morality of representation, and it has been powerfully theorized from a feminist perspective by Catherine MacKinnon in her book (1987), *Feminism Unmodified: Discourses on Life and Law*, Harvard University Press, Cambridge, Mass. Post, in the article quoted here, draws explicitly upon MacKinnon's arguments in order to think through the difference between individualist and pluralist versions of the freedom of expression.

15. Webster, R. (1990), *A Brief History of Blasphemy. Liberalism, Censorship and the 'Satanic Verses'*, The Orwell Press, Southwold, p. 30.
16. Ibid., p.53. Cited from *Observer*, 22 January 1989.
17. *Le Monde*, 2 March 1989.
18. Lee, S. (1990), *The Cost of Free Speech*, London, Faber and Faber, p. 77.
19. *Figaro*, 25 February 1985.
20. *Libération*, 28 January 1985.
21. *Le Monde*, 30 December 1987.
22. *Le Monde*, 11 March 1989.
23. It also holds true, I believe, even if one takes into account the different status of Muslim men and Muslim women, though in an instance such as the headscarf affair one sees how Muslim women may be doubly or more complexly oppressed. This statement is not intended as a weighing up of the relative harmfulness of sexism as against racism in contemporary France. I merely wish to argue, however, that the type of sexism which is specific and internal to Islam is not monolithic or immutable, and may be less entrenched than is sometimes assumed, and furthermore that greater freedom (and a greater freedom of expression) for all Muslims may be a necessary precondition for Muslim women to confront and overcome that sexism.
24. *Cahiers du cinéma*, April 1985.

Bibliography

Baubérot, J. (1990), *Vers un nouveau pacte laïque*, Seuil, Paris.

Bibliothèque publique d'information (B.P.I.), Centre Georges Pompidou (1987), *Censures - De la Bible aux 'Larmes d'Eros'*, Paris.

Communications, no. 9, 1967.

De Certeau, M. (1975), *L'Ecriture de l'histoire*, Gallimard, Paris.

Dworkin, R. (1985), *A Matter of Principle*, Harvard University Press, Cambridge, Mass.

Haarscher, G. (ed.) (1989), *Laïcité et droits de l'homme - Deux siècles de conquêtes*, Editions de l'Université de Bruxelles, Brussels.

Hollier, D. (ed.) (1989), *A New History of French Literature*, Harvard University Press, Cambridge, Mass.

Krakovitch, O. (1985), *Hugo censuré. La liberté au théâtre au XIXe siècle*, Calmann-Lévy, Paris.

Lee, S. (1990), *The Cost of Free Speech*, Faber and Faber, London.

Long, M., Weil, P. and Braibant, G. (1984), *Les grands arrêts de la jurisprudence administrative*, 8th edn, Sirey, Paris.

Maarek, P.J. (1982), *La censure cinématographique*, Librairies Techniques, Paris.

MacKinnon, C. (1987), *Feminism Unmodified: Discourses on Life and Law*, Harvard University Press, Cambridge, Mass.

Post, R. C. (1988), 'Cultural Heterogeneity and Law: Pornography, Blasphemy and the First Amendment', *California Law Review*, vol. 76:297.

Ross, G., Hoffmann, S. and Malzacher, S. (eds) (1987), *The Mitterrand Experiment*, Polity Press, Cambridge.

Webster, R. (1990), *A Brief History of Blasphemy, Liberalism, Censorship and the 'Satanic Verses'*, The Orwell Press, Southwold, Suffolk.

I owe special thanks to Valdo Kneubuhler of the FEMIS library (Palais de Chaillot, Paris), who allowed me to consult the dossier he has established on *Je vous salue, Marie*.

PART III
SOCIETY

8 Ten Years of Socialist Social Policy: Continuity or Change?

LINDA HANTRAIS

Introduction

The left-wing government formed in 1981 had set itself three all encompassing tasks which they hoped to accomplish through their social policies: they intended to change economic and social structures, improve workers' and citizenship rights and reduce social inequality. According to Keynesian economists, social policy, and more especially transfer payments, serve to some extent as the social arm of capitalism, providing a means of reacting to economic trends and pressures. But, as argued for example by Fournier, Questiaux and Delarue,[1] social policy can also be credited with a more subversive function. By consciously intervening in social life, state welfare may negate liberalism and call into question the basis of the very economic system on which it depends. Three instances in recent French history are cited by the same authors to illustrate the unintended outcome of social policy: in the period following the events of May 1968, in 1974 at the time of the oil crisis and again in 1981 with the political change from a right to a left-wing government, the normal order of events was reversed and social policy was given precedence over fiscal and monetary concerns with adverse consequences for the economy. The economic problems resulting from the introduction of many of the social

175

reforms which had been promised in the early years of left-wing government amply demonstrated that economic and social policies are inextricably linked and that priority cannot be given to social welfare at the expense of economic rationality.

Despite the hiatus between 1986 and 1988 when the centre-right briefly returned to power, by 1991 the Socialists had had almost a decade to put their theories about social change to the test and to demonstrate whether rhetoric and ideology could be transformed into action; a task made more difficult against an international background of economic recession. This chapter focuses on the directions taken during this period by social affairs in the more limited Anglo-Saxon sense of the term, excluding incomes policies, industrial relations, employment law and workers' rights, except insofar as they directly affect social welfare. Issues relating to education, culture and immigration, which can be considered as an integral part of social policy, will be alluded to only briefly since they are dealt with more fully elsewhere in this publication. Rather than providing a strict chronological account of overall developments in social policy, series of events are located within different policy areas, and an analysis is carried out of some of the interlocking themes which have attracted most attention over the past ten years in the social arena. An attempt is also made to evaluate the effectiveness of the policy measures taken in relation to the objectives stated in 1981 and to the socialist ideology on which they were premised.

The context of social change

A decade of socialism, or at least ten years under a Socialist president, coincided fairly closely with the period between the last two national population censuses of 1982 and 1990. Comparative data from the INSEE (*Institut National de la Statistique et des Etudes Economiques*) provide a snapshot of some of the major changes which were taking place during this period and a backcloth against which to situate the impact of political action.

Between these dates the total population of France increased by 4.3 per cent. The proportion of the elderly eligible to receive retirement pensions went up at a faster rate, not only due to the fall in the birthrate and greater

176

life expectancy, which had risen from 70.7 years for men at birth and 78.9 years for women in 1982 to 71.8 for men and 80.0 for women by 1990, but also as a result of the lowering of retirement age. In 1982 13.2 per cent of the population were aged over sixty-five and in 1990 17 per cent, but by the same date 19.9 per cent were aged over sixty, the new retirement age.

Partly as result of this policy change, the proportion of the population of working age in employment had risen only slightly, by about 190,000 a year, since the early 1980s. Had there not been an increase in the proportion of women in the labour force, the size of the working population would have remained stable: at the time of the 1990 census 58.8 per cent of women of working age were economically active, compared with 54.7 per cent in 1982. The number of foreign workers had increased by 4.4 per cent to reach 1.6 million or one worker in fifteen, although the proportion of foreigners, including nationals from other EC member states, remained unchanged at about 6.3 per cent of total population.

The extension of the period of education and training for young people and their later entry into the labour market, together with rising levels of unemployment, also had an impact on the size of the labour force. In 1990 only 9.4 per cent of girls and 14.9 per cent of boys aged between fifteen and nineteen were in employment compared with 16.7 per cent and 23.8 per cent respectively in 1982. After rising above 10 per cent in the middle of the decade, according to ILO figures, unemployment had fallen to 9.2 per cent in 1990, which was still above the level reached at the time of the previous census. The combination of a larger number of elderly people in retirement, of the young in training and the unemployed imposed a heavier burden on employers and the working population who pay for social welfare benefits and services through their social insurance contributions and taxes. To some extent these changes in the dependency ratio were offset or mitigated not only by the growth in female employment but also by its greater continuity. Whereas in 1982 71.1 per cent of women aged between twenty-five and twenty-nine were economically active, the rate had risen to 80.5 per cent by 1990. For the age group forty to forty-four the increase was even more marked: 62.4 per cent in 1982 and 75.8 per cent in 1990.

Other demographic trends which have had an impact on social policy are declining marriage rates, the increase in the number of divorces and of extramarital births and the growing number of cohabiting couples and single-parent families, which can be interpreted as signs of changing family constitution and structure. After falling to 4.7 per thousand inhabitants in 1987 marriage rates had risen to slightly above their 1982 level of 5.8 by 1990 with 5.9 per thousand. Divorce rose from 7.3 per thousand married couples in 1982 to 8.4 in 1990. Extramarital births accounted for 13.5 per cent of births in 1982 compared with 28.0 per cent in 1990. Cohabitation is more difficult to track because it is not formally recognized, but according to a study carried out in the mid-1980s more than two million couples were living together without being married, a figure which has been increasing rapidly, according to Léridon and Villeneuve-Gokalp.[2] The number of single-parent families is estimated to have risen from 4.7 per cent of households in 1982 to 5.2 per cent in 1990.

These trends are not peculiar to the 1980s, nor to France, but many were maintained, if not accelerated, during the years of Socialist government. In some cases they may have been affected by policy, although direct causal relationships are difficult to establish, as demonstrated, for example, by Ray, Dupuis and Gazier[3] in an analysis of the economic impact of public policy. In any event, demographic data can provide useful indicators of the factors which are likely to be shaping attitudes and expectations and consequently the pressures being exerted on policy makers.

The recipe for social change

Social change was the key word of the 1981 electoral platforms of both right and left. After more than thirty years in opposition the left were able to proclaim a more fundamental approach and offer what seemed like new directions in their efforts to change society radically. The electorate had been led to expect greater emphasis to be placed on the quality of life through the improvement of living and working conditions and the reduction of social inequality, with the assurance that the cost would be met by the wealthy sectors of the population. In the campaign leading up to the presidential and parliamentary elections of 1981 the Socialist Party put forward 110 proposals for reforms which the left would carry out if brought to power. About a third concerned social affairs, setting out objectives and targets for improving social housing, public services, social security benefits, women's rights to equal pay, family welfare, health care, job creation schemes and working hours, for lowering retirement age and providing better facilities for education and training as well as greater equality of opportunity.

Two major themes were to dominate policy in the early 1980s: national solidarity and social equality. One of the first apppointments made by the new government was of a *Ministre de la Solidarité nationale*, subsequently changed in 1982 to the *Ministre des Affaires sociales et de la Solidarité nationale*, with control over one of the largest budgets and responsibility for all state welfare. The use of the term *solidarité nationale* symbolized a return to the redistributive ideology of the social security system when it was first instituted nationally in the immediate post-war period. The ministry's priorities were to fight against unemployment, poverty and marginalization. Solidarity in this context implied a commitment to draw up contracts between social partners in an attempt to deal with the causes of problems and not merely their effects. The implication was that resources should be redistributed from the richer to the poorer sectors of society by raising low incomes and reducing differentials in income and wealth. The self-employed were also to pay more through taxes and social insurance contributions, which can be interpreted as a response to the resentment traditionally felt towards this category of workers since the cost of their benefits has to some extent been borne indirectly by the social insurance funds of wage earners.

Reviewing three years of social policy in 1984 the Prime Minister, Pierre Mauroy, claimed that the 1981 election pledges had been fulfilled.[4] Most of the 110 proposals drawn up for the 1981 campaign had, he maintained, been acted upon, although in many cases the action took the form of statements of intent or proposals for further discussion. Social justice coupled with financial solvency and solidarity within a context of economic stringency were presented as the main characteristics of the period. Mauroy's successor, Laurent Fabius, confirmed the government's intention to promote social justice and encourage economic activity and he spoke about solidarity in the fight against poverty. At the end of the first term in office of the Socialists in 1986 Laurent Fabius was claiming that his government had achieved the objectives they had set themselves in 1984: they had continued the task undertaken by his predecessor and consolidated the achievements of the previous government.

179

When the Socialists returned to power in 1988, the health of the economy was the government's main concern. Michel Rocard identified four areas for special attention: education, the economy, international affairs and employment. *The Ministère des Affaires sociales* was replaced by a *Ministère de la Solidarité* (without *Nationale*), *de la Santé et de la Protection sociale*. In 1991 Edith Cresson created a *Ministère du Travail, de l'Emploi et de la Formation professionnelle*, while *Affaires sociales* was linked in a partnership with a more nebulous concept: *Intégration*, defined by Marceau Long in the first report of the *Haut Conseil à l'Intégration*, set up in 1990, as:

> A process specifically designed to encourage the active participation of varied and diverse elements in the social life of the nation, while accepting the continued existence of cultural, social and moral specificities, and holding to the belief that this variety and complexity enriches the whole.[5]

The rethinking of priorities was signposted in other ways. The pragmatic politician, Pierre Bérégovoy, took over the *Ministère de la Solidarité nationale et des Affaires sociales* from the more idealistic Nicole Questiaux in July 1982, signalling the realization that sound financial control was a necessary ingredient for managing social welfare. He moved on to become *Ministre de l'Economie, des Finances et du Budget* in Laurent Fabius' government in July 1984 and was subsequently confirmed in this position both by Michel Rocard and Edith Cresson, before taking over from her as Prime Minister in 1992.

The overall shift in Socialist policy during the 1980s away from social affairs reflects the changing concerns of governments in the face of harsh economic realities and the gradual acceptance of socialism as a variant of capitalism rather than an alternative to it. An attempt can be made to track these changes by analysing the development of some of the proposals for social reform announced in 1981 and enacted in the early 1980s before social policy was subordinated to economic priorities. The three social insurance funds and the scheme for unemployment afford an appropriate framework for assessing social policy over a decade of socialism.

Immediately on taking up office, following a pattern set by previous governments, the left rewarded the electorate and fulfilled one of their election pledges by increasing both the minimum wage (*salaire minimum interprofessionnel de croissance*), which was raised by 55 per cent, and the non-contributory guaranteed minimum state pension (*minimum vieillesse*), which went up by 65 per cent for a person living alone and by 51 per cent for a couple. Rates continued to rise over the next few years, albeit more slowly. A comparison between 1981 and 1986 showed that the minimum state pension had increased by 81 per cent for one person and by 64 per cent for a couple.[6]

A very popular reform of the early 1980s was the lowering of the age of retirement to sixty for all workers. The initial proposal had been for women to retire at the age of fifty-five, but this suggestion was not pursued, presumably due to pressures for equal treatment of men and women. From 1983 wage earners who had contributed to a pension fund for 37.5 years became eligible to retire on a full pension, a right which was progressively extended to the self-employed in 1984 and to farmers in 1986. Those who retired at sixty were not however eligible initially for reductions on public transport until they reached the age of sixty-five (subsequently reduced to sixty-two in 1985).

Because the age cohort eligible for retirement in the early 1980s was relatively small as a result of the low birthrate during the First World War, the economic impact of this policy was not so great in 1982 as it will be when the generations of the post-war baby boom begin reaching the age of sixty at the end of the century. Currently their contribution as workers is helping to boost the size of the workforce and pay for pensions. The smaller age cohorts of the 1970s and 1980s will have to pay for the welfare of a much larger group of elderly people. By the nature of their terms of appointment politicians are inevitably more concerned with the immediate effect of policy on their standing with the electorate. The long-term repercussions of lowering the age of retirement did not prevent the left from introducing a reform which would later be very costly and was out of step with what was happening elsewhere in the Western world.

When the centre-right won the elections in 1986 they contemplated restoring the age of retirement to sixty-five. They were reluctant to change the law since the reform had been so popular, as demonstrated at the end of 1983 by a public opinion survey commissioned by the Ministry for Social Affairs: more than 90 per cent of those interviewed were in favour of the 1983 change and felt that the opposition parties should not revert to the former age of retirement if they returned to power. Another survey in 1991 by the SOFRES confirmed the electorate's continued support for the reform which was presented as the most popular of all the policy changes made by the Socialists over the decade. The adverse effects of lowering the age of retirement were already being felt by the pension funds at the end of the 1990s. A *Livre blanc sur les retraites* published in 1991 clearly pinpointed the social problems created by an ageing population. Rather than proposing a move towards a fully funded alternative, however, the authors more cautiously suggested how the current pay-as-you-go pension schemes might be adapted.

Controlling the cost of health care

The two social insurance funds which have most difficulty in balancing their budget are old age pensions and health. The population aged sixty-five and over are the main consumers of medical care, accounting for twice the average spending on health and two-thirds of spending on hospital treatment, which in the early 1980s made up half of all spending on health and nearly two-thirds of the budget for health insurance. The ageing of the population therefore constitutes a drain not only on the resources available to support pensions but also on funds for medical care. The demand for ever better and more expensive treatment and more sophisticated equipment has also sent costs spiralling upwards at a time when resources have been reduced by the growing number of unemployed and of pensioners who in many cases are not contributing to the fund. It was Pierre Bérégovoy who, in 1984, attempted and failed to slow these rising costs through the introduction of a social insurance contribution on unemployment benefits and pensions for recipients of higher replacement incomes.

In their election platform the Socialists had committed themselves to improving health care. Policy in this area had two main objectives: the reduction of inequality in access to treatment by raising benefits and the implementation of tighter financial control over resources. Despite a commitment to careful budgeting extra funds were given almost immediately to the service for staffing and the provision of equipment: within six months 12,500 new jobs had been created and twenty-eight scanners had been installed in hospitals. A health charter was presented to the Council of Ministers in 1982, setting out policy guidelines rather than a catalogue of measures to be implemented. After only a year in office the stated aim of the government was to reconcile economic constraints with services which would be more responsive to needs. The instruments to be used to achieve these ends were information gathering on the state of health of the nation, campaigns to promote better standards of health, improved care and rehabilitation. Although the charter reaffirmed the government's commitment to the independence and pluralism of the medical profession, the importance of general practitioners and staff training, it was followed by the abolition of private beds in public sector hospitals as the first stage in a plan to get rid of private medicine completely by 1986. In recognition of the sort of service which the French public wanted, by 1984 however talk was no longer of abolishing the private sector. The process was in any case reversed by the centre-right when it returned to power, and by the end of the decade the Socialists seemed to have abandoned the idea.

Despite its opposition to the proposal when it was put forward by the previous government in 1983, a daily charge for in-patient treatment in hospitals (*forfait journalier*) was introduced. It was not reimbursed by social security although it could be covered by private insurance (*mutuelle*) or for those in receipt of social assistance (*aide sociale*). Nearly a decade later, the intention was to increase the charge rather than remove it. Other early left-wing plans included a reform of medical training to create a single route of access to medicine in universities but with special status for general practice, one of the areas of particular interest to the Communist Minister of Health, Jack Ralite.

Proposals for far-reaching reform of hospitals were launched in 1983 and pursued further when the Socialists returned to power. In 1984 a new system of budgeting had been introduced for the hospital service in order to achieve greater accountability. Instead of paying the bill at the end of the budgetary period, an allocation was made to each establishment within which they were expected to operate. The government intervened to exercise greater control over medical training and the choice of specialists. By 1986 they were maintaining that financial stability had been achieved. The medical insurance fund was said to have a surplus. These claims of sound financial management by the Socialists were, not unexpectedly, disputed by Jacques Chirac. By the early 1990s as costs were again rising steeply, plans were being considered for reforms which would improve quality and access without the fund running into deficit. The 1991 budget was balanced by further increasing social insurance contributions, thereby imposing a heavier burden on the wages bill for employers. Negotiations between the medical funds and the medical profession were focused on an agreement by doctors to limit the number of drugs prescribed and unnecessary visits in return for being allowed to raise their fees. Most of the measures being taken could be described as an attempt to reach compromise and maintain stability rather than change the principles on which the system operated as might have been expected when the left came to power.

Family policy versus demographic issues

Concern about motherhood, family building and demograhic trends are issues which have come to be associated with parties of the right. Already in the 1960s the Socialists had established themselves as a party interested in women's rights rather than the family. When the left came to power in 1981, women's rights as well as workers' rights were high on the agenda. Following the appointment of Yvette Roudy as the *Ministre délégué auprès du Premier Ministre chargé des Droits de la Femme*, campaigns were launched to heighten awareness of women's issues. Women's rights were tackled by a series of measures, leading in July 1983 to the widely publicized *Loi Roudy* which was aimed at achieving greater equality of opportunity for women at the workplace by instituting positive action programmes. The public sector, true to its reputation for acting as a trailblazer, had already given a lead in 1982 when a law was passed to prevent gender segregation in recruitment and to ensure that the situation was carefully monitored. Policy statements made explicit reference to the intention to take account of maternity and family life so as to avoid women being put at a disadvantage by the presence of young children. From 1984

184

married women were obliged to sign tax returns, men and women were given equal rights in managing their common property and that of their children, and in 1985 they became responsible for each other's debts.

The focus of Socialist family policy was initially on the need to take account of changes in family structure and the greater diversity of family forms. Attempts by the previous government to encourage larger families, and in particular the third child, seen as the key to solving the problems associated with demographic decline, were countered by policies designed to redress the balance between children within families. Allowances were adjusted so that it became less advantageous to have three children: they were raised by 93 per cent for two children and 53 per cent for three. Policy statements presented the government's commitment to a more neutral approach, a concept which it is extremely difficult, if not impossible, to put into practice, as demonstrated by Ray et al.[7] and Sullerot.[8] The original proposal in 1981 to introduce a single rate of allowance for all children including the first was dropped.

Between 1981 and 1983 the spending power of families, particularly those with two children, had improved, but subsequently the real value of family allowances began to fall.[9] By 1982 benefits were already increasing more slowly than consumer prices. A comparison of the rates of allowances in 1981 and 1986 showed that a substantial improvement had nonetheless been achieved during five years of socialism: family allowances had increased by 112 per cent for two children and 71 per cent for three; the single-parent allowance for mothers (or fathers) with one child had been raised by 103 per cent and for two or more children by 52 per cent for each child.[10]

The ninth economic plan for 1984 to 1988 outlined the Socialists' revised approach to family policy. The state was to assume an enabling role, giving couples freedom of choice and allowing them to decide for themselves between a range of options. Previous attempts by policy-makers to encourage couples to adopt a particular family model or to deter them from doing so were criticized as anti-democratic and ineffectual. Three major objectives were defined and they aptly summarize the thrust of family policy from 1983. It was far from being neutral either in terms of its redistributive effects or the incentives it gave couples to encourage them to increase family size. Firstly the government committed themselves, for egalitarian as well pronatalist reasons they claimed, to supporting young families and large families. Secondly they aimed to help couples to combine family life and economic activity by removing obstacles to family building. Thirdly they set out to create an environment conducive to childbirth in an effort to increase the birthrate.

Two new benefits, the *allocation au jeune enfant* and the *allocation parentale d'éducation* were introduced in 1985. The first replaced as many as nine different allowances including pre- and post-natal benefits and the family supplement (*complément familial*), which had been instituted in 1977, although this allowance was kept for a transitional period for older children in large families. The *allocation au jeune enfant* was paid from 1 January 1985 to all families at a flat rate for each child from the third month of pregnancy for nine months irrespective of the parents' income. Payment was to continue after this period for eight out of ten families for a further thirty-two months on a means-tested basis, in effect creating a benefit for the first child in lower income families.

Provision for parental leave had been made in 1977 for firms employing at least 200 workers, with the guarantee of reinstatement in their previous employment after two years. The left extended parental leave to firms with 100 employees in 1981 and then to all employees in 1984. Initially the proposal was for unpaid leave which could be granted to either or both parents of children under two years of age, with beneficiaries maintaining their own rights to social insurance benefits. In November 1984 an allowance was introduced if the parent concerned had been in employment for two or more years. The *allocation parentale d'éducation* provided 1,000 francs a month for parents who decided to take two years of parental leave after the birth of their third child. When the scheme was introduced the allowance was payable only to parents with three or more children for a period of 24 months. On their return to power the Socialists extended parental leave up to the child's third birthday.

In their election platform the Socialists had committed themselves to improving childcare facilities, and the number of places in *crèches* had risen steadily between 1981 and 1986. They continued to support the allowance created in 1972 towards child-minding costs and extended it to all parents employing an approved and properly trained childminder in 1990. Nor did the government abolish the new allowance introduced by the centre-right in 1986 towards childcare costs for all parents employing a child-minder in their own home (*allocation de garde d'enfant à domicile*).

The level had been set high enough to cover the employer's contribution to social insurance and was likely to be of greatest benefit to high income earners because they more often use this form of childcare than other social groups.

The main difference between the family policies pursued by the left and the right concern their overall priorities, pro-natalism versus equality, and the instruments used to achieve their objectives. The Socialists had sought initially to reduce the tax advantages which accrue to high income earners with large families and to assist low income earners with several children, whereas the right placed greater emphasis on the third child through family allowances and tax incentives. The Socialists also emphasized the need to accommodate the diversity of family forms. An early proposal, announced by the President in 1982 and which eventually became law in 1984, was that divorced women who were not in receipt of maintenance would be given help to recover the shortfall in their income from their former husband. By 1986 in recognition of the growing problems associated with marital breakdown and extra-marital births, particular attention was being focused on helping women in single-parent families to get back into employment.

Despite the decision in 1990 to extend the age limit for family allowances to eighteen years and the introduction of new benefits, the family insurance fund, unlike old age and health, ended the decade with a surplus, as had frequently been the case under previous governments.

Social versus economic measures to curb unemployment

In the wind of change which swept the left into power the electorate had been given to believe that an easy and painless solution could be found to the problems of growing unemployment. The new government soon discovered that its promises could not be kept. From 1.6 million in 1981 unemployment rose to almost 2.5 million by March 1986 and 2.6 million in 1991, representing less than 8 per cent of the workforce at the beginning of the decade and just under 9 per cent at the end, after peaking at 10.5 per cent in 1986–87.

Throughout the 1980s a concerted effort was made to create jobs, improve training and relieve the hardship associated with unemployment.

As the social policies formulated failed to curb the problem and contributed to the growing budgetary deficit of the social insurance funds, economic solutions were increasingly sought by tackling the source of unemployment rather than its consequences.

At the beginning of the 1980s the public sector gave the lead, creating 180,000 new jobs between 1981 and 1983, ostensibly in order to improve public services (health, education, post and telephones, transport, etc.), as promised in the 110 proposals during the election campaign. Legal restrictions were placed on employers preventing them from making workers redundant for economic reasons without official permission (*autorisation administrative de licenciement*). In 1982 working conditions were improved by the introduction of contracts governing short-term and part-time employment, guaranteeing levels of pay and entitlements identical with those of full-time employees. Working hours were reduced to thirty-nine, with an agreement to move towards a thirty-five hour week. Again the public sector gave the lead by reducing hours without loss of pay. Private industry was expected to follow suit, with additional incentives for reductions to less than thirty-nine hours. In 1985 and again in 1989 the restructuring of worktime was on the policy agenda, but the emphasis had shifted from reducing the length of the working day, week or year, to ways of increasing flexibility for employers in a situation where job security had become a major issue; the proportion of temporary jobs and short-term contracts had increased from 2.5 per cent of all waged employment in 1977 to about 7 per cent in 1989.

A fifth week of annual paid leave was made statutory in 1982, proving to be another very popular reform with the electorate. The lowering of the age of retirement and schemes for early and progressive retirement were encouraged, with the explicit objective of freeing up jobs for the unemployed. Under one such scheme the state undertook to contribute 30 per cent of the salary for the previous twelve months for workers aged fifty-five or more who decided to continue part-time on the condition that the firms concerned would recruit new workers.

Although the restructuring of worktime had a symbolic value, echoing as it did the Popular Front's legislation on working hours and paid annual leave in 1936, these measures were intended to make more jobs available for young people entering the labour market. In the event the calculation proved to be mistaken, and employment continued to rise far beyond the two million mark which had been seen as a figure to be avoided at all costs. More young people were having problems in finding their first job, and more people of all ages were out of work for longer periods of time and were therefore no longer eligible to receive unemployment benefits.

Another approach to the problem of the unemployed was aimed initially at the young. In 1984 the government created TUC (*travaux d'utilité collective*). The TUC were intended for the sixteen to twenty-one year old age group who were unemployed and not already registered for training courses. *Tucistes* were given the status of part-time trainees for a maximum of twelve months, during which they were covered by social insurance and earned a minimum income of 1,200 francs for eighty hours. They were placed in public sector organizations to do community work with a social or cultural purpose. Pay and social insurance contributions were covered by the state. Jacques Chirac's government pursued a similar course, introducing incentives for small firms which offered young people their first job, by exempting them from employers' social insurance contributions for two years. After their return to power the left replaced the TUC by CES (*contrats emploi-solidarité*) which were similar in form and purpose to the TUC but were extended to older age groups. In an analysis of the scheme towards the end of 1990 after it had been in operation for almost a year, it was found that more than 69 per cent of beneficiaries were young people and 66 per cent were women. About 16 per cent had been out of work for more than three years, and about 25 per cent subsequently found only temporary employment.

One of the most widely acclaimed schemes introduced by the Socialists was a response to the problems of poverty resulting from long-term unemployment. In his *Lettre à tous les Français* in 1988, the outgoing President had undertaken to help the growing number of people below the poverty line, the new poor, by guaranteeing a minimum income to be funded from taxation. As François Mitterrand began a new seven-year term of office, it was imperative for the government to demonstrate that election pledges would be kept. Jacques Chirac's government had introduced agreements (*conventions d'insertion*) between the state and local authorities at the level of the *département* with the object of helping to reintegrate the destitute into the community, offering part-time work in return for a small income (*compléments locaux de ressources*). Beneficiaries had to be resident in the area for more than two years, not in receipt of unemployment benefits and without any other source of income. Building on and extending these precedents, the RMI (*revenu minimum d'insertion*), as it was called, was one of the first proposals to be considered by the new Council of Ministers in July 1988 and was treated as a top priority. It became law in November of the same year for a trial period of just under four years during which it was to be carefully monitored.

Conceptually the RMI offers an interesting example of a differential payment since it was designed to supplement other sources of income up to a defined level. Initially it was set at 1,750 francs a month for one person, with an additional 650 francs for a second person. Beneficiaries had to be aged over twenty-five, or if younger had to have dependent children. They automatically obtained access to social insurance cover and housing benefits. Unlike social assistance which aims to offer support to those who fall through the net due to illness, physical or mental handicap or old age, the RMI did not pay attention to cause but responded directly to need. Its object was to reinstate beneficiaries in society and, in particular, in the workforce, which meant that they had to undergo training or take work offered by the local authority, thereby acquiring a social identity and regaining their autonomy.

Initially between 350,000 and 400,000 people were thought to be eligible for the RMI, although as many as 20 per cent of the population are considered to be at risk and likely to fall into poverty because of ill-health, accident or unemployment. By July 1989 when the scheme had been in operation for less than a year, 268,000 people had registered for the RMI. By the end of 1991 almost a million households and two million individuals had benefited from the scheme.[11] Nearly 80 per cent of beneficiaries in 1989 were single people living alone. Half were under thirty-five years of age, and most of them had no source of income other than the RMI or family allowances.

From the early years of implementation it was difficult to judge whether the RMI would provide a lasting remedy to the problem of poverty and whether the scheme could operate effectively on the scale intended, given its high operating costs. Whatever its success in mitigating the effects of poverty, the RMI may still be cited as a good example of an attempt to bridge the gap between a system of social insurance premised on a work relationship and social assistance which identifies social drop-outs without

190

trying to rehabilitate them. Notwithstanding the difficulty of assessing its impact on unemployment, it may be seen as one of a panoply of measures in an area which was an equally important priority for policy at the beginning of the 1990s as it had been a decade earlier.

Paying for reform

The deficit of the French social security system has become legendary, and one of the major objectives of Ministers for Social Affairs of whatever political complexion would seem to be to find new ways of balancing the budget without incurring the hostility of their political supporters. The left were no exception and by July 1982, after the spending spree of their first few months in office, the Council of Ministers was meeting to discuss ways of making savings. Their task was made more difficult over the decade by rising unemployment, the ageing of the population, the increase in the number of broken marriages and of single-parent families and by the social reforms introduced in the early 1980s. The method of funding social security in France also limits room for manoeuvre, since the main source of income is from employer and employee contributions. Within the EC France is one of the countries with the highest proportion of social security income from contributions.[12] It is also amongst the EC member states devoting the highest proportion of its gross national product (PIB) to social welfare spending with just under 28 per cent in 1990, compared with less than 26 per cent in 1981.

Various commissions were set up by the left to examine the reform of social welfare. They were given the task of looking at ways of revising contributions, for example by extending them to sources of income other than wages and by reducing the burden on employers. In the ninth economic plan proposals were made for spreading contributions across all household incomes to avoid the unfair burden which falls on the industrial and commercial sectors. The authors of government commissioned reports submitted in 1981 (Maillet) and 1982 (Peskine) had highlighted the well-rehearsed problem resulting from the ceiling on contributions, the low level of contributions paid by some sectors of the population and the low input from the state. The preferred solution of the unions was to levy higher contributions on employers and the self-employed who were considered not to be paying their fair share. The Socialists were aware of the political risks involved in increasing the wages bill and the likely effect on unemployment. Instead they reduced contributions to compensate employers for the increase in the minumum wage and, as an incentive for job creation, paid the employer's social insurance contributions when they created new jobs for the unemployed. The plan set in motion early in 1983 to reduce social security spending resorted to stop-gap measures such as delaying the introduction of higher benefits and some of the reforms scheduled for the health sector and cutting back on further spending on hospitals. As a result, by the end of the year the government was congratulating itself on having balanced the budget. By July 1984 they were boasting about their sound financial management of social security and health, and in 1986 they announced triumphantly that they had achieved a budgetary surplus for three successive years, a record which they were unable to sustain between 1988 and into the 1990s.

A much debated alternative to increasing social insurance contributions, which would bring France more closely into line with her neighbours, would be to shift the burden of the cost of services onto taxation. As the social security funds have always remained relatively autonomous, governments have been reluctant to adopt this solution. Plans were set in motion in 1981, and restated in 1982, to move towards the funding of family allowances from taxation in an attempt to reduce the level of employers' contributions. Ten years later the proposal had still not been carried through. In principle such a move should be more easily acceptable than for other areas of social benefits in that family allowances constitute an anomaly, funded as they are for historical reasons solely from employers' contributions. Today the relationship with wages has become tenuous, if non-existent, but the link with taxation already exists in that tax relief in the form of the *quotient familial* can be claimed by couples with dependent children. This deduction is particularly advantageous for couples on high incomes with several children; a fact recognized by the left in 1982 when a ceiling was set on tax relief for children as the first stage towards substituting some of the new allowances for tax relief and as a means of confirming their intention to support vertical redistribution. However, the tax deductions for childminding introduced in 1991 as part of a package of measures to help reduce unemployment ran counter to this commitment.

To some extent the cost of public spending was shifted to the tax system and to the wealthier sectors of society, as pledged in the Socialists' election platform. A new wealth tax (*impôt sur les grandes fortunes*) was established from 1 January 1982, applying to an estimated 200,000 individuals with property worth more than three million francs. Subsequently after being abolished by the right, it was reintroduced in 1988 by the Socialists, symbolically renamed as the *impôt de solidarité sur la fortune*, and was to serve as the main source of funding for the RMI. In 1983 high income earners saw their marginal rate of taxation rise to 65 per cent for income of more than 270,000 francs a year for a single person and 541,000 francs for a couple. At the same time the tax threshold was raised, so that low income earners with less than 28,000 francs were exempt from tax, as were single people in receipt of the minimum wage, which was set above 3,000 francs a month. In 1983 a surtax was levied on the highest incomes in order to contribute to the cost of funding unemployment benefits, to which employers responded by threatening to withdraw from the organization in control of the unemployment fund, the *Union Nationale Interprofessionnelle pour l'Emploi dans l'Industrie et le Commerce.*

When the centre-right returned to power, it tried to grapple with the social security deficit, which the Socialists claimed to have eliminated, by introducing a payment of 0.4 per cent on all incomes, although in their election pledges they had promised to reduce the tax burden. Employee contributions for retirement pensions were raised by 0.7 per cent on incomes below the social insurance ceiling. The bill for health care was to be reduced by cutting the number of exemptions from charges for medicines and increasing the daily rate paid by patients in hospitals. The strength of feeling and support by the French for their social insurance scheme was amply demonstrated in 1987 when a proposal for reducing medical benefits and rethinking retirement age was met by strong opposition from unions and other interest groups who demonstrated in the streets. The government tried to defuse the situation by setting up a Committee of Wise Men to examine possible long-term solutions to the financial problems of the social welfare system. The Committee reported in October 1987. One of its main proposals was for a contribution to be levied across the board on all incomes. Although like tax, it would be administered by an independent body.

With the presidential elections so close at hand, the centre-right did not devote its efforts to initiating what were likely to be contentious reforms. They had however paved the way for the Socialists who adopted a proposal in October 1989 very similar to that formulated two years earlier by the Committee of Wise Men. A *contribution sociale généralisée* (CSG) of 1.1 per cent was levied on all incomes from 1 February 1991 on the grounds that it would be a fairer means of redistribution. This was not a new idea for the left. Already in the early 1980s they had talked about introducing a *contribution sociale de solidarité*, and in 1986 an additional 0.4 per cent had been levied on taxable incomes. The CSG went further than these earlier proposals in that all sources of income were taken into account, whether they were wages, fees, pensions, unemployment benefits or dividends, interest or rents. Unlike income tax in France, the CSG was collected at source, and no tax relief could be claimed. Low incomes under the tax threshold were exempted. Although parliament was required to fix the rate of the CSG each year, Claude Evin, who was the *Ministre de la Solidarité, de la Santé et de la Protection sociale* when the new payment was introduced, stressed at the outset that it should not be seen as a tax. The CSG was heralded as a means of achieving greater social justice since it spread the basis of payment to sources of income which were not previously covered by social insurance contributions, thereby fulfilling one of the election pledges made in 1981.

In its first year of operation the CSG was expected to contribute 3 per cent to the social security budget, but an equivalent reduction in the level of social insurance contributions and the removal of the 0.4 per cent levy were to result in the equalization of funds. As all the income from the CSG was to be paid into the family allowances fund, it went some way towards shifting the cost of these benefits away from employers, as had also been suggested by the Committee of Wise Men, but it did not contribute directly to the funds (health and old age) which were having most difficulty in meeting their costs.

Continuity or change?

In many policy areas the left were not breaking new ground. Previous governments had deployed similar means in dealing with unemployment, poverty and social security deficits. The recipe for social change adopted in the early 1980s was however based on idealistic and unrealistic assumptions about the willingness of certain sections of the population to meet the bill for the changes introduced and without regard for the repercussions on the competitiveness of French industry in international markets. By reducing the length of the working week without a reduction in wages, the effects on the costs of production were predictable, and the expected upturn in the number of jobs was not forthcoming.[13] The increase in the minimum wage, the minimum state pension and social benefits could not be achieved without levying higher social insurance contributions or taxes. By lowering the age of retirement the bill for both contributory and state pensions was increased overnight. The pay-as-you-go principle used in France meant that the burden fell on the working population. By raising family allowances and creating new benefits for families near the poverty line, by extending training for young people and reducing the social insurance contributions paid by employers, the drain on resources contributed to the deepening economic recession. By initially increasing benefits to the unemployed at a time of rising unemployment, resources were stretched to breaking point. Payment by the state of social insurance contributions to *tucistes* and other beneficiaries of job creation schemes resulted in more government spending, and the creation of jobs in the public sector increased the wages bill.

The inability of the economy to absorb these pressures soon became apparent, and as early as 1982 the government was being forced to make U-turns. Some of the reforms promised were postponed, for example the shift towards a new system of funding for family allowances, or abandoned, as in the case of proposals to abolish private beds and remove the daily charge in hospitals. Further rises in pensions and allowances were deferred, and unemployment benefits were reduced.

Social equality was another recurring theme in the discourse on change in the early 1980s, symbolizing the legacy of the French Revolution. The Socialist election platform had raised expectations about the new egalitarian society which would be created. Women's rights were high on the agenda, and a strong impetus was given to policies to ensure greater equality of opportunity. By the end of the decade funds had been reduced, and the political capital to be gained from women's issues had been spent. Greater equality was one of the objectives of the family policy outlined in 1982. By raising the allowance for two children more than that for three, the intention was to move away from the explicitly pro-natalist orientation of the policies pursued by the centre-right and to equalize benefits. By 1983 pro-natalist concerns were again a priority, and over the decade the family policy of left and right progressively became less easily distinguishable from one another as they responded to the many of the same pressures.

The shifts in policy which came to characterize the decade are reflected in the discourse of the Socialists. Whereas social justice and the reduction of social inequality through national solidarity were the leitmotifs of the early 1980s, a decade later the proclaimed objective was no longer to achieve greater equality but to give individuals the opportunity to better their own situation by enabling dropouts to get back on board but without necessarily reducing differentials. Several reports published in 1990, for example that by the *Centre d'Etudes des Revenus et des Coûts*[14] on incomes, demonstrated that almost ten years of socialism had not resulted in a more egalitarian society. According to the CERC, the gap between high and low incomes had widened, and inequalities between unearned incomes were even greater. While the reasons for marginalization had changed, poverty had become more widespread and the poor had become poorer. The talk after a decade of socialism, as outlined in the budgetary priorities for 1992, was of greater efficiency in the provision of training, the strengthening of the industrial base together with the fight against urban deprivation through better social housing, improved access to the legal system and a 45 per cent increase in the funds allocated to the RMI.

It has been argued that by the time the Socialists came to power it was too late for them to try to reshape the welfare state as they had promised in their election pledges.[15] The party had underestimated the economic constraints they would have to face and the problems of restructuring a social security system which was founded on, and firmly entrenched in, strong corporatist interest groups. After a honeymoon period of not much more than a year when social reform was high on the agenda, the Socialists quickly accomplished the ideological U-turn which was needed to redress the economy. The price to pay was the subservience of social policy to economic forces.

The disillusionment of the electorate over the failure of the Socialists to change society as they had claimed they would may to some extent explain the victory of the centre-right in 1986, and again in 1993. In many respects the Socialist governments of the 1980s built on and developed existing policy as they found that radical change was impeded by the legacy of previous generations. Interestingly, the breathing space given to them between 1986 and 1988 was followed by some of their more imaginative policies, such as the RMI and CSG, reflecting the Socialist ideology which had almost disappeared from view elsewhere. Michel Rocard, the then Prime Minister aptly summarized the conclusion reached by the Socialists in 1989 when he stated: 'The economic agenda determines the social agenda: it's impossible to share out wealth which doesn't exist.' But, he conceded: 'The social agenda determines the economic agenda: it's impossible to create lasting prosperity without cohesion, in the workplace and in the nation.'[16]

In the final analysis historians with the benefit of hindsight may well find that the Socialists were perhaps most successful in some of the areas which traditionally characterize the right, such as the management of the economy, where in the course of the decade they helped to bring France more into line with the rest of Europe. At the beginning of the 1990s over six million French people were, for example, shareholders, and privatization was being presented as a viable way forward for industry and a legitimate means of raising additional public funds. Socialism would seem to have been less successful (some would say it had failed) in the areas where its strengths were thought to lie: it had not succeeded in reducing inequalities, improving the quality of life in the inner cities and stemming the growth of unemployment, which had been the main priorities when the left came to power in 1981.

Notes

1. Fournier, J., Questiaux, N. and Delarue, J.-M. (1989), *Traité du social. Situations, luttes, politiques, institutions*, 5th edition, Dalloz, Paris.
2. Léridon, H. and Villeneuve-Gokalp, C. (1988), 'Les nouveaux couples: nombre, caractéristiques et attitudes', *Population*, vol. 43, no. 2, pp. 221-374.

3. Ray, J.-C., Dupuis, J.-M. and Gazier, B. (1988), *Analyse économique des politiques sociales*, Presses Universitaires de France, Paris.
4. *Lettre de Matignon*, no. 107, 22 May 1984, p. 1.
5. *Lettre de Matignon*, no. 330, 11 March 1991, p. 3.
6. Reported in 'Point sur...', *Lettre de Matignon*, no. 184, 10 February 1986.
7. Ray, Dupuis and Gazier, *Analyse économique des politiques sociales*.
8. Sullerot, E., 'Le statut matrimonial: ses conséquences juridiques, fiscales et sociales', *Journal Officiel*, 25 January 1984.
9. Steck, P. (1985), 'Les prestations familiales de 1946 à 1985. Ruptures ou constances?', *Revue françaises des affaires sociales*, vol. 39, special issue, July-September, pp. 63-98.
10. 'Point sur...', *Lettre de Matignon*, no. 184, 10 February 1986.
11. *Lettre de Matignon*, no. 362, 9 December 1991, p. 2.
12. Durin, F., Pollina, L. and Seys, B. (1990), 'Le système de protection sociale', INSEE, *Données sociales*, INSEE, Paris, p. 417.
13. Barou, Y. and Rigaudiat, J. (1983), *Les 35 heures de l'emploi*, La Documentation Française, Paris.
14. Centre d'Etudes des Revenus et des Coûts (1990), 'Les Français et leurs revenus: le tournant des années 80', Les Documents du CERC, no. 94.
15. Freeman, G.P. (1990), 'Financial Crisis and Policy Continuity in the Welfare State', in Hall, P., Hayward, J. and Machin, H. (eds), *Developments in French Politics*, Basingstoke, Macmillan, pp. 188-200.
16. M. Rocard, *Discours devant les Clubs 'Convaincre'*, 5 November 1989.

Bibliography

Barou, Y. and Rigaudiat, J. (1983), *Les 35 heures de l'emploi*, La Documentation Française, Paris.
Centre d'Etudes des Revenus et des Coûts (1990), 'Les Français et leurs revenus: le tournant des années 80', Paris: *Les documents du CERC*, no. 94.

Durin, F., Pollina, L. and Seys, B. (1990), 'Le système de protection sociale', *Données sociales*, INSEE, Paris.

Fournier, J., Questiaux, N. and Delarue, J.-M. (1989), *Traité du social. Situations, luttes, politiques, institutions*, 5th edn, Dalloz, Paris.

Freeman, G.P. (1990), 'Financial Crisis and Policy Continuity in the Welfare State', in Hall, P., Hayward, J. and Machin, H. (eds), *Developments in French Politics*, Macmillan, Basingstoke.

Léridon, H. and Villeneuve-Gökalp, C. (1988), 'Les nouveaux couples: nombre, caractéristiques et attitudes', *Population*, vol. 43, no. 2.

Lettre de Matignon: no. 107, 22 May 1984; no. 184, 10 February 1986; no., 330, 11 March 1991; no. 362, 9 December 1991.

Ray, J.-C., Dupuis, J.-M. and Gazier, B. (1988), *Analyse économique des politiques sociales*, Presses Universitaires de France, Paris.

Steck, P. (1985), 'Les prestations familiales de 1946 à 1985. Ruptures ou constance?', *Revue française des affaires sociales*, vol. 39.

Sullerot, E., 'Le statut matrimonial: ses conséquences juridiques, fiscales et sociales', *Journal officiel*, 25 January 1984.

9 A New Educational Ethos? The Great Non-Debate

PETER COLLIER

Introduction

'The past is another country', as L.P. Hartley said, 'they do things differently there'. And I found it a strange experience indeed to travel back through the Socialist decade in France, using as my time machine 500 copies of the *Nouvel Observateur* retrieved from the garage and distributed chronologically over the dining table.[1] The *Nouvel Observateur*, it seemed to me, was the best source of informed public opinion, as well as a semi-official expression of reigning broad left orthodoxy, even, perhaps especially, when that alternative society found itself saddled with power in the 1980s. Moreover, as regards education, the *Nouvel Obs.* often voices the views of the 'proletariat', that is, the intellectual *lumpenproletariat*, the not-so-nouveau poor who educate the children of the ruling classes, and who are the most jealous guardians of the Republican and Socialist establishment. And yet again, because its commercial success represents the publicly marketable face of socialism: what people want to know about the school system, what they are prepared to spend their money on reading about it.

Above all the *Obs.* provides a useful gauge of the public's perception of problems and its hierarchy of values. It echoes faithfully week after week, with some reflective and analytic distance, the crises that rack public opinion in France, from a dramatic but brief 'fait divers' like the sinking of the Rainbow Warrior, to a long-running ideological conflict like the design of the new opera house at the Bastille. And nowhere is the *Observateur* more sensitive to the tastes and anxieties of its intellectual constituency than in its treatment of matters educational.

My first act was to sort through the decade to feel the quantity rather than the quality. I was surprised to find that whereas education was a constant concern in 1980 and 1981, it slipped steadily below the horizon for the rest of the decade, with momentary blips of interest when the private schools mobilized their consumers (I mean voters) in 1984, and when the *lycéens* took to the streets in 1986 or 1989. The number of articles per year, out of a possible 52, slumped from 20-odd at the start of the decade to 4 or 5 at the end. So much for education as a national priority in the eyes of the intelligentsia.

But when I tried to reduce the actual anecdotal ebb and flow of ten years of debates and policies to the space of a chapter, the events seemed to rush by as inconsequentially and self-deflatingly as the frames of a Claire Brétecher cartoon, or a series of channel 5 video clips. I decided therefore to use the present tense, inspired by Malcolm Bradbury's *The History Man*, in an attempt to slow the tide of history, to freeze the frames of memory, while retaining the frenzy of the passing moment.

A chronicle of mishaps, misunderstandings and misrepresentations

I open my first, musty copy. I wonder what year we are in. It's April, but it could be any year, because education is in a mess, and the primary teachers have just taken to the streets to protest against the shortage of posts. It could be any year, but in fact, it's 1980, and although we don't know it yet, it's the last year of (official) capitalism in France. Only one pupil out of five manages to make it through the secondary system from *sixième* to *terminale*. Two-thirds of these successful eighteen-year-olds become *bacheliers*, and 80 per cent of these then enter higher education. That still makes 845,000 students, nearly half of whom are already out in the world working for a living by their final year. Two-thirds of all university students, however, drop out without a degree. We are reminded, meanwhile, that the elite are not in the universities: there are 23,000 students in the *Grandes Ecoles* (roughly equal to the combined undergraduate population of Oxford and Cambridge). Half of these students are training to be engineers. The one university that has (somehow) managed to introduce selection at entrance, Paris-Dauphine, which specializes in economics and business studies, has 3,700 candidates for 650 places. In May, in an attempt to improve the statistics, the hard-line right-wing Minister of Higher Education Alice Saunier-Seité expels foreign students who fail their DEUG, and, in a display of belated impartiality, she sacks a foreign professor, too, Maria Antonietta Macciocchi, from the University of Vincennes-St. Denis, because she has not got a *permis de séjour* (and not, of course, because she lectures on her compatriot Gramsci). In July, Saunier-Seité overrules dozens of university presidents in order to invalidate dozens of courses at *licence*, *maîtrise*, and doctoral level which she disapproves of. But there are still 66,000 hopeful candidates for the 3,500 CAPES and *agrégation* places, underlining the continuing intellectual prestige and professional advantages of the teaching profession in France. In September the *Nouvel Obs.* quotes Pierre Bourdieu's *Reproduction*, accusing the French education system of practising selection through failure, 'la sélection par l'échec', and thus penalizing the lower classes behind a semblance of egalitarianism. In December it's the students' turn to demonstrate. It is a year like any other.

Now it is 1981. Unsurprisingly, the primary teachers are on strike again for more money. But then Socialism In Our Time arrives. It is the private sector, mainly Catholic, that fears the Mitterrand revolution, although Alain Savary, the new Minister of Education, announces in June that he will hold friendly negotiations. The SNI, the primary teachers' left-wing union, outflanks him on his left, by vetoing the presence of private-school teachers on examination boards for this year's new school-based (instead of nationally-validated) diploma, the *brevet des collèges*. The secondary teachers' union, the *SNES*, joins them in their campaign to try to halt non-graduate recruitment to teaching in secondary *Collèges* (via the the non-prestigious post-experience qualification, the PEGC), in order to universalise the postgraduate competition, the CAPES (*Certificat d'aptitude au professorat de l'enseignement de second degré*). The fact that many private school teachers have not taken the latter State certificate might occur to some readers. Watch this space: with 16 per cent of French pupils in private education (double the proportion in Britain, despite popular mythology) we are on to a massive vote-loser here. In September the Socialist reform machine gathers speed, with new money for ZEP (Educational Priority [i.e., deprived] Zones) and more money for new posts. The Socialist government calls in the scholars, so as to have a rational revolution: a first expert, Louis Legrand, is asked to report.

The Nouvel Observateur reports on a paper by Pierre Bourdieu in an obscure sociological review, *Actes de la Recherche en Sciences Sociales*, which argues that the *Grandes Ecoles* are depriving the university of money and talent, but his attack on the stranglehold on teaching operated by these hyperselective institutions goes largely unnoticed. Pierre Bourdieu, professor of sociology at the *Ecole des Hautes Etudes*, has just become professor of sociology at the *Collège de France*, as successor to Raymond Aron. Despite using new sociological concepts like 'habitus' and 'field', and wielding a rebarbative panoply of statistics and graphs, Bourdieu can still hardly disguise the hidden agenda to his enquiry. He is a vigorous critic of the whole structure of education in France, showing in *Reproduction in Education, Society and Culture*,[2] first published in 1970, that teaching involves the arbitrary imposition of the cultural values of the dominant classes, that the transmission of these values involves a kind of symbolic violence, that the curriculum is used to impose orthodox knowledge and a hierarchy of skills, that meritocratic selection to *lycées* is a self-fulfilling prophecy whereby only those working-class children who can speak the language of upper-class culture succeed, and (since they are hyperselected and unrepresentative) continue to appear to advertise the success of the egalitarian meritocracy. Examination scripts are marked as if they displayed eternal personal essences rather than momentary states of knowledge, and the competitive examinations for entry to the *Grandes Ecoles*, or into teaching or administration, emphasize formal style to the detriment of substantive content. The workers eliminate themselves from the whole system, and the system thus appears vindicated by their failure.

In 1982 we discover that there are 900,000 students in higher education, but the university is failing or losing half of them. A *Collège de philosophie* is founded, which looks like a safe ghetto for interdisciplinary studies, especially as (like the *Collège de France*) it can enrol no full-time students and deliver no qualifications. It is hardly a compensation for the massive snub delivered to the education industry when Mitterrand took

203

Research and the *Bibliothèque Nationale* away from the Ministry of Education, and gave them to Jean-Pierre Chevènement and Jack Lang at the Ministries of Industry and Culture. Lower down the system, too, things are less than perfect, because there are 150,000 illiterate Frenchmen (estimates of illiteracy range from 14 per cent of recruits to National Service to 25 per cent of pupils in *sixième* in some CES, i.e. secondary *collèges*). Prime Minister Pierre Mauroy asks another expert, Laurent Schwarz, to report. In *Bilan de la France : l'enseignement, la recherche, la technologie* he finds that there are too many teachers holding the PEGC, and that teachers need sabbaticals; but although Schwarz quite logically suggests abandoning the PEGC to raise the quality of secondary teaching, he unfortunately recommends selection at entrance to university as a way out of university chaos. Alain Savary ignores this reactionary suggestion, and most of the other recommendations made by Schwarz, who can only reiterate them by publishing them later in book form (*Pour sauver l'université*, 1983).[3] By September Alain Savary is ready for his great reform, announcing 12,000 more teaching posts despite a reduction by 40,000 in the number of pupils at school. In order to renovate the whole pedagogical scene, he calls for school inspectors to stop merely grading teachers, and to take on a new role as animators. He also calls for a longer teaching year, with 32 instead of 25 weeks in the university year. But as soon as October dawns his plans lie in tatters for he finds he does not have enough teachers for his classes. Public disaffection with universities is illustrated by recruitment to the IUTs (*Institut universitaire de technologie*), originally designed in 1966 as vocational institutions specializing in the training of technicians, rather like British polytechnics, but already there are 12,000 candidates for 600 places at the Paris IUT in the avenue de Versailles, which is the kind of application ratio we see at a *Grande Ecole* like ESIEE, where there are 2000 candidates for 100 places in electrical engineering. For the IUTs have been allowed to introduce selection at entrance to their intensive two-year courses. Another expert, Antoine Prost, is given a brief to report on the *lycées*. In December Savary decides that the best way to satisfy the militant laicism of the State teaching body is to integrate the Catholic *école libre* into the State system, and give its teachers the status of civil servants, like State teachers. It is a terrible gamble. The private teachers just *might* want the security and status of their State colleagues, and help the government force the hands of the church and the parents...

As 1983 dawns we forget this problem for a moment. In January the Louis Legrand report, commissioned after the Socialist victory in 1981, is published. It suggests removing the privileges of the most prestigious secondary teachers, the *agrégés*, who earn more money for fewer hours' work than other teachers doing the same job (15 hours per week, as opposed to 18 hours for holders of the CAPES and 21 hours for the non-graduate teachers). Legrand suggests that all teachers should now do 16 hours teaching plus 3 hours extra-curricular team-preparation, and 3 hours tutorial work. This tendentious emphasis on practical to the detriment of theoretical work in the *collèges*, not to mention the promotion of low-powered activities like team teaching and tutorials, provokes a massive, outraged write-in by the *Nouvel Observateur's* professorial readers. By now we have 25 per cent of an age group in higher education, but 37 per cent of them drop out after year 1, and 50 per cent after year 2. In March Savary tries to give university presidents more autonomy and budgetary control (reversing the interventionist policy of Alice Saunier-Seité), but he attempts to square the circle by simultaneously giving more votes on University Councils to *Maîtres-Assistants* and *Assistants* (Lecturers and Assistant Lecturers), in the hope that they will use these votes to introduce vocational training courses, rather than free-floating *licences*, for third-year students. Anyone able to read understands that this is a policy of selection, so in May a massive student strike scuppers the whole project, even though selection was only to be operative at the end of the second year, after the DEUG. Despite support by the *Nouvel Observateur's* Jacques Julliard for selection according to merit, which he grounds in the principle of Republican fairness, selection at entry is absolutely ruled out by Savary himself (no doubt with a little help from Mauroy and Mitterrand). Savary is forced to withdraw his proposal, and will have to console himself later in the traditional way by publishing his programme in book form (*En toute liberté*, 1985). In September we are obliged to remember private schooling. President Mitterrand, and the readers of the *Nouvel Observateur*, are reliably informed that the bishops, their 15,000 teachers, and their 16 per cent of French voting parents, will reject assimilation by the State. Unfortunately, it would now be unthinkable to retreat.

In January 1984 Parliament is busy wondering what to do about the rivalry between the doctorate seen as training for research, associated with the short *thèse de troisième cycle*, and the doctorate as lifetime's grail-hunt, the endless *Doctorat d'Etat*. Their grotesque solution, to introduce a third, 'nouveau', doctorate will soon be tacitly ignored. In February Antoine Prost reports to the hapless Savary. It is Prost's turn to request greater autonomy for individual schools, and tutorial activities by teachers, but he dwarfs these suggestions with the staggering proposal to treble the number of 18-year-olds reaching the level of baccalaureate by the year 2000. The implications may be interpreted through the *Observateur's* usual barrage of statistics: 70 per cent of *sixième* pupils reach *troisième*, 46 per cent *seconde*, 27 per cent get their bac. Did he say treble? Change under 30 per cent to 80 per cent in 15 years? (Prost, in conversation with the author, has insisted on the fact that the rationale behind his suggestion, made at the instigation of employers, was to improve the quality and status of the skilled work-force by providing systematic non-intellectual vocational training parallel to the baccalaureate, but we shall find that he was to be creatively misunderstood as suggesting a massive expansion of the clientèle for the actual baccalaureate diploma). At all events, Savary affects not to notice. He pushes on with the upgrading of primary teacher-training, saying in April that from 1986 *instituteurs* will study for 2 years after the *DEUG* in an *Ecole Normale*, giving them a four-year graduate education. But then the parents show their strength. Two massive demonstrations, one at Versailles in March, and the second in Paris in June (with a congregation of half a million or a whole million, depending whether you believe the police or the *Nouvel Observateur*) prove that the really important problem for *la France profonde* (however *profondément socialiste*) is to stop the State getting its hands on its private teachers. (After the Versailles event the perceptive *Nouvel Obs.* announces that the crisis is over, but reckons without the ideological purity of the Socialists, who refuse to allow local financing for schools. The Loi Debré of 1959 had authorized State subsidies to private schools as long as the State retained control over appointments, but in practice it had proved very difficult to intervene in the choice of teachers, and the Loi Guermeur of 1977 had largely put an end to ideological conflict by rendering official the actual tendency of private schools to pocket the State's money and make their own appointments. Under the new proposals, the State and local councils would pay school running costs as well as teachers' salaries, but any creation of extra posts would be subject to budgetary control). Mitterrand looks for a way to retreat from appearing to be responsible for a humiliating showdown, but is prevented by Parliament from holding a referendum, because the constitution only allows referenda on the 'organisation des pouvoirs publics'. Mitterrand cleverly tries to have a referendum to change the constitution on referenda, so that a face-saving referendum on education will be allowed, but the referendum on the referendum is vetoed as unconstitutional by the Senate. Luckily for all left-thinking parents the *Nouvel Observateur* runs its own referendum (a two-part pull-out in June and July) a rather unFrench holiday work-assignment. In August the results, for those awake enough to read them on the beach, confirm that *Nouvel Obs.* parents and teachers approve selection, dislike zoning (which forces all children to attend their local school), and deplore the decline in spelling and discipline. Despite or because of the fact that their constituents' anxieties are all about having their children well taught and getting them into good jobs, Minister of Education Savary and Prime Minister Mauroy are swept away half-way through the *Observateur* survey, to be replaced by Jean-Pierre Chevènement and Laurent Fabius.

In order to understand the paradoxical support for private Catholic education by a left-wing lay electorate we should perhaps follow Antoine Prost's own analysis in 'The Educational Maelstrom' [4] when he points out that the private schools have more autonomy than the state schools: parents are not forced by zoning to send children to schools they have not chosen, and heads can appoint teachers of their own choice, whereas no State school head can control the Ministry's appointment of his teachers, a bunch of unrelated individuals often prised against their will from the farthest corners of France. The private teachers know perfectly well that if they became *fonctionnaires* they would gain security but they would lose their teaching freedom as well as their religious autonomy. More importantly, even irreligious parents can avoid zoning, and choose a traditional education, by opting for a private school, which is only accidentally, as it were, Catholic.

In October 1984 there are 930,000 students in the higher education system. In November the *Nouvel Obs.* interviews Pierre Bourdieu, whose latest book, *Homo Academicus*,[5] suggests a totally different series of problems and priorities. *Homo Academicus* extends to the university sector the critique already levelled at the secondary sector in *Reproduction*. It builds on the iconoclastic picture of higher education painted in *The Inheritors*,[6] first published in 1964, which had become briefly famous in 1968, but since forgotten. Scholastic success depends on the social status of the parents, and teaching appointments are (perhaps unconsciously) weighted in favour of candidates who reflect the conservative values of the appointing professors, yet the few working-class children who manage to get through the system create the impression that it is open to all talents. Examination marks judge the ability to reflect social values, and lower-class students are judged to be essentially less intelligent because of their failure to master middle- and upper-class rhetoric and sophistry. Teachers waste time writing manuals and journalistic articles rather than engaging in pure research. The *Grandes Ecoles* cream off the best students without teaching them properly how to engage in scientific activity. University professors manipulate the great length needed by young lecturers to complete a *Doctorat d'Etat*, in order to delay their own replacement. But the unplanned, galloping growth in junior teaching posts created a mass of discontented and militant junior teachers, who saw no hope of eventually following in the steps of the tiny number of tenured professorial mandarins, still intent on cloning and inhibiting their successors, and maintaining a closed system based on elitism and inertia.

Few readers are going to plough through *Homo Academicus*. But those who read the interview Bourdieu gives to the *Nouvel Obs.* will be struck by the extraordinary fact that this heretic has just been asked to provide the President of the Republic with an official report on education. The interview repeats Bourdieu's suspicions that the reigning egalitarian ideology is largely demagogical, as well as his attack on the *agrégés* for their sterilizing effect on teaching and research. He rejects both right and left ideologies as not being based on scientific or pedagogical values. He identifies their individual or collective resistance to educational and scientific market forces. He disarmingly states that politicians do little more than inflect fields of forces. He speaks scathingly of marxist planning, bureaucratic committees and specialist reports, preferring to encourage ad hoc progress towards a more Fourierist society. Yet despite this critique, Bourdieu seems to show pride in admitting that he and the *Collège de France* have been asked to report direct to the President of the Republic on science and science teaching.[7]

208

If Bourdieu's interview sounds vaguely Thatcherite, the published report, 'Propositions pour l'enseignement de l'avenir élaborées à la demande de Monsieur le Président de la République par les Professeurs du *Collège de France*',[8] tempers its marketeering with a more utopian generosity. Bourdieu and his colleagues acknowledge the need for vocational relevance, their plea is for a professional as well as a liberal education. They propose to challenge the existing hierarchy of skills, so that the pure theory favoured by the most prestigious sections of the baccalaureate and the *Grandes Ecoles* is not allowed to devalue technical and applied learning, and that this very divide between pure and applied and intellectual and manual should be challenged: science needs to relate theory to practice in order to function at all. Sidestepping the hot coals of private schools and selection, the report argues that there is not necessarily a clash between private and public sectors, or between democratic quantity and selective quality; for Bourdieu's aims are no longer the traditional ones. In terms of intellectual values, his main thrust is to downgrade encyclopaedic knowledge, in order to inculcate the critical spirit, to guard against extreme ideologies, whether based on religion or reason (should we think of Christianity or Islam, capitalism or marxism ?), as well as to be able to criticize social manipulation, say through electoral processes or opinion polls. This social-scientific approach is meant to provide a kind of 'intellectual karate' against advertising, politics and religion. And Cultural Relativism should be inculcated right from the primary school. Immigrants should be encouraged to study their own native languages, otherwise they will not be able to learn French properly. Citizens need to be able to understand statistics (apparently by studying weather forecasting and the reliability of second-hand cars). Cultural history should encourage an interdisciplinary approach to, say, the history of painting and maths in the Renaissance. Yet pupils still need basic culture and knowledge and skills; a sort of national curriculum.

Bourdieu is highly suspicious of school classification, and official judgments. They judge only a momentary condition of the candidate. Bourdieu also attacks what he calls 'selection by failure', but not selection itself, although wisely enough very little is said about this. In fact the need is for more and better-trained teachers, with more resources, such as data banks, research libraries, videos, computers, and money. Bourdieu suggests enhanced status for teachers, but the corollary of this is a more active appraisal of them, by outside specialists, empowered to award in-service training, sabbaticals, and promotion. Burnt-out teachers would then be allowed to move out of teaching into administration and/or culture at the end of their careers. An Open University and evening classes are also needed to encourage professional training and adult education. Schools should liaise with the outside world: firms, artists, libraries, journalists. Establishments should have real autonomy, especially over courses, assessment, and budgeting (and, apparently, selection...), but their funding should derive from various sources. There should be a competitive market between secondary schools.

Yet this rivalry between institutions is to be tempered by State safeguards against unfair competition, whereby the State must give subsidy and support to any culturally valuable activities in danger, which implies tutorial funds, extra payments, ZEPs etc. Bourdieu's programme is an uneasy mixture of egalitarianism, social engineering, and the enterprise culture. Yet if any country could manage to make Bourdieu's vision materialize, it would be France. France has been amazingly successful, under a series of right and left-wing governments, in reconciling State infrastructure and standards with private enterprise and insurance in health care, for instance, compared to the paralysis induced in Britain by the clash between conservative ideological warfare and Labour's attempts to disguise its remaining socialist ideals.

However, in 1985 it is not Jean-Pierre Chevènement's task to engineer utopia, but to reassure the public (it is after all the year of the general election, with the right doing well in the opinion polls), and his key slogan is 'instruire d'abord'. Prime Minister Laurent Fabius's boldest act is to order the separate boys' and girls' *Ecole Normales Supérieures* to merge and go mixed, and allow their students to take the *Doctorat d'Etat* instead of the *agrégation* if they wish (we may remember that Bourdieu has labelled the *Doctorat d'Etat* even more retrograde than the *agrégation*). In May, Chevènement, who by now has had time to read the *Collège de France* report, decides to drop Savary's more dangerous ideas, like tutorial teaching, let alone Bourdieu's, and decides to promote the old-fashioned *brevet* in the *troisième*. However, he is obviously looking for something more striking and exciting, and, sleep-walking his way into history, he cheerfuly decides to adopt Antoine Prost's Americano-Japanese fantasy about trebling the number of baccalaureate-level students, without

210

wondering what the structural, social and financial consequences will be. And although he announces the objectives of bringing 80 per cent of the population up to the level of the bac, he does nothing much about it for the time being. He does de-zone secondary schools so that parents can choose nice schools for their children and bus them out of dubious areas (the opposite of Savary's ZEPs). Paying lip-service to Bourdieu's *Collège de France* report, Chevènement offers every school a microcomputer: 'l'informatique pour tous'. He rejects Bourdieu's appeal for university autonomy (although that was the great achievement of Edgar Faure's 1969 education bill, until reduced by the attacks of Giscard d'Estaing's minister, Alice Saunier-Seité). He accepts a *comité national d'évaluation* for teacher appraisal, but without awarding it any resources, and he accepts the principle of competition between institutions, and... selection of candidates. We wonder whether this U-turn may have helped the Socialist government lose the 1986 election – if the public wanted a right-wing policy, why not elect a right-wing government to implement it?

In 1986 we are all officially capitalists again. Fittingly, it is one of the few remaining French citizens with no baccalaureate, René Monory, who becomes Minister of Education, a phenomenon much stranger than the accidental rise of the bac-less John Major to the post of Prime Minister in philistine Britain. Monory publishes no white paper on education (perhaps because he fears being outvoted in Parliament or outdemonstrated in the streets) but he confirms the end of the PEGC route to teacher recruitment, endorses the policy that all secondary *collège* teachers should pass the CAPES, announces plans to provide 110,000 extra *lycée* places, and decides to maintain the new *brevet des collèges* for 1986. We learn that a quarter of an age group are entering higher education, but that of these only a third are getting through to the DEUG, a quarter to the *licence*, and a fifth to the *maîtrise*. In fact, because of resits, it is impossible to say whether there is a 70 per cent or only a 50 per cent drop-out rate in the *premier cycle* (undergraduate studies), but this becomes irrelevant, given the spectacular sabotage by student demonstration of Higher Education Minister Devaquet's plan to introduce selection at entry and an annual fee of 900 francs (£90). Monory allows Devaquet and his plan to be sacrified to public opinion in December, although in many ways his conservative scheme is very similar to Savary's Socialist plan, with progressive reduction of teaching time in *lycées*, and a longer teaching term.

In 1987 we are nearing 40 per cent of an age group passing their bac, but there are still 80 per cent rejects at the end of the first year of medical studies and 60 per cent drop-outs or failures in the DEUG. None of this is called selection. Devaquet, having been disavowed by his Minister and his pedagogical constituency, has to use the columns of the *Observateur* to argue his dismay at the freedom being allowed universities to select students and to validate their own degrees. Yet already Dauphine requires a *mention* in the baccalaureate (a credit or a distinction), and the Paris Law Faculty (Assas) and 13 other universities use a 'numerus clausus', popularly known as bus-queue selection, and the Minitel provides an amateurish information and orientation service for candidates, called RAVEL. It seems strange to an English observer that nobody on the left or the right thinks of an UCCA system, which would, after all, be very *Jacobin*. But of course, as long as nobody is officially selecting, there is no call for a centralized selection agency. We learn in passing that the staff-student ratio is 1 to 50 but this does not appear to be an issue. The shamelessly selective IUTs are creeping upward in prestige and popularity: there are 64,000 IUT students overall, and at the Paris IUT there are now 13,500 candidates for 750 places. Monory is faced with a massive recruitment crisis; he finds it totally impossible to train any maths teachers, and offers to train candidates as 'old' as 40, and even candidates with no diplomas, as long as they have had three children.

In 1988 the conservative revolution flops, and we get our left-wing government back again. Michel Rocard is Prime Minister, Lionel Jospin Minister of Education. In February the *Nouvel Obs.* repeats the news that 25 per cent of pupils in *sixième* are unable to read, which, together with the confirmation that 10 to 15 per cent of military service conscripts are virtually illiterate, depending on their home locality, helps explain why *Nouvel Obs.* articles in September reveal that major parental anxieties focus on reading and maths. Before dismissing this concern with the three Rs as traditionalist reaction, we should remember how central mass literacy is to the Republican and Socialist ideal, the creation of a community of reason. This concern helps to explain the harsh, relentlessly criterion-based regime of French education, where considerable cohorts of pupils are forced to repeat whole years of schooling until they can pass the standardized end-of-year exams and be allowed to proceed to the next grade. In May it is the 20th anniversary of the 1968 revolution, which started in the University of Nanterre, and in an extraordinary counterpoint the *Nouvel Obs.* fills a large number of pages in two successive numbers in May and June with a hit parade of universities for the benefit of the year's 270,000 new *bacheliers*. The *Obs.* overtly adopts a consumerist model: classing universities by consumer (student) satisfaction with information and teaching, by success according to drop-out rates at the end of the first and second years, by their staff numbers. Handling the questionnaire and processing the data are safely entrusted to the renegade Parisian university, Dauphine, which has successfully rejected the government ban on selection. The survey shows that the *DEUG rénové* (where student progress and difficulties are monitored, and tutorial guidance ('le tutorat') and/or academic recycling ('l'orientation') are offered to those experiencing problems), is gaining ground. Students, oddly, seem to have most confidence in those universities which keep them informed, write reports on their work, and appear to maintain strict standards by failing large numbers of candidates in end-of-year exams. Nobody seems to think or notice how sad and illogical it is to have to equate quality with failure.

In January 1989 Jospin announces a large-scale project: declaring that his education bill will be short, devoid of ideology, based on a broad overview and with practical conclusions, he promises more money for teachers' pay, an instant budget increase for the current 1988–89 exercise, in order to reduce class numbers, but also longer term plans to introduce quality control, and appraisal of teaching. Once again, it is time to call for shorter hours, merit payments and better buildings, more team teaching, more group work, not to mention a national curriculum council. But once again the plans are swiftly answered by another teachers' strike: shorter hours for pupils mean either lower quality teaching or more work for teachers, who will have to organize their studies and prepare study programmes more carefully. In February the *Nouvel Observateur*, re-launching the debate, receives a mountain of hate mail from militant teachers, who are sick of the government, sick of being teachers, and sick of the *Nouvel Observateur*... Meanwhile the rush to be selected out of the allegedly non-selective university system continues: 50,000 pupils are crammed into the *après-lycée* 'preparatory' classes for the *Grandes Ecoles*. *Polytechnique* has 2000 candidates for 300 places, *HEC* 3000 for 250 places, *Centrale* 8000 for 300 places, *Sciences Po* 4000 for 400 post-bac places and 1500 for 450 post-*licence* or post-*maîtrise* places, the *Ecoles Normales Supérieures* 2000 for 200 places.

With the Catholics placated, the private school battle seemed to have been safely lost. But suddenly we remember that a large number of French schoolchildren are Muslims. Autumn 1989 is the term of the 'foulard'. The attempt by some Moslem girl pupils to wear the Islamic headscarf in school is seen by the left as a challenge not only to the religious neutrality of the State but also to the education system as social leveller and creator of opportunities. The *Nouvel Observateur*'s journalists and the established left show a rare moment of clear and unyielding solidarity, with such charismatic figures as Régis Degray (former companion of Che Guevara, turned presidential adviser) and Elisabeth Badinter (a prominent feminist writer, but also the wife of Mitterrand's first Justice Minister, Robert Badinter, who abolished the death penalty) supporting lay education as a guarantee of female equality, and encouraging the journal to stiffen Lionel Jospin's over-conciliatory response to fanaticism.

But Jospin has his eyes on the long term. Mitterrand sees education as a matter of national importance and prestige. Jospin has established a series of think tanks. No doubt remembering the 1984 débâcle (where lack of insight into popular educational demands had brought down the government), he appoints Bourdieu chairman of the section studying curriculum reform. Bourdieu's unjustly snubbed report for Mitterrand in 1985 seems to contain the kind of millenial vision that might find Jospin a place in the history books. In addition, Bourdieu's critique in *Homo Academicus* of the causes of the 1968 student revolution (published, significantly, in 1984), would seem to suggest implicitly (the goal was not openly formulated in the book) that salvation must lie in a programme of controlled expansion. Bourdieu had shown that it was the deteriorating staff-student ratio and lack of material resources that had fostered the revolt of 1968: the real *agents provocateurs* of the May 1968 revolution were neither student conspirators nor brutal riot police, but the careless government that failed to match its random expansion of student numbers with any commensurate increase in resources: was this read by Jospin as a warning for 1988–89? At all events Jospin's commitment to massive, planned expansion, accompanied by adequate resources, seems both to answer the appeal of *Homo Academicus*, and to set the agenda for Bourdieu and his team.

A committee chaired by Pierre Bourdieu, Professor of Sociology at the *Collège de France*, and counting among its members Jacques Derrida, Director of Studies in Philosophy at the *Ecole des Hautes Etudes*, seems a very good omen of government commitment to action and change. (Bourdieu has told the author how excited he felt at the first plenary session, when Jospin addressed the gathering in the following terms: 'Messieurs, nous sommes réunis pour tout changer. Tout est à remettre en cause, tout est possible. Je vous écoute'.) But is it perhaps a sign of some caution that Bourdieu is asked to comment on the curriculum rather than structural reforms? At all events, he, Derrida and co. manage to report on structures nonetheless. Their report, 'Principes pour une réflexion sur les contenus de l'enseignement',[9] calls for active methods of teaching, a rapid turnover of teaching material, and continuous assessment adapted to such practices. They wish to encourage practical experimentation, critical and reflexive thinking, teach how to use dictionaries and graphs, prepare manuscripts, learn communication skills, develop rational work and research methods, with the constant aim of reducing cultural inequality. Teachers should use the curriculum only as a guide and not as a rule. They should also clearly define and fairly test attainable objectives, after checking the transmissibility of essential knowledge with the help of sociological research.

As with the 1985 *Collège de France* report, there is a whole programme of new teaching practices: avoiding encyclopaedic knowledge, making technical applications an integral part of learning, developing pupils' and teachers' interests and orientations, say for interdisciplinary courses; alternating theory and practice, individual, group and tutorial teaching, thus using both classrooms and teachers' talents more efficiently, involving local firms and artists. The development of group teaching, and interdisciplinary projects, and the provision of optional as well as compulsory subjects, particularly in the realm of thematic or image-based courses, drawing on media resources, mean that teachers will need to be paid for research time, and will need sabbaticals and in-service training to help them adapt. There is an air of vague utopia deriving from the fact that the report deals with the whole field from primary to university. Also perhaps from the fact that it contains none of Bourdieu's usual attacks on the *agrégation*, the *Doctorat d'Etat* or the *Grandes Ecoles*. And it does not mention selection.

But the arrival of 1990 ushers in a mood more of hysteria than of Fourierist utopia. Bourdieu's report joins the other great wannabes of the 1980s. As the shadow of the year 2000 falls there has to be a *plan d'urgence* to cater for the 350,000 extra students, who, although still ten years away from university, are already nearly out of primary school. There are to be four new Paris universities, 6-20 in the provinces, 1500 new university posts and a national colloquium (*Université 2000*) but still no fundamental reform of the *premier cycle*, despite its 40 per cent failure rate. In March Jospin raises the question of closing schools on Saturday morning instead of Wednesday afternoon (slightly over half of the *Nouvel Observateur's* parents would prefer to change), and relaunches the ideas of team teaching, teachers' appraisal, and more flexible school rhythms in primary schools, including less *redoublement*. In May another expert, Robert Ballion, produces his report on the *lycées*. He has discovered that de-zoning has led *lycées* to advertise and compete. In June the great debate of *Université 2000* is convened. Nothing new is said. In October Jospin announces extra teaching resources and ancillary personnel, but it is too late, the *lycéens* take to the streets again: they want better buildings and teaching as well, and they even, for the first time, call for selection. In November the *Observateur's* Jacques Julliard calls for better professional education (which Prost had tried to promote in 1984). The *Observateur*, seeing the millenium looming, starts to get cold feet, and calls the 80 per cent baccalaureate target one of Jean-Pierre Chevènement's most outlandish ideas. Is there a whiff of *fin de régime* to this comment?

In 1991 there are 40 per cent of each year-group entering higher education, yielding 575,000 students in the *premier cycle*, but although officially only a third drop out (because quite a few pass at their second or third attempt), the *Nouvel Obs.* mounts a Bourdieu-style critique of the social injustice and wastage involved, and explains that only a third of DEUG students (i.e., 70,000 out of 200,000) actually pass their diploma each year. The most extraordinary revelation of all is that students are now openly dropping *into* University for a year, because this will give them a better chance of a competitive place in an IUT afterwards. In March Jospin takes a small but significant step towards the greater 'professionalisation' of higher education, by announcing the creation of 50,000 extra IUT places for 1994. But the number of new universities planned seems to have shrunk already, to four in Paris, two in the Pas-de-Calais, and one at La

Rochelle. Prime Minister Michel Rocard is replaced by Edith Cresson and in April Lionel Jospin is replaced by Jack Lang.

It is still too soon after their departure from government in 1993 to tell which problems and achievements of the 1980s were due to the Socialists, and which will last. The *Nouvel Observateur* is not encouraging. It greeted Jospin's last ditch attempt in 1992 to break the stranglehold of the scientific *Bac C*, and spread pupils more evenly, with a hysterical and irrelevant campaign to safeguard the 5 per cent of pupils choosing a Latin option – nothing to do with class distinctions, of course. Moreover, during Chirac's brief passage, Monory continued with very similar policies, and came to grief over similar issues. And the Socialists themselves were hardly revolutionary, hemmed in between strong teachers' unions whose members vote socialist but who resist reform, and volatile students whose power to paralyze universities and overthrow governments has frightened all parties since 1968. Primary education, which has not hit the headlines, has enormously developed sporting and cultural activities, and reduced the incidence of rote learning, but little has changed in the *lycées* and *collèges* despite the superficial egalitarianism of a common institutional framework for all pupils until the *brevet*. The attempt to control private education failed, but the lay tradition of State schools was successfully defended. The *écoles préparatoires*, the *Grandes Ecoles*, the CAPES, the *agrégation*, the *Doctorat d'Etat*, continue much as before. An attempt to introduce a new doctorate has failed to dislodge the *thèse de troisième cycle* and the *Doctorat d'Etat*, although one might see a surreptitious weakening of the traditional hierarchies of higher education in the transformation of primary and secondary teaching into an all graduate teacher-training profession, and the relatively slow expansion of *agrégation* posts. Undergraduate studies, above all, continue to be caught between the theoretical goal of open access and the seeming impossibility of financing and structuring such a system fairly and efficiently.

Conclusion

One of the striking things about the specialist reports on education was their degree of unanimity: all the experts (Legrand, Schwarz, Prost, Bourdieu, Ballion) have a similar vision of the ideal education system, with only some minor variations on the degree of selection, orientation and vocationalization envisaged. But together with this homogeneity within an intellectual constituency goes a refusal to discuss between professional interest groups. The teachers have systematically rejected all attempts to accept the kind of anglo-germanic system envisaged for secondary education. The students have resisted all restructuring of universities that seemed to imply lack of choice, thus reducing themselves more and more to the choice between different kinds of failure. The parents want their children to be disciplined, to learn to spell, and to get good jobs. Perhaps the major problem faced by the Socialist government was that it was simply not possible to allow totally free study for pupils, absolute professional comfort for teachers, thorough grounding in fundamental intellectual disciplines, and perfect vocational relevance simultaneously in any known system. Another problem, but which does not seem to be acknowledged, may lie in the universalism of the debates. The *collèges*, *lycées* and universities, the baccalaureate and the doctorate(s) are constantly treated, by professional researchers like Bourdieu as much as by government ministers, as part of one vast unit which has to be handled in the same movement. It seems to me significant that the great, silent revolution in French primary teaching (over the last *two* decades, under official capitalism as well as official socialism), introducing a more humane 'tiers temps', with its 'activités d'éveil', but maintaining the rigorous standards of intellectual development and thorough knowledge for which it was famed, has been possible because primary schooling escaped being considered as part of this global system. And, according to Yvette Delsaut in *La place du maître*,[10] the successful revolution in training primary teachers (who from November 1991 were to be recruited after the *licence* and trained to *maîtrise* level in *Instituts Universitaires de Formation des Maîtres* – IUFM) has been almost entirely dictated by the demographic shift of candidates from teenage working-class boys aspiring to better themselves to adult middle-class women looking for a socially acceptable function.

Otherwise the great problems seem to continue. Is universal access to higher education compatible with selection? Are scientific research and effective undergraduate teaching compatible with the survival of the narcissistic and elitist rituals of the *agrégation* and the *Doctorat d'Etat*? Can the universities survive without selection and/or the staffing and

218

building resources granted to the *Grandes Ecoles* and the IUTs? Can the secondary teachers continue to promulgate a theoretical ideal of knowledge and insist on luxurious professional conditions? Will university students ever realize that their insistence on random freedom to study anything anywhere at any time has never been an option (the *baccalauréat* used to be a highly selective filter until after the second world war); is not imposed in law (viz the *Grandes Ecoles*, the IUTs, all faculties of medecine), or in fact (viz its surreptitious breaches, Dauphine and Assas); that 'la sélection par l'échec' drastically impoverishes the educational conditions and opportunities of even those students who pass?

Perhaps the greatest problem of all has been beyond the control of any Western government. The massive demographic slide into higher education as a basic universal qualification, the enormous increase in female participation, added to large scale unemployment, has led to simultaneous and uncontrollable expectations and disappointments, and has meant that enormous amounts of money have had to be poured into the system merely to stand still. Yet France has recruited and built, while Britain has cut and frozen. They have expanded faster, and from a larger base. The Socialist regime poured vast sums of money into promoting mass access *and* improved quality. By the year 2000 Britain's 30 per cent target for entrance or eligibility for higher education will be dwarfed by France's 80 per cent. Britain, even more than France, needs to listen to Bourdieu's warning in his November 1984 interview with the *Nouvel Observateur*:

> De toute façon, on ne pourra pas rester indéfiniment dans la situation actuelle. Car il me semble avoir compris que lorsque les rats sont soumis à un traitement assez semblable à celui qui est fait aujourd'hui aux professeurs et aux chercheurs, distribuant au hasard les décharges électriques et les grains de blé, ils deviennent fous.

Notes

1. *Le Nouvel Observateur*, 1980–92.
2. Bourdieu, P. and Passeron, J.-C. (1970), *Reproduction in Education, Society and Culture*, Minuit, Paris; trans. Nice, R. (1977), Sage, London.

3. Schwarz, L. (1983), *Pour sauver l'université*, Paris.
4. Prost, A. (1987), 'The Educational Maelstrom', in Ross, G., Hoffmann, S. and Malzacher, S. (eds), *The Mitterrand Experiment*, Polity Press, Cambridge.
5. Bourdieu, P. (1984), *Homo Academicus*, Minuit, Paris; trans. Collier, P. (1988), Polity Press, Cambridge.
6. Bourdieu, P. and Passeron, J.-C. (1964), *The Inheritors*, Minuit, Paris; trans. Nice, R. (1979), University of Chicago Press, Chicago and London.
7. *Le Nouvel Observateur*, 2 November 1984.
8. 'Propositions pour l'enseignement de l'avenir élaborées à la demande de Monsieur le Président de la République par les Professeurs du Collège de France', Paris, 1985 (Archives du Collège de France).*
9. 'Principes pour une réflexion sur les contenus de l'enseignement', Commission présidée par Pierre Bourdieu et François Gros, Mars 1989 (Archives du Collège de France).*
10. Delsaut, Y. (1992), *La Place du maître: une chronique des Ecoles normales d'instituteurs*, L'Harmattan, Paris.

* I wish to express my gratitude to Pierre Bourdieu for drawing my attention to these documents. I would like to make it clear that my interpretation of comments made to me by Antoine Prost and Pierre Bourdieu is my own responsibility entirely, and does not imply their endorsement of my opinions.

Bibliography

Albertini, P. (1992), *L'Ecole en France*, Hachette, Paris.
Bourdieu, P. and Passeron, J.-C. (1964), *The Inheritors*, Minuit, Paris; trans. Nice, R. (1979), University of Chicago Press, Chicago and London.
Bourdieu, P. and Passeron, J.-C. (1970), *Reproduction in Education, Society and Culture*, Minuit, Paris; trans, Nice, R. (1977), Sage, London.
Bourdieu, P. (1984), *Homo Academicus*, Minuit, Paris; trans. Collier, P. (1988), Polity Press, Cambridge.

Delsaut, Y. (1992), *La place du maître: une chronique des Ecoles normales d'instituteurs*, L'Harmattan, Paris.

Dubet, F. (1991), *Les Lycéens*, Seuil, Paris.

Legrand, L. (1983), *Pour un collège démocratique*, La Documentation Française, Paris.

Le Nouvel Observateur, 1980–92.

'Principes pour une réflexion sur les contenus de l'enseignement', Commission présidée par Pierre Bourdieu et François Gros, Paris: Archives du Collège de France, 1989.

'Propositions pour l'enseignement de l'avenir élaborées à la demande de Monsieur le Président de la République par les Professeurs du Collège de France', Paris: Archives du Collège de France, 1985.

Prost, A. (1983), *Les lycées et leurs études au seuil du XXIe siècle*, Centre national de documentation pédagogique, Paris.

Prost, A. (1991), *Education, société et politique. Une histoire de l'enseignement en France de 1945 à nos jours*, Seuil, Paris.

Prost, A. (1987), 'The Educational Maelstrom', in Ross, G., Hoffman, S. and Malzacher, S. (eds), *The Mitterrand Experiment*, Polity Press, Cambridge.

Savary, A. (1985), *En toute liberté*, Hachette, Paris.

Schwarz, L. (1983), *Pour sauver l'université*, Paris.

10 Immigration Politics in Mitterrand's France

JAMES G. SHIELDS

Introduction

Of all the issues which exercised successive Socialist governments under
François Mitterrand, none proved more vexing than that of immigration.
Having acceded to office in 1981 pledged to eliminate discrimination,
establish a new equality between French nationals and foreigners, and put
an end to the insecurity which the immigrant community had come to know
under the previous regime, the Socialists were forced to temper their
humanitarian rhetoric and scale down their aspirations in this domain. Far
from being the period which saw France's immigrants absorbed into a
'new citizenship', the 1980s and early 1990s witnessed an increasing
tendency towards exclusion, evidence of an anti-immigrant sentiment
stoked by economic recession and compounded by the emergence of race
and national identity as major public concerns. While the problems
experienced by immigrants in the 1970s (ghettoization, cultural alienation,
educational handicapping, unemployment, disenfranchisement and racism)
have persisted where they have not worsened, the response of successive
Socialist governments from 1981 onward was fitful and ambiguous. At the
political level, a sustained polemic centred on voting rights for immigrants,
revision of the Nationality Code, and the conditions for entry, residence

and expulsion of foreigners; at the popular level, violence against immigrants, notably those of North African origin, increased dramatically, while racial intolerance discovered a new freedom of expression. As public opinion polls sought to chart the ebb and flow of xenophobic sentiment, the electoral success of the Front National (FN), with its crude anti-immigrant message, provided some measure of the climate in which the immigration 'debate' was now conducted.

This chapter examines the way in which immigration was transformed in the 1980s from a social and economic issue into a subject of intense political controversy. It considers the background to early Socialist policy on immigration, the nature of that policy and the changes brought to bear upon it in the mid-1980s. The rise of the FN, demonstrating the new mobilizing power of the race and immigration issues, is seen as part of a general radicalization of French politics, a hardening of attitudes which characterized all of the major parties and left the Socialists in government at some remove from their more expansive promises of 1981. The chapter seeks to assess the impact of the 1980s and early 1990s in modifying the political perception of immigration and in restricting the range of policy choices open to France's political elite as they prepared for the Mitterrand succession.

Immigration in France from De Gaulle to Giscard d'Estaing

During the first two decades of the Fifth Republic, France underwent massive change, evolving from a still largely rural economy in the 1950s through the rapid industrial and urban expansion of the 1960s to the economic recession of the 1970s. Over the course of that period, and as a direct consequence of these developments, the immigrant community in France altered substantially. Under the presidencies of De Gaulle (1958–69) and Pompidou (1969–74), immigration was seen as a cheap and flexible means of bolstering the labour force within a thriving industrial economy.[1] The classic profile of the immigrant during these years was that of the unskilled male, from poorer European countries (Italy, Portugal, Spain) and, increasingly, from the Maghreb (Algeria, Morocco, Tunisia), recruited for manual labour in the construction, steel, mining and car industries notably. The presence of such immigrants, dictated by economic factors and availability of work, was seen as a temporary phenomenon; their arrival and departure operated, in principle, according to a 'rotational' logic whereby they would return at the end of a given period to their countries of origin and be replaced on a similar basis by similar personnel.[2]

As these labour migrants, living frequently in hostels close to their places of work, had little impact upon France's permanently settled immigrant communities, and as they provided a short-term solution to the country's demographic deficiency, the conditions for their entry and residence were far from stringent. The *Office National d'Immigration* (ONI), set up in 1945 to regulate the flow of foreign labour required for post-war reconstruction, found itself increasingly by-passed in the 1960s by employers observing the sole imperative of supply and demand.[3] Borders were not policed with rigour, and little was done to combat the common practice of illegal immigration, since 'regularisation' procedures could be retrospectively applied to any worker who had gained entry illegally or on a tourist visa. Not only was the government's attitude in this area one of *laissez-faire*: clandestine immigration was openly condoned in the 1960s by the Gaullist Minister of Social Affairs, Jean-Marcel Jeanneney, as a means of keeping the labour pool buoyant.[4] A report presented to the Economic and Social Council in 1969 by Corentin Calvez estimated that, by 1967, only one worker in five was arriving through the official channel of the ONI.[5] Nor were any significant steps taken to integrate these new migrant workers into French society; rather, they were treated as an expendable economic resource and, as such, consigned to marginal status, deprived of political rights and of social prospects beyond the immediate environment of the workplace.[6]

The reasons for such indulgence on the one hand, and such neglect on the other, arose from a distinction commonly observed by the authorities of the day, and upheld by the Calvez Report, between 'a permanent immigrant community, based on the settlement of families with a view to their assimilation, and a temporary immigrant workforce tied in more with economic requirements'.[7] There were, within this perspective, two (and only two) categories of immigrants: those willing and able to integrate fully within French society, and those who were sooner or later expected to return to their countries of origin. Europeans, Calvez argued, were 'easily assimilable' and should be encouraged ultimately to become French

224

citizens, whilst non-Europeans (notably those of North African origin) constituted an 'unassimilable island' suited at best to temporary immigration in response to the changing needs of the labour market. In making this distinction, the Calvez Report set out a principle to which subsequent governments of the 1970s would adhere in defining their immigration policy. Thus, in 1977, Giscard d'Estaing's Secretary of State for Immigrant Workers, Paul Dijoud, outlined with unsparing lucidity the choice confronting France's immigrants: 'We must make it possible for those foreign workers who so desire, to be wholly integrated within the national community, which will normally entail their naturalization, or for those who do not so desire, to preserve their socio-cultural links with their country of origin on the understanding that they will ultimately return there'.[8]

The two key notions here, of course, are *integration* and *return*, leaving no middle ground for an immigrant community which might wish to remain in France but not to be wholly absorbed into French society. Though it drew upon an already threadbare rationale, Dijoud's remark signalled a hardening of attitude by the Giscard administration and anticipated a new official resolve to force the pace with which immigrants (or the least 'assimilable' among them) might be returned to their countries of origin. The year 1974, when Giscard came to office and halted the policy of importing foreign labour, marked both an end and a beginning: the end of primary immigration to France, and the beginning of a process transforming a largely transient immigrant population into a permanently settled community, as increased numbers of dependents and families sought to join their migrant spouses and parents in France. Though such family reunification was officially suspended in July 1974 and only authorized by a number of subsequent circulars and decrees, it heralded a definitive change in the composition and character of immigration in France. The Decree of 29 April 1976 recognized family reunification for the first time as a right, on condition that the applicant had been resident in France on a valid permit for a full year, that he had a steady and sufficient income, and that he could provide housing fit to accommodate the family members in question.[9] In 1976, the non-European immigrant community was more or less equally divided into workers and non-working family members. Between 1976 and 1978, given the ban on foreign labour, over 95 per cent of non-European immigrants admitted to France were family members.[10]

225

Those who chose to return to their countries of origin, by contrast, were more often single males than family groups, which accentuated further the new trend towards a more settled, family-oriented immigrant population.[11]

Whereas immigrants had been viewed up to this point as an economic asset, working for modest wages and contributing more to social security funds than they derived in return, the progressive arrival of dependents placed conspicuously new demands on public and welfare services.[12] As the economic recession deepened, moreover, greatly increased numbers of immigrant workers found themselves joining the ranks of the unemployed.[13] Faced with these developments, and with the concerted opposition of the left and of immigrant support groups to a ban on family reunification, the Giscard administration had recourse to two measures which indicate clearly the official perception of the immigrant community during these years. The first of these measures, introduced in 1977 by Dijoud's successor as Secretary of State for Immigrant Workers, Lionel Stoléru, was a financial incentive scheme (*Aide au retour*) designed to encourage immigrant workers to return to their countries of origin. This was intended initially for the unemployed, but was subsequently extended to those in regular employment, even though an official study in 1976 had estimated that a mere 9 per cent of the largely menial jobs occupied by immigrants would be readily taken up by French workers.[14] The scheme was a failure. Fewer than 100,000 migrant workers and family members took advantage of it, the majority of them Spanish and Portuguese rather than the North African immigrants for whom it was primarily intended.[15] While it freed relatively few jobs for native French, the *aide au retour* programme thus contributed to the growing preponderance of non-Europeans within the immigrant community, with all the ethnic and cultural difficulties which that was seen to imply.[16]

The second notable measure introduced during this period was the law (named after the then Minister of the Interior, Christian Bonnet) voted on by the National Assembly and Senate in December 1979 and amended by the Constitutional Council in January 1980.[17] By redefining more tightly the conditions for entry and residence, granting wider powers to the police to deal with illegal immigrants and making expulsion a more expeditious procedure, the Bonnet Law added to the growing insecurity felt by France's immigrants. In its clear aim of empowering the state to take heavy-handed action against the foreign population in France, it was accused of enshrining in legality a racial discrimination which negated the various initiatives launched in the 1970s to tackle the problems faced by immigrant workers and their families.[18]

Enter Mitterrand : the 'new deal' for France's immigrants

Such, in brief, was the background to the election of François Mitterrand as President in May 1981. Winning an absolute majority in the subsequent legislative elections, the Socialists came to power with all the ideological baggage accumulated over a quarter of a century in opposition. As part of the 'new society' envisaged under the left, the Mauroy government, which included four Communist ministers, was committed to improving the conditions of France's immigrant community (estimated at between 3.68 and 4.46 million, between 6.8 and 8.2 per cent of the total population in 1982),[19] while maintaining tight control over new arrivals. The objective was to defuse racial tensions and shift the emphasis away from the purely economic towards the social, cultural and political, seeing immigrants as part of the fabric of French society rather than an increasingly problematic adjunct.[20]

Three of Mitterrand's *110 Propositions*, the manifesto on which he stood for election to the presidency, concerned immigration. Under the rubric *New Rights For Immigrants*, these three propositions contained the essence of the immigration policy which a Socialist government under Mitterrand would be enjoined to implement. In short, they gave an undertaking to protect immigrants against discrimination and arbitrary expulsion; to guarantee foreign workers the same rights as those enjoyed by French nationals; to grant immigrants full rights of association and a limited voting right in local elections; to control the influx of foreigners to France and step up the fight against illegal immigrant labour.

In the light of these proposals, the Socialists, of all the parties in 1981, seemed to offer the most liberal and the most comprehensive programme on immigration. Above all, they recognized that the great majority of immigrants residing in France were there to stay, that they represented a new demographic reality and that increasing numbers of so-called immigrant children already knew no home other than France. Wary of the colonialist overtones in the term *assimilation*, the Socialists spoke of *insertion* and *intégration*, of encouraging immigrants to play a fuller role within the local and national community, while allowing them to retain their own cultural heritage. By contrast to the discriminatory rationale which had prevailed in official thinking since the Calvez Report, they held that ethnic minorities should be accommodated without the obligation to relinquish their distinctive identity.

Having secured their mandate, the Socialists wasted no time in pursuing their twin-track strategy of controlling all new migration to France and seeking to integrate better those immigrants already living and working in the country. Between July and December 1981, a number of measures were introduced which laid emphasis upon the latter aspect of Socialist policy. Having halted all deportations pending under the Bonnet Law, the Mauroy government decreed certain categories of immigrants (such as children born in France of foreign parents and those who had lived there since the age of ten) exempt from expulsion. In all other cases, expulsion was to be a judicial rather than an administrative procedure, in accordance with a pledge dating from the Common Programme signed by the Socialists and Communists in 1972.[21] Arbitrary *contrôles d'identité*, which had become a regular feature of policing the immigrant community under Giscard, were no longer permitted. The *aide au retour* scheme was abolished. The right of legal immigrants to family reunification was reaffirmed and some of the procedural obstacles to this were removed. A law granting full rights of association now allowed immigrants to set up their own organizations without the prior approval of the Interior Ministry – a requirement which had endured since 1939. This law cleared the way for a proliferation of groups and associations, established to defend the rights and promote the culture of immigrant communities in France.

Of all the measures introduced during this early period of Socialist rule, none proved more contentious than the amnesty, or *régularisation exceptionnelle*, offered to all illegal immigrants who had entered France before 1 January 1981 and who could give evidence of stable employment. Conceived as a means of prising open the twilight world of clandestine labour and of fostering new confidence between immigrants and the authorities, this constituted the most symbolic break with the preceding administration's policy, defying the spirit and letter alike of the Bonnet Law. It was also seen as an important humanitarian gesture which would clear the way for the firm control which the government was already resolved to exert over illegal immigration in the future. Of an estimated 300,000 clandestine immigrants in France, some 130,000 chose this route to legal status.[22]

The momentum set up by these reforms was sustained in other ways during the early years of the Socialist administration. Since education was recognized as an area in which the immigrant community was at a particular disadvantage, the government set up 'zones of educational priority' (Z.E.P.), allocating additional staff and resources to certain educational districts with high concentrations of immigrant children. A *Conseil National des Populations Immigrées* was set up as a consultative body to which all matters concerning immigrant workers and families could be referred. The need to apply for renewal of residence and work permits, and the fact that these did not always expire simultaneously, had served as a continual reminder to immigrants of their precarious, alien status. In July 1984, the government took the important step of introducing a single residence and work permit, valid for ten years and automatically renewable.[23]

A failure of political nerve : the Socialists in retreat

All of these liberalizing reforms marked the Socialists' distance from the restrictive attitude of the preceding administration. Even during this early period, however, there was evidence of hesitation and ambiguity in the implementation of government policy. The regularization of a large number of *sans-papiers*, on the one hand, and the clamp-down on illegal immigration through tighter border controls and increased sanctions against employers, on the other, gave confusing signals to the French and immigrant population alike. Though critical of the Barre government's anti-libertarian stance, the Socialists nonetheless retained the Interior Minister's authority to expel any foreigner deemed to constitute 'a serious menace to public order'[24] – a sanction which kept the threat of expulsion hanging over any immigrant who might fall foul of the authorities, effectively curtailing the range of activities in which immigrants might feel free to engage. The most striking inconsistency of all, however, arose over Mitterrand's Proposition 80. By advocating that immigrants with five years' residence or more should be granted a vote in municipal elections, as a means of better integrating them into the local community and forcing elected officials to take account of their needs, the incoming President had argued in effect for a new conception of citizenship, a citizenship of *residence* defined independently of *nationality*. Though bound in principle by this proposal, the Mauroy government saw fit to drop it from its list of priorities, relegating it instead to a 'long-term objective'.[25] This failure of political nerve was a clear capitulation to a hostile public opinion and to the concerted opposition of the parliamentary right, who argued that enfranchisement at any level was indissolubly linked to nationality. (and who, in any case, had a clear political motive for opposing the reform, since immigrants in countries where they enjoy a degree of electoral participation tend to be strongly left-leaning in their vote.)[26] The shelving of Proposition 80 showed the government for the first time in retreat on its immigration policy, and anticipated a series of measures which, between 1981 and 1984, realigned considerably the axis on which this policy turned.

While the ban on primary immigration was strictly maintained, the Mauroy government proceeded, at intervals, to tighten the legislation on entry and residence, the conditions governing expulsion, and the procedures for family reunification. Identity checks, halted in 1981, were brought back into force as a means of detecting undocumented immigrants. Though expulsion remained in the hands of the judiciary, the Law of 10 June 1983 permitted the urgent deportation of illegal immigrants by court order, effectively denying them the possibility of lodging an appeal. While family reunification was reaffirmed as a right, the Decree of 4 December 1984 stiffened the requirements and stipulated that the formalities be conducted in the country of origin rather than in France. The 'right' to reunification could be refused if the applicant had lived in France for less than a year, if he could not give evidence of 'stable and sufficient resources', or if his accommodation failed to meet the required standard; it could equally be refused if the presence of the family was deemed to constitute a threat to 'public order', 'public health' or 'public security'. Only after the authorities had been satisfied on all of these grounds would families now be granted permission to enter the country.[27]

The joint effect of these measures was to make expulsion more summary and entry more difficult, since many families had previously come into France on tourist visas prior to 'regularizing' their status on the spot. A

230

further significant measure was the Decree of 27 April 1984, which reinstated under another guise (*Aide publique à la réinsertion*) the voluntary repatriation scheme abolished in 1981.[28] Though the government could protest that its offer to subsidize programmes of vocational training for immigrants seeking to reintegrate in their countries of origin set this scheme apart from Stoléru's *aide au retour*, an important point of principle had been conceded.[29]

This progressive retreat by the Socialists from their early liberal policy must be understood with reference to the changing character of the immigration debate in France in the 1980s. By legalizing the status of so many clandestine immigrants, the Socialists had sought to resolve an endemic problem; instead, however, they sparked off an acrimonious debate which, sharpened by the new restrictions on expulsion, allowed the opposition right to accuse the government of *'laxisme'* and of encouraging illegal immigration. If the proportion of French people opposed to a limited franchise for immigrants appeared, according to certain polls, to have diminished since the 1970s, those registering opposition still represented a substantial majority of public opinion, which again allowed the right to call into question the legitimacy of the government's proposals. While the Gaullist and Giscardian parties echoed the emergent FN in evoking the difficulties posed by a large Muslim Arab community, public opinion surveys showed a marked disapproval of the government's pro-immigrant initiatives. In a SOFRES poll conducted in March 1983, 46 per cent of respondents judged that 'the left had done too much for immigrants' (as opposed to 34 per cent dissenting). Among left-wing sympathisers alone, a full 38 per cent of those polled declared that government policy had been over-liberal in this regard.[30]

Even as this poll was being conducted, change was underway. As early as March 1983, at the height of the municipal election campaign, the Socialist Interior Minister, Gaston Defferre, pinned his hopes for re-election as Mayor of Marseille on his promise to control immigration. By the time Laurent Fabius replaced Pierre Mauroy as Prime Minister in summer 1984, the Socialists had few illusions about the need to hold (and to be *seen* to hold) to a rigorous immigration policy. As the government's emphasis shifted from *insertion* to *maîtrise*, the new Prime Minister, in a televised interview in September 1984, credited Le Pen with asking the 'right questions', even if he proposed the 'wrong answers'.[31] The following

231

month, in an issue of the *Lettre de Matignon* devoted exclusively to immigration, the Prime Minister's office articulated the resolve of the new government to resist any 'uncontrolled and unassimilable influx of immigrants' to France.[32] A year later, in a televised debate with Jacques Chirac which rehearsed the agenda for the 1986 legislative election campaign, Fabius made no reference to the ideological imperatives which had informed early Socialist discourse and policy. Instead, he conceded that immigration was 'unquestionably a problem', before proceeding to vaunt his government's record on expulsion and subsidized repatriation.[33]

The politicization of race

The blunt fact is that the Socialists in 1981 had under-estimated the potential for anti-immigrant feeling in France and had miscalculated their ability to carry public opinion with them in their reforms. Seizing the opportunity to attack on this front, the right made great play of the alleged links between immigration, unemployment and the breakdown of law and order, while bringing the debate to focus increasingly on the issues of national identity and citizenship. The municipal elections of 1983 mark a turning-point in the politicization of race and immigration issues in France, as the mainstream right joined forces with the extreme right to belabour the government for failing to enforce law and order and to control immigration. These elections helped to define the new terms of the immigration debate in France, as the number and concentration of foreigners were explicitly equated with the mounting insecurity in certain towns and urban enclaves. The municipal elections of 1983 also saw the first open alliance, in the industrial town of Dreux near Paris (with its 28 per cent of immigrants), between the Gaullist RPR, the Giscardian UDF and the extreme-right FN – a party which won 16.7 per cent of the vote in Dreux on a virulent anti-immigrant platform, with its campaign slogans 'The French First' and '2 million unemployed means 2 million immigrants too many !'.[34]

The equation between immigrants and unemployment was not, of course, new. By 1983, however, this crude rationale was couched in a more openly racialist discourse and extended to cover not just unemployment but a whole cluster of problems grouped under the term *insécurité*, providing a mobilizing theme in a context of advanced economic recession. At the same time, the profile of the immigrant community itself was changing. The liberalization of broadcasting by the government in 1981 had spawned a host of local radio stations in France articulating the views of foreign minorities and raising awareness of the immigrant community. More significantly, the removal of restrictions on the setting up of immigrant associations had fostered new opportunities for activism and demonstrations of solidarity within the immigrant population. From the organized strike action of immigrant workers in the car industry, through the violent protests of immigrant youths in Les Minguettes (Lyon), to the marches by second generation North Africans, or *Beurs*, the immigrant community in the early 1980s was in the process of forging a more assertive and, for some, a more threatening image.[35] Nor was this 'threat' perceived solely in social terms: it had a decidedly ethnic dimension. In 1946, North Africans accounted for only 2.3 per cent of the foreign population in France, 88.7 per cent of whom were European; by 1982, the proportion of Europeans had fallen to 47.6 per cent, while that of North Africans had risen to 38.5 per cent.[36]

On 26 October 1985, *Le Figaro Magazine* adorned its cover page with a bust of Marianne draped in Muslim attire and the question: 'Will we still be French in thirty years?' Inside was a 'dossier' on immigration which predicted that, by the year 2015, France would be submerged by an alien (Muslim Arab) population and culture. Though the Minister for Social Affairs, Georgina Dufoix, responded by refuting the statistics and conclusions of the authors, accused of 'recalling the wildest theories of Nazism',[37] the theme was one which had already gained currency through the rise of the FN. Harping on the changing character of immigration, Le Pen's party portrayed the North African community not only as a drain on the economy and a major factor in the breakdown of law and order, but also, and more ominously, as a threat to national identity and to the very survival of 'Frenchness' itself.[38] The electoral results of the FN (some 10-15 per cent in every national election since 1984) attest to the success with which it exploited anxiety over this issue and mobilized anti-immigrant sentiment amongst a large cross-section of the French voting public. By pushing race and immigration to the fore as major public concerns, the FN altered the dynamics of political debate in France, forcing the parties of right and left to redefine their immigration strategies within a changing pattern of electoral competition.[39]

Immigration, it was clear, had come of age as a national political issue in France. While it would be a gross oversimplification to attribute the success of the FN to immigration alone,[40] there is a strong correlation between the presence of immigrants and levels of support for Le Pen's party. Three regions out of twenty-two (Ile-de-France, Rhône-Alpes, Provence-Alpes-Côte d'Azur) account for some 60 per cent of all resident foreigners in France; it is in these regions, around the urban centres of Paris, Lyon and Marseille, that the FN has established its most powerful electoral bases.[41] In Marseille, where tensions over immigration are especially acute, Le Pen outdistanced all candidates, including the incumbent President Mitterrand, with 28.3 per cent of the vote in the first round of the 1988 presidential elections – a result reflected throughout the main *départements* of Provence-Alpes-Côte d'Azur (Alpes-Maritimes: 24.2 per cent; Bouches-du-Rhône: 26.4 per cent; Var: 25 per cent; Vaucluse: 23.1 per cent).[42] Analysis of voting motivations, too, has consistently shown immigration to be an overriding priority for the FN electorate.[43] Though anxiety over the economic and demographic impact of immigrants is far from new in France, it was given a keener edge in the climate of the 1980s, with a beleaguered left in government and the extreme right emerging as a potent electoral force.

As the debate over demographic trends and the defence of 'national identity' gathered pace, a bitter polemic developed around the questions of nationality and citizenship. Stoked by a number of publications bearing the imprimatur of the 'New Right',[44] the polemic focused on the question of whether the Nationality Code should be revised so as to prevent children born in France of immigrant parents from acquiring French citizenship as an automatic right. As it stood prior to the legislative elections of 1993, the Nationality Code accorded French citizenship either, at birth, to the offspring of at least one French parent (Article 23: *jus sanguinis*), or, at the age of eighteen, to children born of foreign parents in France who were resident in the country during the five years preceding their majority (Article 44: *jus soli*), unless they chose explicitly to refuse it. While the FN argued that birthright alone should be the qualification for citizenship, the RPR and UDF called for an end to the passive nature of the *jus soli* and its replacement by an active, voluntary principle: a formal application for

234

citizenship made to a tribunal and contingent on a commitment to honour the 'moral contract' entered into thereby.[45] The parliamentary elections of 1986 saw this become a central plank in the RPR-UDF programme for government, as the traditional right sought to counter the FN's electoral appeal. Undertaking to forge 'a national community strengthened in its identity', the *Plate-forme pour gouverner ensemble* held out to immigrants the stark choice: 'integration or subsidized repatriation'. As for political rights, these were to remain linked to a national status which should no longer be granted by 'purely automatic means' but which should be 'requested and accepted'.[46]

Chirac, Pasqua and the hardening of government policy

The reform of the Nationality Code anticipated in 1986 proved, in the end, a fiasco. Faced with stern opposition from the parties of the left, immigrant associations, student organizations and a section of the French clergy, the Chirac government, which had replaced the Fabius administration in March 1986, set up a special commission (the *Commission des sages*) to look into the whole question of nationality. Before the Commission had even reported its deliberations, it had been decided that the issue was too sensitive to pursue in the run-up to the presidential elections of April-May 1988. Though the Chirac government was forced to back down on its nationality reforms,[47] it did succeed in radicalizing the legislation relating to immigrants and in creating a more repressive climate. In a bid to clamp down on illegal immigration and to combat a wave of Arab-inspired terrorism in September 1986, the RPR-UDF government extended the powers of the police to conduct random identity checks and to detain suspects. Controls on non-EC foreigners entering France were tightened by a new visa requirement, while the conditions governing political asylum were made more stringent. The most telling item in the new panoply of legislation was the Pasqua Law of 9 September 1986.[48] This law made expulsion once again an administrative rather than a judicial matter, thus expediting the process and undoing an important Socialist reform of 1981. It also stipulated that any 'threat to public order' constituted grounds for expulsion, refusal of entry or non-renewal of a residence permit, leaving decisions in this ill-defined area at the discretion of the police and local prefecture.

Negating the spirit of the early Socialist reforms in favour of immigrants, the Chirac interregnum of 1986–88 shifted the emphasis away from integration towards exclusion and repatriation. The truth is, however, that for all the hardline character of the Chirac-Pasqua reforms, they merely gave more radical expression to objectives and policies already espoused in principle by the left, namely tight controls on entry and residence and a resolute commitment to combating illegal immigration. After their return to power in 1988, the Socialists maintained the same firm line. Le Pen's unprecedented success (14.4 per cent) in the 1988 presidential election kept immigration high on the political agenda and ruled out any softening of government policy. In November 1988, the new Minister of the Interior, Pierre Joxe, drew cheers from the opposition benches when he declared to the National Assembly that France could not become 'a refuge for all the disinherited of the developing world'.[49] Unsurprisingly, the Joxe Law of 2 August 1989, in amending the provisions of the 1986 Pasqua Law, re-establishing judicial control over expulsion through a departmentally-based *Commission du séjour des étrangers*, kept the same restrictive objectives.[50] Despite the creation in December 1989 of the *Haut Conseil à l'Intégration*, with its brief to advise on all means of integrating immigrant communities, and the strengthening of anti-racist legislation through the Gayssot Law of 13 July 1990, the successive governments of Michel Rocard, Edith Cresson and Pierre Bérégovoy showed no enthusiasm for returning to the discourse and policies of 1981. Instead, they sought to defuse the immigration issue and to harness cross-party consensus around a policy of firm control – though the *affaire du foulard* in autumn 1989, reopening the whole debate over French identity, showed how fragile such 'consensus' was.[51]

Little wonder that, when the five main human rights and immigrant support organizations in France held a 'March against racism and for equality of rights' on 25 January 1992, the Socialist contingent was pointedly shunned. While the parties and trade unions of the left turned out in force to swell the estimated 50-100,000 demonstrating on behalf of immigrants and asylum-seekers, the Socialists found themselves relegated to the rear of the march, which was symbolically led by refugees who had fallen foul of recent government restrictions on asylum. Billed as a protest against Le Pen, the event quickly took on the aspect of an anti-government demonstration, with banners, slogans and chants to that effect. Reporting in *Le Monde*, Philippe Bernard captured the irony of this 'astonishing spectacle', of this 'world turned upside down', describing 'the massed and diverse ranks of the left denouncing fascism and hatred, while defying a government... of the left.'[52] That the Socialists ended up thus participating in a demonstration directed largely against themselves was a measure of how confused their relationship with their ideological heritage and their traditional left-wing constituency had become on the immigration and asylum issues.

Towards a culture of intolerance : the immigration 'debate' into the 1990s

By reneging on their initial commitment to immigrant rights, shifting their focus from the defence of the many to the prosecution of the few, the Socialists failed to provide a counterweight to the pressure exerted by the right and, more particularly, the extreme right. Increasingly, they saw the initiative for formulating immigration policy wrenched from their grasp, as they found themselves obliged to respond to an agenda set by others. It is here, in the effect which it exerted not just on the opposition right but on the Socialists themselves, that the real significance of the FN lies. The publication in November 1991 of the party's policy document on immigration marked a new stage in the radicalization of the debate over immigrants and race in France. In a 50-point agenda drawn up by its deputy leader, Bruno Mégret, the FN called for: the repeal of legislation to combat racism and antisemitism in France; the reform of the Nationality Code, restricting citizenship to a birthright; the review of all naturalizations granted since 1974 (a retroactive measure for which Vichy alone provides a precedent); the practice of 'national preference', putting French nationals first in line for employment, immigrant workers first in line for redundancy; the levying of a special tax on employers using immigrant labour; the restriction of family allowance and other welfare benefits to French nationals alone; the conversion of immigrant hostels into housing for 'needy French'; the expunging of foreign ('cosmopolitan') ideas from school textbooks and the fixing of quotas for immigrant children in French schools; a ban on the building of 'places of worship foreign to French identity' and severe new restrictions on Islamic teaching in France; the introduction of a 5-year prison sentence for any immigrant refusing to comply with identity verification procedures; the deportation of all illegal immigrants, those convicted of criminal offences and the unemployed, using boats and planes chartered by the state; the setting up of detention centres under police surveillance for immigrants served with a deportation order.[53]

A case-study in discrimination, this policy statement by the FN challenged the founding principles of the Fifth Republic, defying a Constitution which guarantees equal access for all to employment and welfare support, irrespective of race or creed.[54] The foregoing were not, however, the policy options of an extremist fringe alone. While Le Pen continued to enjoy the regular support of some 10-15 per cent of the electorate, opinion polls suggested that up to three times as many agreed with his stance on immigration. Such was the concern over this fact, and over the incidence of racist violence in France, that a National Consultative Commission on Human Rights was instructed to investigate the problem. In March 1991, the Commission published its findings in a 245-page report. While 94 per cent of those polled considered racism to be widespread in France, 42 per cent admitted to harbouring some element of racial prejudice themselves; while 24 per cent judged that there were 'too many Jews' in France, fully 71 per cent stated that there were 'too many Arabs'. The evidence, concluded the Commission, was that France was witnessing 'an increasingly marked tendency to racism in attitudes and everyday behaviour'.[55]

In this way, taboos which have prevailed in France since the overthrow of Vichy are being swept away. Nor is such a development due to the FN alone. Though Jean-Marie Le Pen embodies the most extreme expression of this xenophobic tendency, other political leaders must bear their share of responsibility. During a dinner-debate in Orléans in June 1991, the leader of the Gaullist RPR, Jacques Chirac, demonstrated the extent to which an overtly racialist discourse now passes for part of the immigration 'debate' in France. Judging the country to be suffering from an 'overdose' of immigrants, Chirac proceeded to illustrate his argument thus :

238

Take the French worker who lives in an apartment block in La Goutte d'Or [a district of Paris with a high immigrant population], who struggles along with his wife to make about 15,000 francs, and who sees, across the landing, a crowded family with a father, three or four wives and twenty-odd kids, who receive 50,000 francs in social security benefits, without working, of course... Add to that the noise and the smell, and it's enough to drive the French worker mad.[56]

Uttered by the leader of the most powerful party of the right, by a politician who had twice held the office of Prime Minister and who remained a strong contender for the presidency, these words provoked a storm of protest from anti-racist movements and political opponents alike. Appearing next evening on French television, however, Chirac recanted nothing of his remarks, claiming that they were based on reports he had received 'hundreds of times' from those confronted with such realities. Setting himself up thus as the defender of so many nameless victims, Chirac, in a style redolent of Le Pen, declared defiantly that he had decided to 'tell it like it really was'. To counter what he saw as the extreme right's 'monopoly' of this problem, he set about outlining his own policies, articulating a list of measures which could have come straight from the programme of the FN :

... control immigration... put an end to family reunification... conduct a thorough review of the right of asylum... open up a debate on the right of foreigners to welfare benefits that are not linked to contributions... reform the Nationality Code... stop talking about votes for immigrants.[57]

With all their demagogic tone, these remarks signalled a new determination by Chirac to challenge the leader of the FN on his own ground. The method was not new; nor was Chirac alone in employing it. Caught between a Socialist government in electoral decline and an extreme right in the ascendant, leaders of the traditional right yielded increasingly to the temptation to outbid Le Pen, thereby seeking to recover the support which he drained from them. When ex-President Valéry Giscard d'Estaing, head of the centre-right UDF, published in *Le Figaro Magazine* of 21

September 1991 an article entitled 'Immigration or invasion?', he was surely aware of the public reaction it would provoke. Unlike his Gaullist counterpart in Orléans, Giscard was not addressing an assembly in the heat of a debate: he had the opportunity to refine his terms and express himself with studied precision. In recognizing immigration to be a 'sensitive issue' in which 'words had to be used with caution, because of their emotive or historical charge', Giscard proceeded to conclude that:

> ...the type of problem which we face is changing from being one of *immigration* ('the arrival of foreigners wishing to settle in a country') to being one of *invasion* ('the act of entering and spreading with sudden effect', according to the definition given by Littré).[58]

Despite this exhibition of lexical scruple, Giscard, by using a term so fraught with dread connotations to describe 'a problem destined to weigh heavily upon our future', had adopted an idiom whose sense could not be so easily attenuated. Having thus conjured up the threat facing France, the ex-President (and presidential hopeful still) went on, much as Chirac had done three months earlier, to outline *his* package of solutions. Echoing Le Pen's warning of the dangers to 'French identity' posed by a large immigrant population, Giscard advocated the restriction of nationality to a 'bloodright', calling for a referendum on the issue and for the necessary constitutional reform which would allow this to take place. In addition, he argued for a 'zero quota' of immigration until the next census, the automatic expulsion of all illegal immigrants, heavier penalties for those employing illegal immigrant labour, a review of the legislation allowing immigrants to bring their families into France, an increase in the power of mayors to grant or refuse housing to immigrants, and (not least) the implementation of a 'vigorous policy of birth promotion', in France and Europe alike, in order to redress the 'demographic implosion' by reserving a special child quota allowance for indigenous families.

Giscard's extension of the final point here to French *and* Europeans is significant. For he was not referring in this article to 'immigrants' any more than Mégret or Chirac, in the extracts cited above, were referring to 'immigrants'. They were each in turn referring to the 1.5 to 2 million-strong North African community, for whom the term *immigré* has become a ready designation (even though, in the 1982 census, Portuguese, Italians and Spaniards still accounted for a greater proportion of the foreign population than Algerians, Moroccans and Tunisians). In political discourse and media reporting across the board, the representation of the foreigner, both visual and mental, has crystallized around the same imagery: the 'immigrant' in France is differentiated by colour (dark), culture (Arab), and religion (Islamic). The issue is not simply about jobs, housing and welfare benefits, however important such material factors are in a context of recession: it is about notions of cultural integrity and the preservation of a national, and European, identity. At a time when Europe is dissolving its internal borders, seeking to enshrine in Community legislation a distinction (in terms of free movement and voting rights) between first and a second-class migrants, the term 'immigrant' has come to carry less of a *national* and more of a *racial* connotation. The notion that there is a cultural and, beyond that, a biological European heritage is crucial, certainly, to the FN's construction of the immigrant and the distinction which it draws between European and non-European nationals. What is explicit in the discriminatory discourse of the FN lies implicit within much of French public discourse on immigration today: from the 'smells' evoked by Chirac, through the 'invasion' described by Giscard, to the 'threshold of tolerance' (*seuil de tolérance*) acknowledged finally by the Socialists as a factor in the integration of immigrant communities, it is the same *discours de stigmatisation* which has come to characterize the representation of the (non-European) immigrant in France.[59]

For this reason, it is important to recognize that the parties of the mainstream right have not been drawn alone into the trap of endorsing Le Pen's politics. In the summer of 1991, the French Communist Party (PCF), which has never occupied secure ground on the immigration issue, published a two-page tract entitled *Immigration: The Communists' Opinion*. In it, the PCF evoked an immigrant community swollen by an organized trade in clandestine foreign labour, harbouring untold numbers of illegal residents and contributing to the problems of delinquency, drug addiction and violent crime. Since immigrant families were often among the largest and the poorest, the tract argued, they constituted a drain on limited welfare resources, making access to such resources difficult for needy French families. Though it was targeted primarily against government policy in all of these areas, and though it held the right and extreme right to account for the mounting racism in France, the tract provided a prime example of how the immigrant issue has become a political weapon to be used by each party against the others. Condemning the tract out of hand, the prominent anti-racist organization, the MRAP, expressed its 'stupefaction' that the PCF could appeal thus to a race-conscious prejudice against the immigrant community.[60]

Such contributions to the immigration 'debate' serve to confound the distinction between left and right and to underline the political capital made by all sides from the issue. In a televised interview on 8 July 1991 (at the very moment when the MRAP was engaged in its *passe d'armes* with the PCF), the then Socialist Prime Minister, Edith Cresson, went so far as to countenance the use of charter flights to return illegal immigrants and those refused asylum to their countries of origin. Given the notorious precedent for this (the expulsion of 101 Malians under the Pasqua Law in October 1986), it was not surprising that the Prime Minister's suggestion provoked an outcry from anti-racist organizations and a number of her political colleagues. By concentrating attention on the single issue of illegal immigration, portraying the clandestine foreign worker as one of the major problems facing France, she demonstrated once more the extent to which the tone and substance of Socialist discourse had evolved since 1981. The point was taken up by the then president of SOS-Racisme, Harlem Désir, who urged the government 'not to make immigrants, even illegal immigrants, the scapegoats for the country's social problems'.[61] Such objections notwithstanding, when the government announced its new package of immigration measures in July and September 1991, the emphasis was on tracking down and deporting illegal immigrants, imposing heavier sanctions on employers of clandestine foreign labour, and removing from political asylum-seekers the right to a temporary work permit. As for the pledge to grant immigrants a vote in municipal elections, it was quite simply never restored to the agenda, despite the note of personal regret sounded by Mitterrand in the *Lettre à tous les Français* which served as his platform for re-election in 1988.

Conclusion

The 1980s and early 1990s marked a new phase in the politics of immigration in France, challenging the Socialists on some of their most cherished ideals. Though the Mitterrand administration remained formally committed to justice and equality for the immigrant community, and to the eradication of intolerance and racial discrimination, it lost the initiative in terms of formulating policy and commanding public approval for liberal reforms. While in opposition during the 1960s and 1970s, the Socialists were able to elaborate a clear and coherent platform on immigrant rights and anti-racism; between 1986 and 1988, they rediscovered something of this earlier clarity of purpose in their stance against the Pasqua Law and the reform of the Nationality Code. In government, however, they were much less sure of their ground, caught between the conflicting tensions of ideological principle and managerial pragmatism.[62] While their record on immigration reform in the early 1980s was far from negligible, the gains achieved were subsequently eroded under pressure from the political right and from public opinion. By the time of their defeat in the legislative elections of March 1993, the impression was that the Socialists no longer had a project for the immigrant community which was substantially distinct from that of the mainstream right. Though differences in rhetoric and emphasis persist, the policy options open to any government, of left or right, are now much more severely restricted than they appeared in 1981. Tight control over all new entrants (including refugees and asylum-seekers), the eradication of clandestine foreign labour, the provision of a voluntary repatriation scheme, and the progressive integration of the permanently settled immigrant population: such are the fixed points around which left and right alike now structure their immigration policies. The FN alone advocates the enforced repatriation of legally resident immigrants – a draconian proposal which permits the other parties, while hardening their line, to pretend to reason and moderation.

Yet the issue is not just one of policy: it is also about discourse, the manner in which immigrants are represented in political debate, in the media, in public opinion polls, and in the popular imagination.[63] The 1980s confirmed the changing trend in the ethnic composition of the immigrant population, bringing home fully the permanent character of France's large North African community. The 'unassimilable island' envisaged by Calvez in 1969 has become an enduring feature of contemporary France; the *mythe du retour* has been dispelled. This simple fact ramifies into a number of highly complex issues (of group identity and conflict, cultural and religious compatibility, political and civil rights) with which future

243

governments will continue to wrestle. The net effect of the 1980s and early 1990s is that such issues must now be addressed in a climate inimical to the advancement of immigrant rights, where a discourse of intolerance has gained currency and where the political agenda has shifted markedly to the right. It is a curious legacy of the Mitterrand era that immigrants in France today find themselves subject to a more pronounced discrimination than when the Socialists came to office, pledged to champion their cause, in 1981.

Notes

1. Freeman, G.P. (1979), *Immigrant Labor and Racial Conflict in Industrial Societies: The French and British Experience 1945-1975*, Princeton University Press, Princeton, pp. 68-98, 176-212 *passim*.
2. Gaspard, F. and Servan-Schreiber, C. (1985), *La Fin des immigrés*, Seuil, Paris, pp. 19-22.
3. Ogden, P.E. (1991), 'Immigration to France since 1945: myth and reality', *Ethnic and Racial Studies,* vol. 14, no. 3, pp. 297-300; Hollifield, J.F., 'Immigration and modernization', in Hollifield, J.F. and Ross, G. (eds) (1991), *Searching for the New France*, Routledge, New York/London, pp. 122-5.
4. Gani, L. (1972), *Syndicats et travailleurs immigrés*, Editions sociales, Paris, pp. 67-8.
5. Calvez, C., 'Le problème des travailleurs étrangers', *Journal Officiel de la République Française. Avis et Rapports du Conseil Economique et Social*, no. 7, 27 March 1969, p. 309.
6. See Minces, J. (1973), *Les travailleurs étrangers en France*, Seuil, Paris, chaps. 6, 9, 13 and 16.
7. Calvez, 'Le problème des travailleurs étrangers', p. 316.
8. Cited in Cordeiro, A. (1984), *L'immigration*, 2nd ed., La Découverte, Paris, p. 88.
9. Decree no. 76-383, *Journal Officiel*, 2 May 1976, pp. 2628-9.
10. Schain, M.A. (1985), 'Immigrants and politics in France', in Ambler, J.S. (ed.), *The French Socialist Experiment*, Institute for the Study of Human Issues, Philadelphia, pp. 169-70.

11. The recorded proportion of the immigrant population in employment dropped from 60 per cent in 1946 to 50.4 per cent in 1962; by 1982, it stood at only 42.3 per cent (Le Moigne, G., 1986, *L'immigration en France*, PUF, Paris, p. 17). On the trend towards greater family immigration, see Tribalat, M., et al. (1991), *Cent ans d'immigration, étrangers d'hier Français d'aujourd'hui. Apport démographique, dynamique familiale et économique de l'immigration étrangère*, PUF/INED, Paris, pp. 73-106.

12. See Grillo, R.D. (1985), *Ideologies and Institutions in Urban France: The Representation of Immigrants*, CUP, Cambridge, chaps. 5 and 6.

13. See Fitzpatrick, B. (1987), 'Immigrants', in Flower, J.E. (ed.), *France Today*, 6th ed., Methuen, London/New York, pp. 87, 98-9.

14. Cordeiro, *L'immigration*, p. 92.

15. Weil, P. (1991), *La France et ses étrangers. L'aventure d'une politique de l'immigration 1938-1991*, Calmann-Lévy, Paris, pp. 109-10; Mestiri, E. (1990), *L'immigration*, La Découverte, Paris, pp. 64-5.

16. See Schain, M.A. (1990), 'Immigration and Politics', in Hall, P.A. et al., *Developments in French Politics*, MacMillan, London, pp. 253-68.

17. Law no. 80-9, *Journal Officiel*, 11 January 1980, pp. 71-2.

18. Ashford, D.E. (1982), *Policy and Politics in France: Living with Uncertainty*, Temple University Press, Philadelphia, pp. 275-6, 279-80.

19. The *Institut National de la Statistique et des Etudes Economiques* (INSEE) recorded 3.68 million immigrants in the March 1982 census, while the Ministry of the Interior (basing its calculation on valid residence permits, with no allowance for deaths, departures or naturalizations) put the figure at 4.46 million in December of the same year.

20. In a publication issued by the Socialists in 1977, reaffirming their commitment to the Common Programme signed with the Communists in 1972, the undertaking is explicit to extend to immigrants 'equality of rights in the economic, cultural and social spheres'. See *Parti socialiste: 89 réponses aux questions économiques* (1977), Flammarion, Paris, p. 43.

21. See the *Programme commun de gouvernement du Parti communiste français et du Parti socialiste (27 juin 1972)*, Editions sociales, Paris, p. 144.
22. Weil, *La France et ses étrangers*, pp. 146-57.
23. *Ibid.*, pp. 176-83. Immigrant workers also benefited from more general reforms effected during the early 'state of grace', such as the raising of the national minimum wage, higher welfare benefits and pensions, a reduction of the working week and increase in the annual holiday entitlement, and the extension of workers' rights through the *Lois Auroux*.
24. *Le Monde*, 2 October 1981.
25. On the government's prevarication and the shelving of this proposal, see Weil, *La France et ses étrangers*, pp. 157-62.
26. See Husbands, C.T. (1991), 'The mainstream right and the politics of immigration in France: major developments in the 1980s', *Ethnic and Racial Studies*, vol. 14, no. 2, pp. 184-6; Hargreaves, A.G. (1991), 'The political mobilization of the North African immigrant community in France', *ibid.*, vol. 14, no. 3, pp. 353, 365.
27. Decree no. 84-1080, *Journal Officiel*, 5 December 1984, pp. 3733-4.
28. Decree no. 84-310, *ibid.*, 28 April 1984, pp. 1272-3.
29. For the Fabius government's presentation of a policy which the Socialists had condemned under the previous regime, see the *Lettre de Matignon*, no. 123, 15 October 1984, p. 3.
30. Julliard, J. (1984), 'L'alerte', in SOFRES, *Opinion publique. Enquêtes et commentaires 1984*, Gallimard, Paris, p. 125.
31. *Le Monde*, 7 September 1984.
32. 'Immigration: vers l'équilibre social', *Lettre de Matignon*, no. 123, 15 October 1984, p. 1.
33. *Le Monde*, 29 October 1985.
34. On the town of Dreux as a case-study in the political exploitation of the immigrant, see Gaspard, F. (1990), *Une petite ville en France*, Gallimard, Paris, pp. 149-205.
35. On the emergence of the *Beurs* as a distinct community and social pressure group, see Hargreaves, A.G. (1989), 'The Beur generation: integration or exclusion?', in Howorth, J. and Ross, G. (eds), *Contemporary France : A Review of Interdisciplinary Studies*, vol. 3, Pinter, London/New York, pp. 147-59.

36. Weil, *La France et ses étrangers*, Annexe VI, pp. 374-5.

37. *Le Monde*, 29 October 1985.

38. Among a host of publications which rehearse this line, see Le Pen, J.-M. (1984), *Les Français d'abord*, Carrère-Lafon, Paris; (1985), *La France est de retour*, Carrère-Lafon, Paris; (1985), *Pour la France: programme du Front National*, Albatros, Paris.

39. See Perrineau, P. (1989), 'Les étapes d'une implantation électorale (1972–88)', in Mayer, N. and Perrineau, P. (eds), *Le Front National à découvert*, Presses de la Fondation Nationale des Sciences Politiques, Paris, pp. 37-62; Ignazi, P., 'Un nouvel acteur politique', *ibid.*, pp. 63-80; Schaïn, M.A. (1987), 'The National Front in France and the construction of political legitimacy', *West European Politics*, vol. 10, no. 2, pp. 229-52; (1988), 'Immigration and changes in the French party system', *European Journal of Political Research*, vol. 16, pp. 597-621; Shields, J.G. (1990), 'A new chapter in the history of the French extreme right: the National Front', in Cole, A. (ed.), *French Political Parties in Transition*, Dartmouth, Aldershot, pp. 185-204.

40. See Shields, J.G. (1991), 'The politics of disaffection: France in the 1980s', in Gaffney, J. and Kolinsky E. (eds), *Political Culture in France and Germany: A Contemporary Perspective*, Routledge, London/New York, pp. 69-90.

41. See Ogden, P. (1987), 'Immigration, cities and the geography of the National Front in France', in Glebe, G. and O'Loughlin, J. (eds), *Foreign Minorities in Continental European Cities*, Franz Steiner, Stuttgart, pp. 166-7, 176-82. For some of the complexities underlying the correlation between the presence of immigrants and the FN vote, see Husbands, C.T. (1991), 'The support for the Front National: analyses and findings', *Ethnic and Racial Studies*, vol. 14, no. 3, pp. 382-416.

42. On the 1988 presidential election, see Shields, J.G. (1989), 'Campaigning from the fringe: Jean-Marie Le Pen', in Gaffney, J. (ed.), *The French Presidential Elections of 1988: Ideology and Leadership in Contemporary France*, Dartmouth, Aldershot, pp. 140-57.

43. See on this point SOFRES (1985), *Opinion publique 1985*, Gallimard, Paris, p. 181; SOFRES (1987), *L'état de l'opinion: clés pour 1987*,

Seuil, Paris, pp. 107, 111; SOFRES (1991), *L'état de l'opinion 1991*, Seuil, Paris, pp. 121, 125.

44. See, for example, Le Gallou, J.-Y. et le Club de l'Horloge (1985), *La Préférence nationale: réponse à l'immigration*, Albin Michel, Paris; Griotteray, A. (1984), *Les immigrés: le choc*, Plon, Paris.

45. See Shields, J.G. (1987), *'Jus soli* and *jus sanguinis*: French nationality in the scales', *Patterns of Prejudice*, vol. 21, no. 3, pp. 34-6.

46. *RPR-UDF: Plateforme pour gouverner ensemble 1986*, p. 14.

47. When the Commission's report, *Etre Français aujourd'hui et demain*, was published in February 1988, it endorsed the government's proposal that Article 44 be amended to include some expression of a desire to become French, but recommended that the principle of *jus soli* be retained intact and that every step be taken to encourage those eligible to accede to this right. On the nationality question, see Costa-Lascoux, J. (1989), *De l'immigré au citoyen*, La Documentation française, Paris, pp. 115-44.

48. Law no. 86-1025, *Journal Officiel*, 12 September 1986, pp. 11035-7.

49. *Le Monde*, 18 November 1988.

50. Law no. 89-548, *Journal Officiel*, 8 August 1989, pp. 9952-4.

51. The *affaire du foulard*, or 'headscarf affair', centred on the question of whether Muslim schoolgirls should be allowed to wear their chadors in class, or whether this constituted a violation of the secular principle upon which French state education is founded. The controversy arose over three Muslim girls excluded from a school in Creil for refusing to remove their veils during class.

52. *Le Monde*, 28 January 1992. The major organizations involved were the *Ligue des droits de l'homme* (LDH), *Mouvement contre le racisme et pour l'amitié entre les peuples* (MRAP), *Ligue internationale contre le racisme et l'antisémitisme* (LICRA), *Fédération des associations de solidarité avec les travailleurs immigrés* (FASTI) and *SOS Racisme*.

53. Mégret, B. (1991), *Contribution au règlement du problème de l'immigration: 50 mesures concrètes*, FN document, Paris.

54. The Preamble to the Constitution of the Fourth Republic, endorsed in 1958 by that of the Fifth, is explicit in outlawing the forms of discrimination which the FN seeks to institute. See Godechot, J.

(1979), *Les Constitutions de la France depuis 1789*, Garnier-Flammarion, Paris, pp. 389-90, 424.

55. Commission Nationale Consultative des Droits de l'Homme (1991), *La Lutte contre le racisme et la xénophobie 1990*, La Documentation française, Paris, pp. 197-8, 216, 222, 234.

56. *Le Monde*, 21 June 1991.

57. See the report of the interview in *Le Monde*, 22 June 1991.

58. Giscard d'Estaing, V., 'Immigration ou invasion?', *Le Figaro Magazine*, 21 September 1991.

59. See the *tribune libre* by Rebérioux, M. et al., 'Les étrangers et la France', in *Le Monde*, 25 January 1992. On the 'threshold of tolerance', see MacMaster, N. (1991), 'The "seuil de tolérance": the uses of a "scientific" racist concept', in Silverman (ed.), *Race, Discourse and Power in France*, Avebury, Aldershot, pp. 14-28. In a televised interview in December 1989, President Mitterrand himself stated that immigration in France had attained the '*seuil de tolérance*' in the 1970s. On this remark and the President's subsequent embarrassment over it, see *Le Monde*, 12 December 1989; 16 July 1991.

60. MRAP, 'Non à la dérive du débat politique', communiqué dated 5 July 1991.

61. *Le Monde*, 10 July 1991. See the concern expressed by Madeleine Rebérioux, president of the *Ligue des droits de l'homme*, to François Mitterrand over the 'repressive' character of government policy (*ibid.*, 14-15 July 1991).

62. See Wihtol de Wenden, C. (1991), 'Immigration policy and the issue of nationality', *Ethnic and Racial Studies*, vol. 14, no. 3, pp. 319-32. See also the reviews of Socialist government policy in *Le Monde*, 3 January 1989; 28 January 1992.

63. In relation to the press specifically, see Bonnafous, S. (1991), *L'immigration prise aux mots. Les immigrés dans la presse au tournant des années 80*, Kimé, Paris.

Bibliography

Ambler, J.S. (ed.) (1985), *The French Socialist Experiment*, Institute for the Study of Human Issues, Philadelphia.

Ashford, D.E. (1982), *Policy and Politics in France: Living with Uncertainty*, Temple University Press, Philadelphia.

Bonnafous, S. (1991), *L'immigration prise aux mots. Les immigrés dans la presse au tournant des années 80*, Kimé, Paris.

Calvez, C., 'Le problème des travailleurs étrangers', *Journal Officiel de la République Française. Avis et Rapports du Conseil Economique et Social*, no. 7, 27 March 1969.

Le Chevallier, J.-M. (1989), *Immigration en Europe: Attention, danger*, Groupe des Droites européennes, Paris.

Cole, A. (ed.) (1990), *French Political Parties in Transition*, Dartmouth, Aldershot.

Commission Nationale Consultative des Droits de l'Homme (1991), *La Lutte contre le racisme et la xénophobie 1990*, La Documentation française, Paris.

Cordeiro, A. (1984), *L'immigration*, 2nd ed., La Découverte, Paris.

Costa-Lascoux, J. (1989), *De l'immigré au citoyen*, La Documentation française, Paris.

Flower, J.E. (ed.) (1987), *France Today*, 6th ed., Methuen, London/New York.

Freeman, G.P. (1979), *Immigrant Labor and Racial Conflict in Industrial Societies: The French and British Experience 1945-1975*, Princeton University Press, Princeton.

Gaffney, J. and Kolinsky, E. (eds) (1991), *Political Culture in France and Germany: A Contemporary Perspective*, Routledge, London/New York.

Gaffney, J. (ed.) (1989), *The French Presidential Elections of 1988: Ideology and Leadership in Contemporary France*, Dartmouth, Aldershot.

Le Gallou, J.-Y. et le Club de l'Horloge (1985), *La Préférence nationale: réponse à l'immigration*, Albin Michel, Paris.

Gani, L. (1972), *Syndicats et travailleurs immigrés*, Editions sociales, Paris.

Gaspard, F. and Servan-Schreiber, C. (1985), *La Fin des immigrés*, Seuil, Paris.

Gaspard, F. (1990), *Une petite ville en France*, Gallimard, Paris.

Giscard d'Estaing, V., 'Immigration ou invasion?', *Le Figaro Magazine*, 21 September 1991.

Glebe, G. and O'Loughlin, J. (eds) (1987), *Foreign Minorities in Continental European Cities*, Franz Steiner, Stuttgart.

Godechot, J. (1979), *Les Constitutions de la France depuis 1789*, Garnier-Flammarion, Paris.

Grillo, R.D. (1985), *Ideologies and Institutions in Urban France: The Representation of Immigrants*, CUP, Cambridge.

Griotteray, A. (1984), *Les immigrés: le choc*, Plon, Paris.

Hall, P., Hayward, J. and Machin, H. (eds) (1990), *Developments in French Politics*, MacMillan, London.

Hargreaves, A.G. (1991), 'The political mobilization of the North African immigrant community in France', *Ethnic and Racial Studies*, vol. 14, no. 3.

Hollifield, J.F. and Ross, G. (eds) (1991), *Searching for the New France*, Routledge, New York/London.

Howorth, J. and Ross, G. (eds) (1989), *Contemporary France: A Review of Interdisciplinary Studies*, vol. 3, Pinter, London/New York.

Husbands, C.T. (1991), 'The mainstream right and the politics of immigration in France: major developments in the 1980s', *Ethnic and Racial Studies*, vol. 14, no. 2.

Husbands, C.T. (1991), 'The support for the Front National: analyses and findings', *Ethnic and Racial Studies*, vol. 14, no. 3.

Journal Officiel de la République Française

Lettre de Matignon

Mayer, N. and Perrineau, P. (eds) (1989), *Le Front National à découvert*, Presses de la Fondation Nationale des Sciences Politiques, Paris.

Mégret, B. (1991), *Contribution au règlement du problème de l'immigration: 50 mesures concrètes*, FN document, Paris.

Mestiri, E. (1990), *L'immigration*, La Découverte, Paris.

Minces, J. (1973), *Les travailleurs étrangers en France*, Seuil, Paris.

Le Moigne, G. (1986), *L'immigration en France*, PUF, Paris.

Le Monde: dossiers et documents (1984), 'Les immigrés en France', no. 115.

Ogden, P.E. (1991), 'Immigration to France since 1945: myth and reality', *Ethnic and Racial Studies*, vol. 14, no. 3.

Parti socialiste: 89 réponses aux questions économiques (1977), Flammarion, Paris.

Le Pen, J.-M. (1984), *Les Français d'abord*, Carrère-Lafon, Paris.

Le Pen, J.-M. (1985), *La France est de retour*, Carrère-Lafon, Paris.

Le Pen, J.-M. (1985), *Pour la France: programme du Front National*, Albatros, Paris.

Le Pen, J.-M. (1989), *L'Espoir*, Albatros, Paris.

Programme commun de gouvernement du Parti communiste français et du Parti socialiste (1972), Editions sociales, Paris.

Rebérioux, M. et al., 'Les étrangers et la France', *Le Monde*, 25 January 1992.

RPR-UDF: Plateforme pour gouverner ensemble 1986 (legislative election manifesto).

Schain, M.A. (1987), 'The National Front in France and the construction of political legitimacy', *West European Politics*, vol. 10, no. 2.

Schain, M.A. (1988), 'Immigration and changes in the French party system', *European Journal of Political Research*, vol. 16.

Shields, J.G. (1987), '*Jus soli* and *jus sanguinis*: French nationality in the scales', *Patterns of Prejudice*, vol. 21, no. 3.

Silverman, M. (1991), 'Citizenship and the nation-state in France', *Ethnic and Racial Studies*, vol. 14, no. 3.

SOFRES (1984), *Opinion publique - 1984*, Gallimard, Paris.

SOFRES (1985), *Opinion publique - 1985*, Gallimard, Paris.

SOFRES (1987), *L'état de l'opinion - 1987,* Seuil, Paris.

SOFRES (1991), *L'état de l'opinion - 1991*, Seuil, Paris.

Taguieff, P.-A. (1991), *Face au racisme*, 2 vols., La Découverte, Paris.

Tribalat, M. et al. (1991), *Cent ans d'immigration, étrangers d'hier Français d'aujourd'hui. Apport démographique, dynamique familiale et économique de l'immigration étrangère*, PUF/INED, Paris.

Weil, P. (1991), *La France et ses étrangers. L'aventure d'une politique de l'immigration 1938-1991*, Calmann-Lévy, Paris.

Wihtol de Wenden, C. (1991), 'Immigration policy and the issue of nationality', *Ethnic and Racial Studies*, vol. 14, no. 3.

11 Cultural Shifts and the Greening of French Society

GINO RAYMOND

Introduction

If a week is a long time in politics, then the period which has elapsed since the foundation of the French Fifth Republic may seem like an eternity which veils the historically fragile relationship between French society and the political structures which govern it. As recent studies of French political culture have recalled, since 1789 there have been ten major changes of regime, and two during the period following the second world war.[1] The realignment between the people and the politics of France that became manifest as the country entered the last decade of the twentieth century may be viewed in a long historical perspective, rendered contemporary by the way cultural changes imposed revisions of the fundamental assumptions that had hitherto characterized French politics, expressing the pressure for a profound redefinition of the latter as France prepared to enter the twenty-first century. The chapter which follows will endeavour to illuminate the way the role of the polity and the political cleavages within it were brought into question, the cultural shifts contributing to this process, and the changing perception of the prerogatives of power which led to the apparently irresistible rise of 'green' politics in France.

A changing political culture

The unwarranted nature of any assumption that there was a stock of clear and commonly held convictions defining the political culture of the French people became ever more apparent as the 1980s drew to a close. Even an ostensible appeal to a historical consciousness of the fundamental ideals defining the French Republic made its most resounding impact on public opinion in terms of history as spectacle, style over substance. In spite of the unwavering focus provided by events, colloquia and the media in the period leading up to the celebration of the bicentenary of the Revolution, a series of polls carried out by SOFRES suggested an abiding and surprising level of ignorance. One-third of those interviewed did not know the nationality of Marie-Antoinette; almost half did not know how Danton died, the role of Saint-Just in the Revolution and whether Robespierre was *Montagnard* or *Girondin*.[2]

The very style chosen for the main events commemorating the bicentenary of the Revolution were seen by some (ironically such as the pop singer and Socialist supporter Renaud) as a compromise with showbusiness and a retreat from the political vision which underlined the libertarian and egalitarian achievements of the Revolution;[3] the kind of vision to which François Mitterrand had been inclined to allude at the beginning of the decade when promoting the idea of 'le socialisme à la française'.[4] The truth was that well before the end of the decade, the literary and cultural establishment sympathetic to the government had, for the most part, chosen to adapt to the conclusion wryly articulated by Bernard Rideau, a former adviser to Valéry Giscard D'Estaing, that politics is not about convincing but seducing the electorate.[5]

For those intellectuals who allied themselves most closely with the government, attempts to articulate in political terms the vision which characterized their ambition in the early 1980s were largely eschewed, especially in the run-up to the presidential elections of 1988, in favour of an apolitical discourse focused on the presidential personality of François Mitterrand. The phenomenon that was to be termed *Tontonmania* and *Mitterrandolâtrie* was given its original impetus in the pages of the periodical for upmarket Socialists called *Globe*, by its editor Georges-Marc Benamou. In an article entitled 'Tonton et nous' ('Uncle and us'), which appeared in February 1986, Benamou declared that for him and his friends

Mitterrand personified the political and cultural consciousness of France, and its hope for the future. The waiting game played by Mitterrand before declaring his intention to seek a second presidential mandate focused the attention of some of his supporters even more exclusively on the redemptive nature of the presidential personality rather than on politics. A new peak was reached in December 1987 when Dominique Jamet made his plaintive appeal to Mitterrand to stand again for the presidency in an article entiltled 'Tonton ne nous quitte pas' ('Uncle don't leave us'), once more in *Globe*, during the course of which he affirmed his belief in Mitterrand as the sole figure capable of healing the divisions in French society.

Evident in the attitude of Benamou, Jamet and others of the same persuasion was a recognition of the need to shift the ground on which support for the figurehead of the Socialist establishment could be solicited because the political operation of that establishment in foreign and domestic matters, and even in the day to day accomplishment of parliamentary business, had significantly damaged the faith of the French electorate in their political system and the parties operating in it. The Socialist government was dogged by scandal first on the foreign front, with the secret service operation in July 1985 to sink the Greenpeace vessel Rainbow Warrior in Auckland, New Zealand, in order to prevent it from interfering with French nuclear testing in the region. On the home front there followed a series of financial scandals involving the illegal funding of PS activities; scandals which were less shocking in themselves than for the willingness of the government to amnesty those involved and thus create the impression that the judicial process was being impeded for politically partisan motives. More recently, a police investigation into the illegal trade-off of public works contracts for undeclared funds to finance the PS and which seemed to have run into the ground in 1989, was brought again to public attention by a legal ruling in January 1992, which led to a re-opening of the file on *l'affaire Urba*, named after the consultancy with close links to the PS and whose name featured in the original police investigation which pointed to a hidden web of financial and business contacts designed to generate funds for the PS.[6]

The disillusionment created by the government's management of political issues could not have been relieved by an aspect of the way the business of government was conducted, and which seemed to weaken the very obligation of accountability to parliament. The provisions of article 49.3 of the constitution of the Fifth Republic effectively allow a government to push through its measures in the face of majority opposition provided that it is not defeated by a censure motion. Between 1988 and 1990 during his period as Prime Minister, Michel Rocard used the provisions of this article on more than 20 occasions. The disenchantment created by the perceived abuse of political power did not, however, serve to discredit solely the Socialists. The amnesty offered to those involved in the illegal funding of political parties could not have been voted through by the Socialists alone on 22 December 1989. By the beginning of the 1990s all of the major parties were touched by a disaffection with political pursuits that were seen in an increasingly negative light, leading to what may be described as a crisis of legitimacy, concerning the proper limits of political power.[7] A tacit admission of the way corrupt political practices impacted on the perception of political life itself was implicit in Prime Minister Pierre Bérégovoy's outline of government proposals on the *moralisation* of public sector finances to the PS congress in Bordeaux in July 1992, and was made clear by the Finance Minister Michel Sapin in a press interview during the following week, when he enjoined those with the responsibilities of political office to maintain an objective distance vis-à-vis their functions and assume the *modestie* now demanded by the French people.[8]

The exasperation of the *rénovateurs* of left and right, faced with what they saw as the mediocrity of the political establishment and their lack of ideas, reflected the scepticism of their constituents regarding left or right-wing plans to effect the kind of change that would impact on their individual lives. The failure of the political parties to retain the trust of the electorate had left a political void characterized by a kind of negative consensus which views freedom in terms of *espaces de liberté*, those areas of personal initiative where politics does not and should not be allowed to encroach; a form of liberty which uses civil society as its host but which fails to appreciate that the interests of the individual and the body politic are coterminous. The negative consensus which began to operate to the detriment of mainstream politics, operated conversely to the benefit of the new forces which made a virtue of their apolitical, or even anti-political attitudes.

In contrast to the declining efficacy of the political discourse of the major parties, a figure like Jean-Marie Le Pen thrived by articulating an emotive discourse aimed at the voter not as a citizen, with all the obligations that

256

implies, but as a victim: a victim of insensitive public bodies; of the economic failure brought by corrupt political parties; of the 'foreign' either in terms of racial otherness or foreign ideas like the European project.[9] Ample opportunity was provided to purvey the cynicism typical of the bedrock of FN supporters regarding the mainstays of the established order, like the civil service and the schools, to a wider electorate.[10] The persistent whiff of corruption created by the financial irregularities touching the PS provided Le Pen with the excuse he wanted for denouncing the government as a bunch of 'thieves, gangsters and racketeers'. When asked for his reaction to Prime Minister Cresson's decision, announced on 18 January 1992, to respond by taking legal action against him, Le Pen justified his pronouncement by arguing his right to express himself in a way that would be understood by the people.[11] Notwithstanding the ostensible condemnations of Le Pen for choosing to forego political discourse in favour of demagoguery, as Jim Shields has shown in his chapter, the major parties had themselves expressed a willingness to edge backwards into a less than rational discourse in order to enhance their popularity vis-à-vis the electorate.

The political establishment had found itself constantly reacting to the mood of the people instead of leading it and, in desperate attempts to catch up with the tide of change, allowed itself to be perceived as resorting to excuses for lapses in the integrity of its officials, or opting for agressive strategies redolent of *la politique politicienne*, with all the negative connotations that entails. The fact that the established parties of left and right were being tarred by the public with the same brush inevitably brought into question whether the political cleavage brought about by the Revolution was as clear as it used to be and whether it remained as mobilizing a dynamic as it once was.

The traditional dividing line between left and right in French political life marked out opposing attitudes regarding the Church, money and, more fundamentally, the conflicting visions of humanity which provided the ideological dimension to the competition for power. Apart from the Catholic mobilization against the proposals put forward at the end of 1983 by the Minister of Education, Alain Savary, in response to what was perceived as a threat to the independence of Church schools, the issue of the place of the Church in French society is no longer a controversial one. Money, however, retains a political significance in defining the adversarial relationship of left to right. To a sizeable proportion of the French electorate, the concentration of wealth in a limited number of hands and the power this confers still adduces the spectre of the illegitimate and dominant influence of a class or interest group being exercised at the expense of the generality, and the poor in particular. The critique of the unfair distribution of wealth remains a left-wing theme and as the 1980s progressed the Socialists gave legislative form to their concerns with measures like the definition of the minimum income required for an individual to be an integral part of society (the *revenu minimum d'insertion* introduced in 1988). As Linda Hantrais has shown, the RMI, aimed essentially at reintegrating the beneficiaries of social assistance into the workforce, was to receive the majority of its funding from a wealth tax also introduced in 1988 (*impôt de solidarité sur la fortune*). The idea of social justice behind the government's attempt to shore up the state system for redistributing wealth to the most needy was evident in the creation of the CSG (*contribution sociale généralisée*) in February 1991; a levy of 1.10 per cent on all sources of income.

Nonetheless, the government's attempt to refute the political constructions put on the introduction of the CSG was evident in its affirmation that this should not be seen as a tax but as a non-punitive measure for achieving social justice since it spread the basis of payment to sources of income which were not previously covered by social insurance contributions. The desire not to appear partisan and the emphasis on the general interest signalled a sensitivity to the fact that though the undue concentration of wealth among unaccountable elites might mobilize concern, on the left as in French society in general, the pursuit of money was no longer perceived as reprehensible, and was in fact readily accepted. Underlying the growing redundancy of attempts to frame the pursuit of social justice in terms of conflicting classes, there lay the intimation of a more profound redundancy that struck at the intellectual roots anchoring the perception of society by the traditional parties of left and right, and which conditioned their discourse.

In grossly simplified terms, the traditional right-wing perception of human nature is one marked by an Augustinian sense of moral imperfection. The corollary of the conviction that humanity is inherently not perfectible is the pursuit of a social order whose aim is not the fulfilment of universalist ideals of justice and freedom, but the relative freedom that may be enjoyed by the individual in a society protected from anarchy or civil war. Conversely, the corollary of the left-wing assumption that humanity is inherently good but corrupted by society is a revolutionary project along lines aimed at establishing justice and well-being for all, as opposed to the few. These assumptions which still help to shape the fundamental dispositions of the major parties in France have in recent years been threatened by the emergence of a rather different, and what has been termed a 'parasitic' notion of liberty.[12] The doctrinal crisis on the right of the political spectrum heightened as the confusion regarding the criteria defining the legitimate order deepened. The traditional notion of freedom to act within the bounds defined by obligation to a social order is undermined by uncertainty as to what that order is or should be. And for both left and right, the idea that the instruments of the state could be used either to integrate the disparate elements of society into an egalitarian whole or to secure the stability of a certain social order, was thrown very much into question by the shifting perceptions of power that emerged among the people of France as the 1980s drew to a close.

Shifting perceptions of power

Challenges to the notion of the French state as one and indivisible, assimilating individual, religious, ethnic and class differences into the mould from which French citizens would emerge, multiplied as the years of Socialist government progressed. Developments in the classroom, at the ballot-box and in the street provided incontrovertible evidence that the republican paradigm established by the Revolution could no longer be relied on to appeal effectively to an electorate that grew in volatility as it became less ideologically rooted.[13] It was notable that one of the most testing challenges to the traditional notion of the French state occurred in the institution which, for Jules Ferry and his followers in nineteenth-century France, was the crucible in which the constituent parts of a secular and egalitarian society would cohere: the school. The debate which raged over the prerogatives of the Republic and the right to *différence* in September 1989 was sparked by the decision of the principal of the Collège Gabriel-Havez in Creil, to exclude three French muslim girls of North African parentage from the school, after the parents had insisted that the

259

girls retain their islamic headscarves in class. The *foulard islamique* provoked an intense debate between those who insisted on the role of the school as a *lieu d'émancipation*, a crucial site for the creation of a free and secular society, and those who challenged the right of the state to suppress *différence* in pursuit of a republican ideal. The ultimate decision of the *Conseil d'Etat* on this matter, though largely supportive of the prerogatives of school principals in such a context, did not bring the wider debate to an end.

For many observers, the viability of a statist ethos based on *assimilation* was brought into question. Faced with the resistance on all sides to the integration of cultural identities based on non-European origins outside of the Judeo-Christian faith, was it now more realistic to talk of *enfermement*, i.e. the peaceful pursuit of separateness within far more supple structures of civil society, instead of the conflictual road to assimilation prescribed by a voluntarist ideology? The process of change in the values and norms of French society had pursued its course during the Socialist years, and in spite of the acknowledged difficulty of measuring the impact of this kind of change, it undoubtedly plays a major role in determining the viability of political doctrines and institutions.[14] The change outlined in the debate on *assimilation* or *enfermement* was not limited to the issues of race or religion, and as the behaviour of the French electorate at the ballot-box culminating in the *élections sanction* of spring 1992 testified, voters were less inclined than ever to allow their preferences to be assimilated into monolithic structures of partisan politics. The emergence of what was dubbed *une France heptagonale*, a political landscape occupied by seven formations (PC, PS, Génération Ecologie, Verts, UDF, RPR, Front National), of whom none was able to garner more than 20 per cent of the votes cast, was a measure of the gulf that had opened up between the political establishment and the people of France.[15] These political preferences reflected the lifestyle preferences of individuals whose choices reacted against the cultural constraints and political rigorism that once dominated French society.

As recent studies of cultural change in modern France illustrate, in spite of opposition from influential voices with a more classical appreciation of the term, 'culture' has developed a near all-purpose elasticity,[16] concomitant with the elasticity which characterizes the definition of the groups which now constitute French society. A two-stage development is identifiable which was marked, firstly, by a burgeoning 'central constellation'; that broad band in French society whose permeable contours encompass continually emerging groups and which is typically constituted by people like teachers, civil servants, managers, engineers, most other salaried non-manual workers and most technicians.[17] Within that constellation, however, there has been a second development which, as the influence of ideology has waned and the links with social origins have stretched, the imperative of fulfilment has become highly individualized and the right most vigorously pursued, as Gilles Lipovetsky puts it, is the right to 's'accomplir à part'.[18] In Lipovetsky's analysis, this process of *personnalisation* has penetrated the disciplinarian realm of politics and appropriated the prerogatives that were once exercised in the collective pursuit of social well-being. The French press in the 1990s abounds with surveys of *la société psy*, as the political means for building a better society are forsaken in favour of an ever-growing variety of methods offering individuals or small groups the prospect of constructing a fulfilled existence for themselves alone.[19] The varied and individualistic consumption of which the foregoing choices are a part, may be seen as a kind of non-political suffrage which reinforces rather than negates a democratic culture,[20] but this cannot compensate for the tension that arises when the rejection of the political establishment is not accompanied by a corresponding decline in the expectation of what it should provide.

According to opinion poll soundings of public reaction to the great reform project of François Mitterrand's first term, i.e. decentralization, the French people retain a paradoxical attitude to the state. Though welcoming the initiatives devolved to the regions and the localities, particularly in the realm of public services, the public perception of the state as provider may have been refined, even redefined, but not fundamentally altered. In addition to the predictable expectation of the state as investor in and keeper of the nation's capital infrastructure, the individuals surveyed also expected the state to be the guarantor of decent and comparable standards of living across the nation.[21] While preferring a more 'modest' state to the one which once cherished the ambition of founding society anew, the individual still burdens the modest state with the expectation that it will find a way to create the conditions that enable individuals to make choices for and by themselves, while at the same time facilitating the emergence of a perpetually challenged sense of common good.[22]

What came to be perceived as the rejection of politics in France in the 1980s was in fact a more nuanced and paradoxical development that surfaced across Western Europe, created by societies straining to contain a greater range of interests than ever before within political structures which those interests judged inadequate.[23] As the appeal of the established parties declined in France, so the appeal of associations and alliances to individuals 'who owe their political positions to no one but themselves' (as described by Alain Schmit, spokesman and leader of one such association, *Charente première*) grew. The names chosen by these movements express on the one hand a wish to distance themselves from traditional partisan politics, but on the other hand a desire to achieve objectives that inevitably necessitate the exercise of political power, for example: *Le Nouveau Monde, Association des citoyens, AGIR, Mouvement national citoyennes citoyens.*[24]

The foregoing contradiction could not be truer of the section of the electorate who entered the political fray for the first time during the 1980s: the 18-24 year-olds. For these first-time voters the political establishment they faced was constituted, to a significant degree, by the generation of 1968 who had learned to combine their Keynesian, collectivist and statist vision with a strong measure of economic orthodoxy in order to manage French capitalism.[25] For the newly enfranchised citizens this compromise was simply another orthodoxy still marked by a totalizing vision that betrayed them while purporting to accommodate their desire for autonomy and specificity. The increasing attraction of the ecological banner to them, as well as other sections of the central constellation of French society, swelled the ranks of the green movements in France. In so doing it would precipitate the inevitable emergence of the tensions that must afflict an engagement with politics that simultaneously rejects the constraints of the system in which it operates.

Green non-politics

In the presidential elections that marked the beginning and the close of the 1980s, the two ecology candidates polled the same level of support of approximately 4 per cent: Brice Lalonde in 1981 and Antoine Waechter in 1988. But this apparent stasis did not reflect the extraordinary rise in consciousness regarding ecological issues which led to what may be called the 'greening' of France. There were a number of scandals and ecological disasters which undoubtedly focused the minds of the French public on the threat to their environment and the shortcomings of their government in the protection of that environment: the less than honourable conduct of the French government over the Rainbow Warrior affair in 1985; the manifest lack of contingency plans exposed by the aftermath of the explosion at the nuclear reactor at Tchernobyl in the former USSR in 1986; and the inevitable element of risk involved in the bulk transport of oil, as exemplified by the catastrophic leakage of millions of tons of crude oil into Prince William sound, Alaska, when the Exxon Valdez ran aground in 1989.

The foregoing examples of incidents that raised environmental awareness may all emanate from outside *l'Hexagone*, but the extent to which this awareness permeated everyday life in France was crucial in laying the platform for the electoral take-off achieved by the ecologists in the municipal elections of 1989, when the marked progression in their support between the two ballots resulted in their returning over thirteen hundred Green local councillors, from a body of Green candidates that was twice as big as the one they were able to field in 1983. The breakthrough was underlined by the results of the European election of 1989 when the ecology movement took a 10.59 per cent share of the vote (helped, undeniably, by a number of factors, chief among which was a proportional representation voting system) and returned nine European Deputies, including two fellow travellers.[26]

Like many ideas aimed at a fundamental revision of received doctrines about society, the ecological cause received a considerable intellectual and political impetus from the events of May 1968, in which individuals like Yves Cochet, a future European Deputy for the ecologists, and Brice Lalonde, played an active part. Though active, Lalonde and Cochet were among those students disinclined to be orientated by the blinkers of a left-wing ideology in their political perceptions and, together with future personalities in the ecological vanguard like Christian Brodhag and Maryse Arditi, they were chief among that generation to be influenced by the intellectual ferment that followed 1968, and which marked the tranformation of an environmental concern into an environmental campaign to prevent the world's fabric from being irredeemably damaged. An early concrete result of this new consciousness was the foundation of the French branch of Friends of the Earth in 1970, by Alain Hervé, Pierre Radanne, Cochet and Lalonde.

A measure of the currency gained by environmental concerns was reflected in the creation in France in 1971 of a Minister for the Environment. As the 1970s progressed the *vague écolo* spread and its ripples surfaced with increasing frequency in *spécials* and *suppléments* in the popular and mainstream political press like *Actuel* and *Le Nouvel Observateur*, as well as the predictably apocalyptic visions depicted in periodicals like *La Gueule Ouverte*. Antoine Waechter was the first of the post '68 generation to mount a serious electoral challenge to the prevailing political orthodoxy when in 1973 and barely in his twenties, he founded *Ecologie et Survie* together with Solange Fernex, in order to promote an environmentalist candidate in the legislative elections of that year. In 1974, notwithstanding their distaste for traditional political campaigning, the ecologists mobilized their votes behind René Dumont in the presidential elections of that year. However, the full acceptance of the weight deployed by the ecologists in the political balance was to be unequivocally signalled much later, when in 1988 Prime Minister Michel Rocard gave the Environment portfolio, not to a member of the political establishment but to a leader of the ecological movement, Brice Lalonde.

The difference between the 1970s and the 1980s was the difference between ecological issues that were the intellectual currency of exchange among a campaigning minority, and issues that became common currency in the commercial, social and political sphere. The extent of this osmosis was highlighted by the term 'green capitalism', coined by the French economic periodical *Dynasteur*. Commercial competition to affirm the ecological credentials of brand names and products was driven by a hard-headed sense of the profit to be made in responding to the demands of a new kind of consumer whose shopping needs would have been unrecognizable a decade earlier: bio-degradable detergents, CFC-free aerosols, recycled paper products and unleaded petrol, to name but a few green products that became commercially viable during the 1980s. Established as a serious issue in commercial terms, the environmental cause also assumed the intellectual seriousness that once guided philosophical reflections on the emancipation of the proletariat. Setting out the new ethical agenda for the children of the *trente glorieuses*,[27] those generations formed during the thirty years of uninterrupted post-war prosperity and who now crowd the central constellation described by Mendras and Cole, thinkers like Félix Guattari pleaded for an end to the infantilism of conspicuous consumption and the development of an *écosophie* which rehabilitates subjectivity and singularity.[28] Thus building on the break with 'ouvrièrisme' and productivism made by André Gorz, erstwhile collaborator of Sartre on *Temps Modernes*, in his farewell to the proletariat.[29]

For all their success in raising awareness of their cause and of their potential as a new force, the ecologists nonetheless entered the 1990s without a recognizably coherent political identity, and therefore liable to being labelled with all manner of political attributes: described as the heirs to communism and to third-worldism by *Figaro Magazine* (14 March 1992); as watered-down leftists in *L'Express* (12 March 1992); some of their supporters were even described as *écolo-fachos* and *écolo-pétainistes* in *Actuel* (October-November 1991).[30]

The narrowly political characterizations of the press, however, failed to furnish explanations that encompassed the sweep of the green movements. Suggestions that they represented a short-term protest movement were refuted by the fact of their organized existence for over a decade and a half. Environmentalist candidates had indeed done well in localities where elections had allowed the voters the opportunity of airing a local environmental grievance, but the scope of green successes nationally prevented these movements from being regarded as a new localism. The analysis of voting patterns had proved the undeniable transfer of votes from socialist to ecology candidates as the socialist constituency declined, but the presence of votes transferred from the centre parties proved that the new force in French politics could neither be called a new leftism nor a new centrism.

That the success of the ecologists should prove so difficult to categorize in typically political terms should not be surprising in view of their own refusal, constitutionally and in the practice of politics, to assume an orthodox political identity.[31] The creation of *Les Verts* in 1984 was the result of a long and contentious debate as to how the ambitions of the ecologists could be realized without fundamentally compromising their principles. The organization formed in January 1984 (*Les Verts, Confédération écologiste-Parti écologiste*) was the first to incorporate the word *parti*, and in a secondary designation which does not feature in current usage when referring to *Les Verts*. It was the outcome of a painful period of gestation which in ten years had seen the creation of six national organizations and at least five electoral umbrella organizations. In spite of this the new alliance in 1984 failed to integrate The Friends of the Earth, and in 1990 would find itself faced with a rival for the same constituency in Brice Lalonde's newly-formed *Génération Ecologie*.[32] Lalonde's new movement espoused the loosely organized and alliance inclined structure which he had originally wished, and failed to see the *Verts* adopt. In contrast, after Lalonde parted from them in the mid-1980s and Waechter and his supporters took over the Verts in 1986, the ecumenical political ecology personified by Lalonde became anathema to Waechter's determination to steer an autonomous course that was neither left nor right.

The root cause of the tension in the ecological camp regarding its political destiny is a vision of humanity which refuses to compromise with the fractured identity and the consequent barriers to fulfilment imposed by the modern state. The person should not be divided and exploited as a worker, a voter, or an inhabitant of a narrowly-defined socio-economic group. Instead, the individual should be perceived as a whole entity engaged in a multiplicity of activities. For the ecologists therefore, it would be tantamount to repeating the error of past movements to isolate their activity in a specialized field called party politics, within structures that limited their action, separated them from civil society, and in a profound manner militated against the achievement of that broader sense of liberty that accommodated an undivided experience of subjectivity and individuality.

Such laudable ideals, however, are severely tested when confronted with the necessity of making choices dictated by the structures of power as they exist, rather than as they ought to be, and this was highlighted in the regional and cantonal elections of March 1992. In their endeavour to persist in the idea that they did not engage in the manoeuvrings and partisan behaviour of traditional parties, the ecologists reversed into what was a classic piece of party political squabbling.

The logic of an alliance between *Les Verts* and *Génération Ecologie* was evident to the *Verts* militants in the Alpes-Maritimes during the campaign for the regional elections, especially in view of the threat from the FN. In spite of this argument, the national leadership determined to abide by its principle of autonomy.[33] The stumbling block was constituted by the

266

refusal, expressed by both sides, to allow the ecological movement to be undermined by political deals and dogmas. Paradoxically, the discord between the two sides was articulated in very familiar political terms. Whereas for the *Verts* leadership co-operation with a movement led by the Minister for the Environment was too much like a passive acceptance of Socialist entryism, for Brice Lalonde the major failure of the *Verts* was their Stalinist sectarianism. The circular logic entailed by the denial of politics was succinctly expressed by Lalonde when he described his movement as 'the party for those who do not want a party.'[34]

Apart, most obviously, from the collapse of the *Parti socialiste* and the consequent landslide for the mainstream right, the great surprise of the legislative elections of March 1993 was the failure of the ecologists to mobilize their support and translate it into seats. The alliance between the *Verts* and *Génération Ecologie* brought them only 7.80 per cent of the votes in the first round on March 21 and foretold their demise in the second round a fortnight later. Nonetheless, the affirmation by the former *Vert* Deputy Dominique Voynet (ejected from her seat in the Jura in the second round) that her party could still celebrate a moral victory sounded somewhat hollow.[35] In reality it was a failure due in no small measure to political mismanagement and resulting from a less than wholehearted alliance.

The vote by 70.70 per cent of the *Vert* delegates meeting in Chambéry on 14 November 1992 in favour of an alliance with *Génération Ecologie* for the legislative elections could not obscure the fact that their leader had to balance conflicting ambitions, not only in the relationship between the *Verts* and *Generation Ecologie* but also within his party. At one extreme, Waechter had had to contend with the aptly nicknamed *Khmers Vert* opposition to any dilution of their principles and ambitions, and on the other he had had to placate those who opposed the idea of an electoral alliance with *Génération Ecologie* which operated to the detriment of the Socialists.[36]

The conflicting ambitions in the relationship between the *Verts* and *Génération Ecologie* became apparent each time pressure was put on Waechter's fidelity to his 'neither left nor right' strategy. An early and striking example of this was provided by the contrasting responses of the new ecological partners to a keynote speech by the former Socialist Prime Minister Michel Rocard, on the future of left-of-centre forces in France. In essence, Rocard's speech at Montlouis-sur-Loire on 17 February 1993 was a call for a 'big bang' in French politics that would lead to a recomposition of progressive forces capable of providing a credible alternative to the right. Initial reports of Brice Lalonde's reaction to the 'outstretched hand' of Rocard suggested a new modesty and openness on the part of the former.[37] Antoine Waechter's reaction to the notion of a new alliance with elements of the political establishment was, however, distinctly more sceptical, as expressed in his acerbic remark on the television channel TF1 on 24 February 1993: 'After treating us with contempt for ten years the Socialists have spent the last ten months courting us.'

Further overtures from the PS were to prove equally fruitless as the legislative elections drew nearer. The suggestion by the PS that its first-round candidates would stand down in favour of better placed ecology candidates in the second round of the impending elections failed to make any serious impact on the prevailing opinion among the ecologists in favour of a 'neither left nor right' policy. The extent to which this attitude led to a negative conditioning of the ecologists' campaign was implied in the immediate post-electoral soundings of public opinion. In one survey, 43 per cent of all voters and 33 per cent of the ecologist constituency felt that the *Vert-Génération Ecologie* alliance had failed to develop sufficient credibility on issues other than the environment.[38] In short, it had failed to convince the electorate that it had climbed out of the single-issue bunker to address their other major preoccupations like unemployment, and paid the price.

Conclusion

The tactical blunders and the subsequent failure to acquire political credibility which characterized the campaign of the ecologists during the legislative elections of spring 1993 were soon underlined by the attitude of the new centre-right government of Edouard Balladur. Far from adopting a triumphalist or dismissive approach regarding green issues, the government displayed considerable zeal in affirming its eco-friendly credentials. At the twenty-fifth congress of *France Nature Environnement* (the federation representing 700,000 members in 170 nationwide branches of *Associations françaises de protection de la nature*) in Paris in May

1993, the Environment Minister Michel Barnier outlined programmes for secondary and tertiary education, including the *Grandes écoles*, aimed at turning every young French person into an *éco-citoyen*.[39] All rhetoric aside, this constituted a clear signal from the new government that it intended to tap the reservoir of environmental concern, especially among prospective first-time voters, which far from subsiding, as a superficial reading of the legislative election results might have suggested, had in fact not been harnessed with political astuteness by the ecologists.

A crossroads has cleary been reached by the ecologists in France: whether to revive the remarkable forward momentum gained in the late 1980s by developing the specialized structures and the clearly designated elite that may enable them to share in the exercise of political power, or whether to persevere with the posture of green non-politics, thereby running the risk of becoming the 'green utopianism' that fills the vacuum left by the demise of the red utopianism of yesteryear.[40]

The success of the ecologists in rallying support in France incorporated some of the archetypal results of the shifts, in sociology and political culture, that became clearly evident as the end of the Socialist years came into view. The greening of French society heralded the emergence of what may be perceived as a new paradigm: a new fault line in society between the post-industrial non-established individuals and the party system, an opposition which opens up a series of new cleavages over the orthodox notions of citizenship, modernity and democracy, which themselves were born out of the political conflicts and social shifts of nineteenth-century France. Although it is impossible to predict the impact on the structures governing France, it is unquestionable that those key notions which define the operation of civil society are being re-appraised by a growing number of its members.

Notes

1. See Gaffney, J. (1991), 'French Political Culture and Republicanism', in E. Kolinsky & J. Gaffney (eds), *Political Culture in France and Germany*, Routledge, London, pp. 13-35.
2. The findings of these polls are summarized by Duhamel, O. (1989), in 'La révolution française est terminée', *Pouvoirs*, no. 50, pp. 121-5.

3. Faubert, S., 'Histoire secrète d'un divorce', *L'Evénement du jeudi*, 13 July 1989.

4. Favier, P. and Martin-Roland, M. (1990), *La Décennie Mitterrand*, 2 vols., Seuil, Paris; vol. 1, *Les Ruptures*, p. 109.

5. Briet, M-O., Hénau, V. and Raynaert, F. (1989), *Pour en finir avec les années 80*, Presses Pocket, Paris, p. 175. The irreverent way in which politics is perceived by these young authors in terms invented by the tastes of fickle consumerism, is as revealing as the observations they make. The revival of the debate concerning civil society is regarded by the authors as little more than an attempt by politicians to refloat their waterlogged discourse.

6. For a personal but nonetheless informative account of the extensive financial wheeling and dealing characterized by the generation of fake invoices ('fausses factures'), see the version of events related by the policeman at the heart of the original investigation: Antoine Gaudino (1990), *L'Enquête impossible*, Albin Michel, Paris.

7. Pfister, T. (1990), 'La triple crise française', *Revue Politique et Parlementaire*, No. 950, pp. 73-9.

8. Robert-Diard, P., 'Un entretien avec M. Michel Sapin', *Le Monde*, 17 July 1992.

9. Mongin, O. (1991), *La peur du vide: essai sur les passions démocratiques,* Seuil, Paris, p. 169. The 'retour du national' in 1980s France was a broader and more subtle phenomenon than might be assumed by focusing exclusively on Le Pen. Numerous groups developed to defend what they perceived as a threatened French identity, from a party in pursuit of a hunting, shooting and fishing rustic ideal to associations for an active citizenry. The pursuit of this allegedly threatened identity by such a diversity of groups was facilitated by the fact that the notion of national identity was so lacking in unambiguously definable content. As M. Lipianski (1991) suggests: 'Cette identité n'a plus un contenu très précis: elle est davantage évoquée que décrite. C'est comme une image effacée dont on ne percevrait plus que le contour. On a l'impression d'un cadre vide ou, du moins, un contenu flou dans lequel chaque groupe peut introduire les valeurs qu'il veut défendre', in *L'identité française. Représentations, mythes, idéologies*, Editions de l'espace européen, La Garenne-Colombes, p. 253.

10. Fysh P. and Walfreys, J. (1992) 'Le Pen, the National Front and the Extreme Right in France', in *Parliamentary Affairs*, Vol. 45, No. 3, July, pp. 309-26, p. 312.

11. Porte, G., 'Je l'ai fait, je l'ai refait et je le referai', *Le Monde*, 21 January 1992.

12. Tenzer, N. (1990), *La société dépolitisée*, PUF, Paris, p. 216.

13. Hayward, J. (1990), 'Ideological change: the exhaustion of the revolutionary impetus', in Hall, P., Hayward, J. and Machin, H. (eds.), *Developments in French Politics*, London, MacMillan, pp. 15-32, p. 32.

14. Inglehart, R. (1990), *Culture Shift in Advanced Industrial Society*, Princeton University Press, Princeton N. J., p. 432.

15. Julliard, J., 'Le miroir brisé du Président', *Le Nouvel Observateur*, 26 March 1992.

16. Rigby, B. (1991), *Popular Culture in Modern France*, Routledge, London, p. 162.

17. Mendras, H. with Cole, A. (1991), *Social Change in Modern France*, Cambridge University Press, Cambridge, p. 31.

18. Lipovetsky, G. (1983), *L'Ere du vide: essais sur l'individualisme contemporain*, Gallimard, Paris, p. 14. As Lipovetsky argues in a later study (1987), nowhere is this 'logique de la différence et de l'autonomie' better expressed than in fashion, which is the most appropriate representation of the fact that 'une valeur mondaine inédite rayonne désormais: le Nouveau', in *L'empire de l'éphémère. La mode et son destin dans les sociétés modernes*, Gallimard, Paris, p.70.

19. See, for example, the rather tongue-in-cheek survey by Gauthier, R., Jauvert, V. and Sigaud, D., 'Douze méthodes pour vivre mieux', *Le Nouvel Observateur*, 9 April 1992.

20. This is Paul Yonnet's contention in (1985), *Jeux, modes et masses 1945-1985*, Gallimard, Paris, p. 376. In a more recent study Michel Maffesoli also advances the argument that instead of panicking when faced with the evidence of 'non-participation politique' and other manifestations of 'désengagement', there may be a more positive way of interpreting this development: 'on peut voir, au contraire, dans cette "non-réponse", autre forme de la *secessio plebis*, une force spécifique, une attitude dynamique par laquelle la vie sociale se

recentre sur l'essentiel,' in (1992) *La transfiguration du politique*, Grasset, Paris, p. 122.

21. Percheron, A. (1992), 'L'opinion et la décentralisation ou la décentralisation apprivoisée', *Pouvoirs*, No. 60, pp. 25-40, p. 38.

22. Crozier, M. (1987), *Etat modeste, état moderne*, Paris, Fayard, p. 309.

23. For a sense of this see the findings of Flickinger, R.S. and Studlar, D.T. (1992), 'The Disappearing Voters? Exploring declining turnout in Western European elections', *West European Politics*, Vol. 15, No. 2, pp. 1-16.

24. 'Les associations dans la bataille électorale', *Le Monde*, 27 June 1992.

25. Ory, P. (1989), *L'Aventure culturelle française 1945-1989*, Flammarion, Paris, p. 224.

26. Hainsworth, P. (1990), 'Breaking the Mould: the Greens in the French Party System', in Cole, A. (ed.), *French Political Parties in Transition*, Dartmouth, Aldershot, pp. 91-105, p. 97.

27. 'Les enfants des "trente glorieuses" ', *Le Monde*, 12 June 1992.

28. See Guattari, F. (1989), *Les Trois Ecologies*, Galilée, Paris.

29. This is the broad thrust of André Gorz's essay (1980), *Adieu au prolétariat: au-delà du socialisme*, Galilée, Paris.

30. One of the ironies for *Les Verts* was that the recruitment of members accelerated rapidly up to the end of the 1980s, only to hit a ceiling. On closer inspection this fact revealed that organizationally the *Verts* suffered from a high turnover of activists and a dearth of politically experienced personnel. See Prendeville, B. (1992), 'The French Greens: United We Stand,' *Modern and Contemporary France*, no. 49, April, pp. 62-4.

31. Though highly effective in politicizing environmental issues, such as the defence mounted in 1990 of 124 acres of French forest on the Rhine near Marckolsheim when it was threatened by the building of an acid factory, in their political practice the *Verts* had often showed themselves disinclined to make a clear and active commitment on hard issues like employment, education and minimum incomes. See Whiteside, K. H. (1992), 'The Political Practice of the *Verts*', *Modern and Contemporary France*, no. 48, January, pp. 14-21.

32. Sainteny, G. (1992), *Les Verts*, Presses Universitaires de France, Paris, p. 25.
33. Saux, J-L., 'Les Verts restent opposés à toute alliance avec Génération Ecologie', *Le Monde*, 15 February 1992.
34. Lalonde, B., 'En quoi nous sommes différents', interview with Schneider, R., *Le Nouvel Observateur*, 20 February 1992.
35. *Le Monde*, 30 March 1993.
36. Saux, J.-L., 'M. Waechter est sérieusement contesté par ses propres amis,' *Le Monde*, 17 November 1992.
37. See, for example, Thenard, J.-M., 'Brice Lalonde rejoint le big bang de Michel Rocard,' *Libération*, 23 February 1993.
38. In *Libération*, 29 March 1993.
39. Cans, R., 'Michel Barnier annonce qu'il veut privilégier l'éducation et la formation à l'écologie', *Le Monde*, 11 May 1993.
40. Pronier, R. and le Seigneur, V.J. (1992), *Génération Verte*, Presses de la Renaissance, Paris, p. 328.

Bibliography

Briet, M.- O., Hénau, V. and Raynaert, F. (1989), *Pour en finir avec les années 80*, Presses Pocket, Paris.

Cans, R., 'Michel Barnier annonce qu'il veut privilégier l'éducation et la formation à l'écologie', *Le Monde*, 11 May 1993.

Cole, A. (ed.) (1990), *French Political Parties in Transition*, Dartmouth, Aldershot.

Crozier, M. (1987), *Etat modeste, état moderne*, Fayard, Paris.

Duhamel, O. (1989), 'La révolution française est terminée', *Pouvoirs*, no. 50.

Faubert, S., 'Histoire secrète d'un divorce', *L'Evénement du Jeudi*, 13 July 1989.

Favier, P. and Martin-Roland, M. (1990), *La Décennie Mitterrand*, 2 vols., Seuil, Paris.

Flickinger, R.S. and Studlar, D.T. (1992), 'The Disappearing Voters? Exploring declining turnout in Western European elections', *West European Politics*, vol. 15, no. 2.

Fysh, P. and Walfreys, J. (1992), 'Le Pen, the National Front and the Extreme Right in France', *Parliamentary Affairs*, vol. 45, no. 3.

Gaudino, A. (1990), *L'Enquête impossible*, Albin Michel, Paris.

Gauthier, R., Jauvert, V. and Sigaud, D., 'Douze méthodes pour vivre mieux', *Le Nouvel Observateur*, 9 April 1992.

Gorz, A. (1980), *Adieux au prolétariat: au-delà du socialisme*, Galilée, Paris.

Guattari, F. (1989), *Les Trois Ecologies*, Galilée, Paris.

Hall, P., Hayward, J. and Machin, H. (eds) (1990), *Developments in French Politics*, MacMillan, London.

Inglehart, R. (1990), *Culture Shift in Advanced Industrial Society*, Princeton University Press, Princeton N.J.

Julliard, J., 'Le miroir brisé du Président', *Le Nouvel Observateur*, 26 March 1992.

Kolinsky, E. and Gaffney, J. (eds) (1991), *Political Culture in France and Germany*, Routledge, London.

Lalonde, B., 'En quoi nous sommes différents', interview with Schneider, R., *Le Nouvel Observateur*, 20 February 1992.

Lipianski, M. (1991), *L'identité française. Représentations, mythes, idéologies*, Editions de l'espace européen, La Garennes-Colombes.

Lipovetsky, G. (1983), *L'Ere du vide: essais sur l'individualisme contemporain*, Gallimard, Paris.

Lipovetsky, G. (1987), *L'empire de l'éphémère. La mode et son destin dans les sociétés modernes*, Gallimard, Paris.

Maffesoli, M. (1992), *La transfiguration du politique*, Grasset, Paris.

Mendras, H. and Cole, A. (1991), *Social Change in Modern France*, Cambridge University Press, Cambridge.

Mongin, O. (1991), *La peur du vide: essai sur les passions démocratiques*, Seuil, Paris.

Ory, P. (1989), *L'Aventure culturelle française 1945-1989*, Flammarion, Paris.

Percheron, A. (1992), 'L'Opinion et la décentralisation ou la décentralisation apprivoisée', *Pouvoirs*, no. 60.

Pfister, T. (1990), 'La triple crise française', *Revue Politique et Parlementaire*, no. 950.

Porte, G., 'Je l'ai fait, je l'ai refait et je le referai', *Le Monde*, 21 January 1992.

Prendeville, B. (1992), 'The French Greens: United We Stand', *Modern and Contemporary France*, no. 49, April.

Pronier, R. and le Seigneur, V.J. (1992), *Génération Verte*, Presses de la Renaissance, Paris.

Rigby, B. (1991), *Popular Culture in Modern France*, Routledge, London.

Robert-Diard, P., 'Un entretien avec M. Michel Sapin', *Le Monde*, 17 July 1992.

Sainteny, G. (1992), *Les Verts*, Presses Universitaires de France, Paris.

Saux, J.-L., 'Les Verts restent opposés à toute alliance avec *Génération Ecologie*', *Le Monde*, 15 February 1992.

Saux, J.-L., 'M. Waechter est sérieusement contesté par ses propres amis', *Le Monde*, 17 November 1992.

Tenzer, N. (1990), *La société dépolitisée*, Presses Universitaires de France, Paris.

Thenard, J.-M., 'Brice Lalonde rejoint le big bang de Michel Rocard', *Libération*, 25 February 1993.

Whiteside, K.H. (1992), 'The Political Practice of the *Verts*', *Modern and Contemporary France*, no. 48, January.

Yonnet, P. (1985), *Jeux, modes et masses 1945-1985*, Gallimard, Paris.

Notes on Contributors

Alistair Cole is a Lecturer in the Politics Department at the University of Keele. He has written extensively on French Politics. He is the co-author of *Social Change in Modern France* (1991, with H. Mendras), and *French Electoral Systems and Elections since 1789* (with P. Campbell); and editor of *French Political Parties in Transition* (1990). His most recent book is entitled *François Mitterrand: A Study in Political Leadership* (Routledge, 1994).

Peter Collier is a Lecturer in French at the University of Cambridge and Fellow of Sidney Sussex College. He is the author of *Proust and Venice* (C.U.P., 1989) and co-editor of a number of collections of interdisciplinary essays, most recently *Literary Theory Today* (Polity, 1990) and *Artistic Relations* (Yale, 1994). His translations include Pierre Bourdieu's *Homo Academicus* (Polity, 1988) and *The Political Ontology of Martin Heidegger* (Polity, 1991); and most recently Zola's *Germinal* (O.U.P., 1993).

Helen Drake took up a lectureship in French and European Studies at Aston University after having gained the experience of working for a major multinational company. She has published a number of articles on various aspects of European integration and is currently co-editing a book on political leadership in contemporary France (Dartmouth).

John Flower is Professor of French at the University of Exeter. He has published extensively on the work of François Mauriac and on the relationship between literature and politics in twentieth-century France. Future publications include a study of Pierre Courtade and a special issue of *Europe* on Paul Nizan. He is also editor of the *Journal of European Studies*.

John Gaffney is Reader in European Politics and Director of the Institute for the Study of Language and Society at Aston University. His works include *The French Left and the Fifth Republic* (Macmillan, 1989), and *The Language of Political Leadership in Contemporary Britain* (Macmillan, 1991). He is currently researching for a book on the rhetoric of political leadership in the twentieth century.

Linda Hantrais holds the Chair in Modern Languages and is Director of the European Research Centre in the Department of European Studies at Loughborough University. She is convenor of the Cross-National Research Group and series editor of *Cross-National Research Papers*. Her research interests include the theory, methodology and practice of cross-national comparisons, particularly with reference to social policy and to Franco-British comparisons of women in professional occupations. Her recent publications include *Managing Professional and Family Life: a Comparative Study of British and French Women* (Dartmouth, 1990).

Nicholas Harrison is a Research Fellow at St. Catharine's College, Cambridge. His current research is centred on the idea of censorship, particularly the way in which political/juridical and psychoanalytical discourses on censorship have intertwined in French literary culture of the twentieth century and have shaped the reception of the writings of Sade.

David Looseley is Lecturer in French Studies at Bradford University. He is the author of *A Search for Commitment: The Theatre of Armand Salacrou* (1985) and of a number of articles on modern French theatre and cultural policy. His most recent book is on politics and culture under Mitterrand (Berg, 1994), the research for which has been funded by the Leverhulme Trust.

Gino Raymond has taught at a number of institutions in Britain and France, and is presently a Lecturer in the Department of French at Bristol University. His research interests encompass both politics and literature and he has published articles on the French Communist Party as well as the dilemmas faced by committed writers in France. His current projects include a historical dictionary of France (Scarecrow Press) and a study of the French Communist Party during the Fifth Republic (Dartmouth).

James G. Shields taught at the Universities of Glasgow, Caen and Aston before taking up his present position as a Lecturer in French Studies at Warwick University. He has written widely on French politics and on early nineteenth-century French literature and thought. He is currently working on a study of the extreme right in contemporary France.

278